New Boots
in New Zealand

New Boots in New Zealand

Nine Great Walks,
three islands & one tramping virgin

Gillian Orrell

www.knowthescorebooks.com

To Mum and Dad

First published in the United Kingdom
by Know The Score Books Limited, 2006
118 Alcester Road
Studley
Warwickshire
B80 7NT

www.knowthescorebooks.com

A CIP catalogue record is available for this book from the British Library
ISBN 1-905449-40-2
ISBN 978-1-905449-40-8

Text design and production by *BookNZ*
Maps by Fran Whild
Cover design by Nick Turzynski
Printed in China through Colorcraft Limited, Hong Kong

Contents

Acknowledgements

I owe a great debt to New Zealand's Department of Conservation (DOC) and to the many DOC officers, conservation workers, hut wardens, track workers and office staff who do such a wonderful job of looking after the natural world through which we trampers tramp. This debt extends to the peoples and government of New Zealand who value and protect their natural environments.

Thank you to the many friendly, helpful and informative New Zealanders who aided my research – particularly to staff at the National Archives, the Alexander Turnbull Library, the Auckland Central City Library and the University of Auckland, and to DOC employees Ken Bradley and Brian Dobbie for answering the questions that no one else could answer.

For their tips, company, assistance and laughter, I am deeply indebted to my fellow trampers, particularly: Gill Davidson and Sarah Gray; Ian Beadle, Matthew Cooper and Dominic Morris; Jane Palmer, Shane Hona and Leon (wherever you are); Steve Carr and Ben Stewart from Wades Landing Outdoors; honorary trampers Stewart and Robyn; and the unforgettable 'Boys from Murupara' – Steve Malaquin, Steve Teddy, Glen Craddock and Jason, Glen, Colin and Blair. My heartfelt thanks also to the friends who helped me on the journey between tracks, but particularly to Kanaka Ramyasiri, and Chris and Kane Dooley.

Thank you to older friends who have shaped parts or all of what follows, not least by diligently reading drafts and being brave enough to give me their honest opinion: Tamsen Harward, Karen Scardifield, Jonathan Medcalf, Emil Bernal, Steve Hill, Helen Willis and Gemma Pearson. Any remaining errors are entirely mine. Thanks too to my publishers, Simon Lowe at Know The Score Books and Ian Watt at Exisle, who believed in this book and made it happen. And humblest thanks to my parents, to whom this book is dedicated, for absolutely everything.

Finally, but crucially, thank you from the bottom of my heart to everyone who has ever tramped or will go tramping in New Zealand whilst leaving no trace that they were there.

Taking care of things

Personal safety

I did not die or sustain any serious injuries in researching and writing this book, but there were many times when I was acutely aware of how easy it would be to do either, or both.

My hope is that as you read this book you will be entertained by what the Great Walks and the backcountry of New Zealand have to offer and that, along the way, trampers and prospective trampers will pick up lots of practical information, almost without noticing it. However, what follows is not a guidebook, nor is it a comprehensive guide on what to take, how to prepare or other ways to avoid the inevitable dangers inherent in tramping.

Sadly, there are regular reports of injuries and fatalities in New Zealand's backcountry. No one imagines that they will be the subject of such a report, yet people still make the seemingly small decisions that can lead to this. Decisions about what food and clothing to take. Or what boots to wear.

Personal safety whilst tramping depends on a number of factors: knowing where you're going; understanding what to expect of the terrain; knowing what facilities will be available – and what won't; knowing how to stay warm, well fed and hydrated; anticipating all possible types of weather (of which New Zealand has a breathtaking and volatile array); understanding basic first aid; taking the right equipment, knowing how to use it … and so on.

If you're preparing to tramp, please make sure you get all the information you need to take good care of yourself out on the track. A great place to start is with the New Zealand Department of Conservation (DOC) website at www.doc.govt.nz/Explore/Safety.asp.

Other useful websites include:
- NZ Mountain Safety Council (www.mountainsafety.org.nz)
- New Zealand weather (www.metservice.co.nz)
- Avalanche warnings (www.avalanche.net.nz)

- NZ Land Search and Rescue (www.nzlsar.org.nz)
- NZ Search & Rescue Council – distress beacon information (www. beacons.org.nz)

Finally – and as importantly – make sure that you notify the local DOC office of your intentions before you head into the bush *and* that you add your details into each intentions book en route. These books are found in all DOC huts, as well as at some car parks and information shelters. You should fill in as much detail as possible about your planned route, dates, times, size of party etc. It is all too easy to get into trouble in the backcountry, where rescue is only possible if someone knows to come looking and knows where to look.

Environmental care

Health and safety does not start and end with the tramper. The natural environment must survive your trip too. The aim is to leave no trace of yourself behind. This is not always achievable, given that you're likely to encounter mud and leave a few footprints in it. But footprints should be all.

The number of different ways in which a tramper can damage the environment that he or she is enjoying is truly depressing. Worse still, few of us instinctively know and understand each of the impacts we can have on the natural environment as we tramp through it.

The good news is that it doesn't take long to learn a great deal. Again, a great place to start is on DOC's website at www.doc.govt.nz/Explore/NZ-Environmental-Care-Code.asp.

For those travelling to New Zealand from other countries, your opportunities to protect New Zealand's natural environments begin even before you arrive. In particular, don't take any food or plants etc. with you and make sure you clean tramping boots and other equipment carefully, so that you don't inadvertently import bits of another country. Fortunately, New Zealand's airports are equipped with customs and agricultural/quarantine officers. On arrival, after your passport has been checked, your shoes and other equipment will be too. If in doubt, declare any potentially muddied items you may have. If you haven't already cleaned them, local officials are fully equipped to do so.

Happy – and responsible – tramping.

New Zealand Locations

NORTH ISLAND

Auckland

Te Urewera
National Park

Lake Waikaremoana
Track

Lake
Taupo

Gisborne

Whanganui National Park

Egmont National Park

Tasman Sea

Whanganui River Journey

Tongariro
Northern Circuit

Abel Tasman Coastal Path

Abel Tasman
National Park

Wanganui

Heaphy Track

Takaka

Tongariro
National Park

Kahurangi National Park

Wellington

Paparoa National Park

Nelson Lakes National Park

Westland/Tai Poutini National Park

Kaikoura

Mount Aspiring National Park

Arthur's Pass National Park

Routeburn Track

Christchurch

SOUTH ISLAND

Milford Track

Aoraki/Mount Cook National Park

Fiordland National Park

Kepler Track

Queenstown

Te Anau

Dunedin

Pacific Ocean

STEWART ISLAND

Rakiura Track

Rakiura National Park

Southern Ocean

1
Wilderness awaits

One dark evening in February I sank down exhausted in front of the nine o'clock news and watched an item from New Zealand appear amongst the headlines. Severe and prolonged rainfall had caused the Whanganui River to flood. Footage showed buildings, animals and people being flung out to sea by a body of water that ought not to be called a river. Cattle were being catapulted along with surprised expressions on their faces. Barns and fences were in hot pursuit of their livestock. Locals were describing this as the worst flood they'd ever known. They looked and sounded like people who had seen many floods, who called a spade a spade and who were used to getting on with things, rather than talking to TV crews.

I watched with open mouth. I almost found the energy to sit up straight. I'd seen flood footage before, sometimes from Japan, sometimes from America, sometimes from the M40. But in the eighteen years since the French secret service sank the *Rainbow Warrior* in New Zealand's waters and then tried unsuccessfully to deny it, I couldn't remember seeing a single story from New Zealand make prime-time headline news in the UK.

New Zealand doesn't have the population density that seems to be required to generate revolution, scandal, mass murders or other events sufficiently depressing or salacious to make headline news in the UK. New Zealand is larger than the UK in land area, with a population roughly half that of London. New Zealanders regularly make it into UK sports news, but rarely the depressing bits that go before. Until the Whanganui River flooded, I had presumed that New Zealand would be mentioned only as a footnote in an item on global warming – when the newsreader would talk gravely about the greenhouse gases produced by millions of sheep and cattle gently burping and farting all over those green hills.

The flooding of the Whanganui River hasn't changed my plans for my trip to New Zealand. However, as just one of New Zealand's many natural hazards, flooding might add some interesting challenges to my scheme. I am travelling to New Zealand to take up one of the national pastimes. I don't mean rugby – I'm far too attached to my ears for that. I'm going to do something for which the locals have invented their own word. I'm going tramping.

In New Zealand no one treks. Or hikes. Or bushwalks. No one even goes on multi-day walks. In New Zealand, everyone tramps. Well, not quite everyone. Now that New Zealand has a city with more than a million inhabitants, there are some New Zealanders alive who have never felt the rush of cold, mountain water into their boots. However, a large number of New Zealanders (or Kiwis, as they are better known) are trampers. Young Kiwi couples tramp into the bush as a courtship ritual. They stay overnight in places that are far enough away from home for privacy, but close enough for them still to have some energy left when they get there. Older Kiwi couples have been known to do the same. Thousands of Kiwis belong to tramping clubs. Every Easter holiday, Labour Day and Queen's Birthday weekend is an opportunity to tramp. Even the New Zealand Prime Minister, Helen Clark, goes tramping.

The basic principle of tramping is to head into 'the bush' for hours, days or weeks at a time, carrying everything you'll need. Many trampers carry tents and camp in remote spots, but New Zealanders have also built a network of basic huts across much of the land. These structures offer a home to any creature with enough energy to reach them and enough intelligence to open a door. Or sometimes a window.

I have never tramped before. I have spent most of the last decade living in London and working in offices where a few flights of stairs and the distance to the drinks machine have been the most strenuous of each day's physical challenges. Yet I refuse to believe that I have become a city wimp. Something deep inside me, which may yet turn out to be my Stupidity, believes that I belong in the great outdoors. Something else inside me, which may yet turn out to be my Arrogance, believes that once I set my mind to do something, I rarely fail.

The hard evidence is mixed. I have climbed Snowdon but I was younger then, I needed a whole day to recover and Snowdon is a foothill compared with New Zealand's mountains. I have run the London Marathon, but I never tell any one my finishing time. Suffice to say that I beat all of the

Wombles (but only just) and a few of the Save the Rhinos campaigners, who run in thick and unwieldy rhinoceros costumes that were originally intended for the opera and weigh 14.5 kilograms. There were many who didn't wear heavy costumes, who walked most of the way and who still finished a long way in front of me. My run was slower than their walk.

Carrying a heavy backpack may not be a problem. I routinely carry one loaded with laptop, files, various heavy plug-in devices and things I needed a year ago but haven't cleared out. Yet, if I walk up the escalators on the London Underground with my laptop on my back and a book in my hand, I feel strangely light-headed at the ticket barriers.

I will be tramping alone. It's difficult to persuade fellow city workers to take a few months off from being paid in order to carry a heavy pack hundreds of kilometres through remote spots, utterly beyond the range of reception for any mobile phone. Besides, I haven't tried. I want to travel alone. After living and working in a city of more than seven million, it's not the presence of other people that will be the biggest challenge, but their absence. And, this way, no one need know the full details if I fail horribly.

I'm starting my attempt to become a tramper with the 'Great Walks'. These tracks showcase New Zealand's diverse and dazzling landscapes. Besides, these tracks and their huts are reportedly well maintained – making it more difficult for novices like me to get lost or injured (or worse) whilst venturing into the wilderness.

Each of the Great Walks takes between three and five days to complete but some are notoriously more difficult than others. I am curious to discover what constitutes not just a great walk, but a Great Walk. I am also curious as to why one of these Great Walks is a canoe journey. Is this something to do with the Kiwi sense of humour?

New Zealand currently has nine Great Walks. Eight are on the two main islands, which the rest of the world tends to think of as the whole of New Zealand (when it thinks of New Zealand at all). These islands are extraordinarily different from each other – one riddled with volcanoes and the other stretched around the long spine of the Southern Alps. They bear the unimaginative titles of 'the North Island' and 'the South Island'.

The South Island wins the prize for largest New Zealand land mass, at around 151,000 square kilometres, or about twice the size of Scotland. (The South Island also walks away with a number of other national prizes such as those for Most Enormous Mountains, Single Highest Mountain and Most Recorded Deaths on Mountains.) The North Island comes second with around 115,000 square kilometres of land. This is roughly the size of England if East Anglia were finally to declare itself a republic.

As befits the relative size of these two islands, five of the Great Walks are on the South Island and three are on the North Island. One of the North Island tracks will take me 145 kilometres along the Whanganui River. Hopefully it won't be flinging cattle out to sea when I get there.

The ninth Great Walk is on Stewart Island, which is the third largest of New Zealand's islands and yet is so much smaller than the two main islands that it warrants a name unconnected with basic points of the compass. Stewart Island has an area of around 1,700 square kilometres, which makes it roughly the size of the Isle of Skye and slightly bigger than Greater London. Its permanent inhabitants number around 400 – about one twentieth of the population of the Isle of Skye and about the size of one Kiwi shared house in London. Stewart Island lies off the southernmost tip of the South Island. Only certain parts of Antarctica would take me longer to reach.

I am going tramping because I want to head deep into the wild landscapes that give New Zealand far more drama than any edition of the nine o'clock news. New Zealand has a string of active volcanoes. Its largest city, Auckland, has forty-eight volcanoes alone – and these are just some of the smaller ones. New Zealand has geysers, and hot springs that have caused people to pass out and drown. It has so many mountains that it elongates its postcards and still can't fit them all in. It has some of the highest recorded rainfall on Earth and storms to outdo any special effects department. Each year, millions of tons of rock and vegetation are pulled off the sides of mountains by rain, wind and gravity. If this weren't enough, New Zealand has around 14,000 recorded earthquakes each year. The road network clings to existence through gorges, canyons, creeks, mountain passes and the worst the weather can offer.

One way to explain the shapes and behaviours of this land is through the activities of gods, half-gods and legendary figures. The Maori tribes of New Zealand recount tales that explain everything from the creation of the Earth to the shaping of certain mountains, the weather and the size and shape of local flora and fauna. One of the Great Walks traverses volcanoes that erupted to provide fire for a Maori elder stranded on an icy peak. Another runs through steep, narrow valleys cut by a skilful god as he learned to use a new axe.

Another way to view the massive frolicking of the land is to take the scientific approach. This says that New Zealand is positioned at the very point where two of the largest tectonic plates on Earth collide. The Pacific and Indo-Australian plates are locked in a scrum. Under the North Island, one side is winning and the other is being pushed down into a hotter place. The result: volcanoes, boiling mud and hot springs. Under the South Island, there is stalemate in the scrum and the front row forwards from both teams are being heaved high up into the air. The result: jagged mountains that are still growing. The scientific approach also tells of glaciers and meteorological forces that shape the land from above, through erosion, landslides, floods and avalanches.

This is a wild land – even before you add the bungy jumps, skydives, jet boats and numerous other ways Kiwis have invented to help visitors get excited here. Kiwis don't need to partake in these activities. They have their own ways of flinging themselves into this wilderness. Tramping is one of them. Hunting and fishing are others, though often combined with a good tramp.

Many of New Zealand's most arresting landscapes are only accessible by foot. A helicopter can sometimes do it, given the right kind of weather, a good pilot and enough money. But to see awe-inspiring landscapes unobstructed, and for as long as you want to stare at them, the only way to go is to tramp.

Then there are the flora and fauna. Not even a helicopter will help here. New Zealand has some of the oldest forest on Earth. About seventy-five per cent of the flowering plants in this forest only live there. It has more species of fern than ought to be distinguishable by the naked eye (about 200 at the last count). Some of its trees are thought to be up to 1,500 years old. Making their homes amongst them are some of the strangest birds, including the world's only alpine parrot and several species that can't even fly. Undisturbed by mammals for millions of years, they became flightless and are now some of the most endangered species on Earth.

This wild land survives in part because this was pretty much the last place on Earth discovered by human beings. It is perhaps not surprising that New Zealand was one of the last countries to be found by European explorers: it is, after all, just about as far away from Europe as it was possible to get before space travel. Historians relate that Europeans only sighted New Zealand in 1642 and left after a few days. They didn't come to stay until after 1769.

European explorers encountered Maori tribes, sometimes quite disastrously, and many people still think of Maori as the native human inhabitants of New Zealand. However, academics who have put a good deal of work into these things relate that New Zealand Maori are descended from Polynesians who first arrived in New Zealand around 800–1,000 years before the Europeans. In other words, the Polynesians arrived first, but no human being is truly native to New Zealand.

Maori and European are still the two main cultural traditions of New Zealand. The country is officially bilingual: government departments, municipal buildings, plants, animals and mountains have both English and Maori names. Kiwis are highly conscious of their dual heritage. A Kiwi doesn't have to be Maori to enjoy sticking his tongue out at an opposing country's rugby team, or rolling his eyes, slapping his thighs and suggesting something more like a war than a game of rugby.

However, Maori and European traditions have had markedly different relationships with the land. For Europeans, mountains and rivers are physical barriers to be overcome or conquered. For Maori, mountains and rivers are ancestors from whom they trace their origins. Europeans divide land into plots for private ownership, whereas Maori tradition encourages people to take care of the land through collective stewardship. Europeans treat land as a resource to be harnessed for human benefit, whereas Maori tradition seems to place greater emphasis on the health and 'happiness' of the land.

The Great Walks are largely inside New Zealand's National Parks, but there are areas of controversy even here. Sometimes part of a track crosses private land. Sometimes local Maori tribes feel that they are not sufficiently involved in the collective stewardship of the land traversed by a Great Walk. How best to look after the land is a subject that still causes no end of debate in parliament and in local pubs and tramping clubs throughout the islands. Walking the Great Walks will take me some way inside this debate.

I have never attempted anything quite like this before. Still, there are lots of reasons for me not to worry: I can go at my own pace; I speak the language;

Kiwis have a reputation for being one of the friendliest nations in the world; I will meet lots of locals on the tracks; and it's highly unlikely that the flora and fauna will cause me any harm. At least, not without my collusion.

I worry anyway. What will I do if I twist an ankle in a remote spot? What percentage of my body weight in chocolate will I need to carry? If I do manage to complete all of the Great Walks, won't it be the middle of winter before I've finished? Is canoeing difficult? What about in winter?

Research about tramping in New Zealand has left me giddy with the knowledge that I know nothing. Waterproof overtrousers, a new backpack and new boots have been acquired, much to the relief of several salesmen in specialist outdoors shops who have begun to take a very keen interest in when I am leaving the country.

I tell myself to worry only about pack weight – because this is at least partially under my control. I need to carry as little weight as possible if I'm to have a chance of tramping (and canoeing) the full 550 kilometres of Great Walks.

On the eve of my flight, the assembled equipment is as follows:

- *Items to prevent hypothermia*: sleeping bag, sleeping sheet, spare jumper, spare socks, thermal underwear, woolly hat, woolly gloves
- *Items to protect sensitive English skin from strongest sunlight in the world*: sun hat, sunglasses, suncream (highest possible factor), lip balm
- *Food-related gear*: mug, bowl-plate, knife, fork, spoon, water bottle
- *Items required to maintain some semblance of civilisation*: soap, toothbrush, toothpaste, red bandana (for concealing long, greasy hair), toilet paper, moisturiser, underwear, towel
- *Light to find my way around huts in the dark*: small torch, spare batteries
- *Cumbersome equipment I wish I didn't have to carry*: asthma inhalers, emergency inhaler attachment (for worst-case, middle-of-nowhere asthma attack that won't take place as long as I'm carrying this), eczema creams
- *Emergency supplies in case all else fails*: ear plugs, first-aid kit, whistle, Swiss Army knife (which I'm sure I'll need for something, I just can't think what)
- *Something to put all of this in*: thirty-four plastic bags (various sizes) and a backpack that is on the small side for the purposes of a five-day tramp, thus forcing me to pack efficiently

- ❧ *Things to be otherwise worn or draped round me*: waterproof jacket and trousers, camera, film, those funny trousers that can be zipped to three different lengths, and a specialist tramping top that will allegedly counteract the odour of sweat.

My housemate arrives home, runs a glance over the items on display at my feet and picks up the single roll of toilet paper.

'You know, they do have toilet paper on the other side of the world,' she says. 'I've not been to New Zealand myself, but I'm told that it is so.'

2

Crossing Tongariro without a bus: The Tongariro Northern Circuit

I have chosen my first track on the carefully considered basis that it's the nearest Great Walk to Auckland, which is where my plane landed. The Tongariro Northern Circuit is also one of the most difficult Great Walks. It is a series of ascents and descents around the volcanic heartland of the North Island. I am assured that one of these ascents is painful even for the fittest tramper. In good weather, the horizon-filling views of volcanoes are supposed to take your mind off the pain. However, the weather here can change more quickly than I can yet pull on my waterproof trousers.

The second day of this four-day track is known as the Tongariro Crossing, which is labelled (and heavily marketed as) 'New Zealand's finest one-day walk'. In a country full of exceptional walks, this is not to be ignored – and people don't ignore it in their tens of thousands. Upwards of 65,000 people walk the Crossing each year and the majority walk it during the summer months, when crampons, ice axes and mountaineering experience are finally dispensable. On an average summer's day, more than 500 people troop along the track. Should I get into trouble on the most difficult and dangerous day of my tramp, at least I won't be alone.

Just before I set out, I sit in the Visitor Centre in Whakapapa Village watching an information video on volcanoes and the things they get up to (and yes, Kiwis do pronounce 'wh' as 'f' with some occasionally interesting consequences). The video is a small treat before a tiring and potentially quite painful four days of hard labour. I don't have to leave until nearly lunchtime, and watching educational TV is an excellent excuse to spend the morning sitting down. What I see, however, makes me think that I shouldn't get up again.

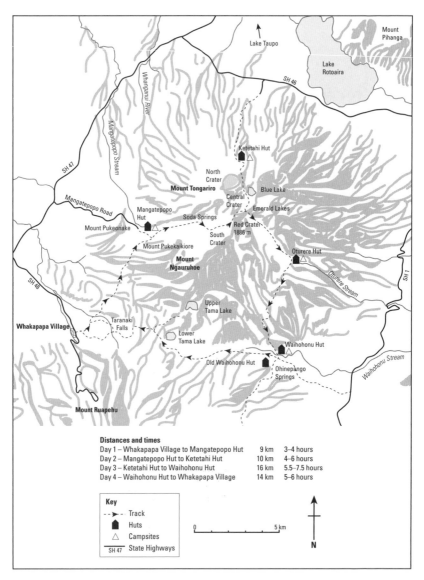

Distances and times
Day 1 – Whakapapa Village to Mangatepopo Hut   9 km   3–4 hours
Day 2 – Mangatepopo Hut to Ketetahi Hut   10 km   4–6 hours
Day 3 – Ketetahi Hut to Waihohonu Hut   16 km   5.5–7.5 hours
Day 4 – Waihohonu Hut to Whakapapa Village   14 km   5–6 hours

Key
- ➤ - Track
⬛ Huts
△ Campsites
SH 47 State Highways

0   5 km

N

The Tongariro Northern Circuit

These volcanoes are big and they are active. Footage from eruptions in 1995 and 1996 (the most recent of many) includes eyewitness accounts from skiers who were on the mountains at the time but who escaped without any injuries – other than the usual ones self-inflicted by skiers. I hear all about how quick and deadly lava flows can be and I pay particular attention to the ongoing attempts we tiny humans make to predict when eruptions will occur and to keep ourselves out of the way of freshly thrown-up rock. By the time the documentary credits fade, I have a new-found respect for the mountain underneath which I'm sitting and for the other mountains I'm about to walk up to and over. I also have a small twinge of excitement in the pit of my stomach at the mere prospect of the earth moving more violently than usual at some point over the next four days. I know it's unlikely that any one of these volcanoes will spit out anything interesting while I am scrambling my way round them, but a girl can dream.

No imminent eruptions are predicted, but I have nevertheless been warned that I could die if I set out on the track within the next forty-eight hours. The risk of being smothered by hot lava or choked by clouds of ash is low. However, the risk of dying from exposure or from being irretrievably blown off the higher sections of the track is apparently high.

For almost a week I have been seeking regular advice about the weather from the DOC outpost in Whakapapa Village. DOC stands for Department of Conservation, although the short form is so widely used that any one who's been in New Zealand for more than a couple of hours should be 'DOC'ing with ease.

They have been watching the progress of a particularly nasty front over the mountains, and I have been waiting. Until today, when, after three days of snow and gales, the front seems finally to have shuffled off and I really feel that, in the company of merely a heavy downpour of rain, it is time for me to set off. The extremely hardy-looking lady behind the counter disagrees.

'As you'll see from the board, we're forecasting severe gales and snow for tomorrow and the next day. You won't be able to make it across the saddle on either day – and the forecast isn't great for the day after that either.'

I stare pleadingly at the nice lady. It is March, and late summer in New Zealand. I glance at the forecast. More snow. More gales. I look back into her eyes. She knows that I want to set out anyway. She tries another tactic, 'Two days ago, two men went out onto the track and were separated in a blizzard.

They were experienced. They had all the right equipment. They were big men. Yet, they both spent a night alone on the mountain and had to be picked up by helicopter the following morning, suffering from exposure.'

'Oh.'

She doesn't have to say the rest. I know that, unlike the volcanoes all around us, I am small and mostly inactive. The day I stretched myself over the five foot mark on the measuring wall is still fresh in my mind. I am inexperienced. I am female. I am on the less acned side of thirty. I am on my own.

I distract her attention, 'How do you pronounce this?' I point to Mount Ngauruhoe on the parkmap.

'Yeah, it's a difficult one. It's *now-roo-hoi.*'

I immediately hear one of the other members of the DOC team pronounce it differently. Then I have an idea.

'There's a hut warden at Mangatepopo Hut, isn't there?'

'Yeah, there are still wardens at all the huts.'

'Well, how about I walk as far as Mangatepopo Hut today? That's only three or four hours away and it's before the alpine section of the track. Tomorrow the hut warden will radio in for the early morning weather forecast. If that forecast is bad, I promise I won't try to go up over the saddle.'

I leave the Visitor Centre in possession of a hut pass for the next four nights and a slightly manic grin. I don't know what's going to happen. All I know is that after five days of waiting I can finally see a volcano appearing on the horizon and I want to go and say hello.

Day one: Playing with fire

It is raining hard and I have no idea how far I'm going to get. I could be about to spend an afternoon walking with a heavy pack in the rain only to have to spend all of tomorrow trapped in a hut at the bottom of an active volcano. Worse still, I may have to wait out two days in the hut, driven mad by boredom and running so low on food that I end up having to walk back here again. Whatever happens, I have to live with the knowledge that at the start of my first tramp, I have already been tempted to break the first rule in the tramping book: never go against DOC advice.

To go tramping in New Zealand and ignore the advice of DOC is a foolish thing to do – more so, even, than letting someone secure a long, elasticated rope to your ankles *with a towel* and then obeying their instruction to jump into a void.

DOC is unlike any other government department I have ever experienced. Its influence on everyday life in New Zealand makes Defra (the UK's Department for Environment, Food and Rural Affairs) look like it chose the wrong gene pool. Defra has more than 13,000 employees, making DOC's 1,500 permanent force seem small. However, that's one Defra employee for roughly every 4,400 people in the UK, but one DOC employee for every 2,700 people in New Zealand – dropping to 2,000 when you take into the account the additional 500 or so foot soldiers that DOC employs each year on a temporary or seasonal basis.

The reach of DOC goes beyond the statistics. DOC staff are stationed around the country in green and yellow huts and offices. Many of these outposts are key focal points in New Zealand's towns, particularly those where the town centre comprises a high street with a supermarket, a few essential shops (which always include at least one outdoors activity shop) and a DOC office. DOC offices often double up as the local visitor centre, which means that most tourists in New Zealand meet many members of the green and yellow army. The centre of Whakapapa Village, where I currently stand, is an extreme example of this: here, the 'village' centre comprises one small store that can physically hold no more than about seven shoppers, and the DOC Visitor Centre, which could accommodate a small supermarket.

Almost without exception DOC staff are passionate about the natural environment. In this they reflect the priorities of a good proportion of the general population – the farmers, the trampers, hunters, fishermen, those who believe in the important spiritual connection between human beings and the rest of the natural world, and those who simply appreciate the mountainous views from their back doors.

The DOC staff I have met so far look hardy, fit and made for the Great Outdoors. They are the distilled essence of Kiwi. Their uniforms comprise practical fleeces, sweaters, shirts, trousers and shorts in browns and greens, with neat DOC logos on their chests. Every fibre of their beings was made to be climbing mountains and fording rivers.

DOC strives to preserve Mother Nature's beauty indefinitely. DOC staff also do their utmost to stop people dying in her sometimes merciless grip. In 2002 a television documentary series in New Zealand followed the work of thirteen conservation officers as they went about the daily business of saving endangered species, fighting fires, conducting research, killing pests, monitoring avalanches, maintaining tracks and many, many more tasks – including search and rescue operations for those less skilled in handling themselves in the bush. I don't know many countries where conservation officers are TV heroes.

Thus, when a number of DOC officers tell me not to attempt the high altitude section of the Tongariro Northern Circuit for yet another couple of days, I pay attention.

Ten minutes down the track, the sun appears and there's just me and my pack in the whole world. My pack isn't as light as it could be because I've decided that I should avoid freeze-dried specialist outdoors food and instead carry the produce of a small market garden.

Raw vegetables have a hold over me, established two years ago when I contracted a 'glandular-fever-like illness' that caused several doctors to stare worryingly at blood test results and keep telling me to stay away from work. They couldn't offer a cure (they could barely offer a diagnosis), but they diligently performed blood tests until I began to think that my main problem might be loss of blood. With nothing better to do between trips to the blood bank, I tried to eat myself better. My eventual recovery probably had nothing to do with raw carrots, but by then I was addicted. Nowadays the memory of illness tells me that I'm likely to find tramping tiring, but it doesn't deter me from going. Instead it makes me want to take several pounds of fresh vegetables along for the ride.

To my shame, the other heavy load I bear is a broken saucepan, 'borrowed' from the kitchen in the hostel where I've been staying. A chance conversation with a fellow traveller in Whakapapa Village had revealed my mistaken interpretation of the DOC guidelines for trampers on the Tongariro Northern Circuit. 'Utensils' apparently encompasses things in which food can be cooked – not just, as I had thought, things with which food is eaten once cooked. Suddenly discovering this whilst staying in a retail vacuum posed something of a problem. The small store in Whakapapa Village sells only basic food at imaginative prices. Anything else must be sourced many miles and over an hour's drive away – and it seemed rather pathetic to have to leave again just after I'd arrived. So I tried to charm the reception staff at the hostel into letting me borrow a saucepan. When this failed, I rooted around the back of the hostel cupboards, found a small saucepan with a handle missing (presumed melted) and asked my conscience to look the other way while I stashed it in my pack.

Over the first few kilometres and under fresh sun, I have soon forgotten that I am carrying much weight at all. I am so excited that I turn off on the first side trip I see, along a springy path by a stream, towards Taranaki Falls. It would be much easier to see these falls from the final section of the track, but I am feeling so keen that I bound along the additional hour's walk. Besides which, I don't know if I will make it to the later section of the track three days from now.

The sun has woken a couple of day trippers and one other lady, who displays the full rigging of backpack and waterproofs. I greet them all with smiles and friendly comments, which perplex the day trippers. They are clearly not Kiwis, who are so far proving to be as friendly and welcoming as their reputation foretells – except when they're trying to discourage you from walking up mountains. We stare up at the water hurtling off the edge of the cliff above us. I feel the first stirrings of relaxation.

Back on the proper track, I get into a rhythm on the gentle ups and downs of volcanic furrows. I trip along – sometimes quite literally – a narrow path over tussock, rock and heather. Heather was introduced here by early twentieth-century Brits trying to recreate highland hunting scenes for their amusement and acclimatisation. The heather did what came naturally to it, and local plant species promptly began to expire. Years later people noticed that this wasn't helpful to the local ecosystem and have been trying to eradicate the heather ever since. Every time I spot a clump amongst the tussock my genes feel the dull thud of the imperialist guilt hangover.

Water, wind and feet erode the track, the ridges it crosses and the plants gripping onto this world of moving rock. Apparently, at higher altitudes in this alpine scrub the plants are so delicate that a single footprint can last one hundred years. I have no desire to create fresh guilt, so I try to stick precisely to the path. This is not easy. The terrain is so fragile that erosion has converted the path into a deep, winding canyon in many places, up to four feet deep, but only about one foot wide. Were I to follow this path, either my hips or my pack would become wedged in the side of the crevasse. Self-rescue would only be possible through starvation, abandonment of my belongings or by digging myself out. I don't even want to think about having to be rescued from this position by someone else. So I do what many other pairs of feet before me have done: I trample on the tussock above and to the side of the official track. Trampling does not feel as good as tramping.

The panorama of vents on view from the top of each furrow provides an outstanding distraction from heather guilt, attempts to avoid being wedged into the canyon path and the endless ups and downs of this terrain. The most mesmerising sight, forward right, is Mount Ngauruhoe. When I stop to stare at this mountain, I can't help but bow my head towards it. I don't even feel daft for doing so.

Mount Ngauruhoe's name is almost as difficult to explain as it is to pronounce. The most often cited explanation is of a revered Maori, Ngatoro-i-rangi, who climbed the mountain but fell victim to the extreme cold at the summit. Close to death, he prayed to his sisters to save him and they sent fire-demons to his rescue. The fire-demons travelled along the line of greatest thermal activity in New Zealand (from White Island through the centre of the North Island) and burst out from the mountain top. Ngatoro was thus saved from freezing to death – and presumably also spared from being blown to pieces, although most versions of this legend make no reference to this. In gratitude, he slew the female slave who had accompanied him and cast her body into the crater (now that's gratitude for you). Her name was Auruhoe and the mountain was named after her. However, another version relates that the slave was called Auruhoe because this was the local Maori name for the mountain. This appears to leaves us back where we started.

Two different explanations come from direct translations of the component parts of the name. Unfortunately, the only point on which the translations agree is that 'nga' means 'the'. One translation says that Ngauruhoe means 'the hair of Hoe' – Hoe being Ngatoro's grandson, and his hair representing the plumes of smoke that escape from the mountain. Another translation says that Ngauruhoe means 'the act of tossing hot stones out of an earth oven', which links Maori cooking techniques with eruptions of rock from the volcano. Much as I love the image of little wild-haired Hoe, my money is on the hot stones.

Whatever the origins of its title, it is impossible not to stare and stare at the vent. It is a perfect cone and exactly what I would have drawn for a volcano when I was ten years old (although it is not currently belching forth the clouds of orange and purple squiggles that I would have enthusiastically included). Its width is vast, but the vertical lines in the solidified lava also make it seem imposingly tall.

Yet Mount Ngauruhoe is the underdog in this volcanic playground. It is a young slip of a volcano; its neighbours – Mounts Tongariro, Ruapehu, Pukekaikiore, Pukeonake and several others – are older, bigger, more complex, or all of the above. This only makes it more appealing to me. Of course, it's also hard to avoid the landscape marketing phenomenon of *The Lord of the Rings* films. I am, after all, standing transfixed by none other than Mount Doom.

I keep having to flick glances its way as I walk. Do I expect to see the vast armies of Sauron marching forth at any time? Do I expect it to blow up in a cloud of special effects and not be there any more? Actually, yes – I am concerned that it will disappear: the cloud coming in with that next front could steal it from me at any point and potentially for the next four days. Every look could be my last.

Back behind the now invisible Whakapapa Village, Ruapehu slowly pushes the remaining clouds off its peaks. If Ngauruhoe is the perfect barnacle shape, then Ruapehu is a mass of barnacles, limpets and corals that would grace the belly of the oldest whale. There is no comparing the size: Ruapehu is immense and is difficult to comprehend in one look, even as it appears slowly from underneath its duvet of cloud. It is also behind me, which means that I keep stopping to look behind as well as in front. I can't help it. I am gloriously alone in a sweeping volcanic landscape and all the mountains are coming out to play.

After three hours I still love the views, but I can't wait to see Mangatepopo Hut in one of them. I wince at the freshly filling blisters on both feet. I thought I'd worn my boots in, but I clearly have much to learn about the art of lace tying. Tight for down; looser for up. Goodness knows what for endless ups and downs over scores of dry stream beds.

The hut finally pops out from behind a piece of tussock. I don't expect there will be any one in tonight other than the hut warden and me, but some company will be good, particularly if this is to be home for the next day or two.

As I approach the door, I see belongings strewn everywhere. Bags and boots cover the wooden porch and excited children swarm out from their hiding place behind the hut. I add my boots to the collection and go inside, where every surface is coated with belongings and where a German tramper sits in a corner, fuming. Five very tall men follow me into the hut.

'Hey, how are you? Where are you from?'

'Erm … England.'

'Oh great! Would you mind talking to the kids about the UK? Just ten minutes or so – and maybe to answer some questions.'

'Yes, OK. Although could I just grab a few minutes to sit down first?'

'Sure. Oh – and sorry there aren't any beds left. There's thirty-five of us.'

Thirty-five. Mostly children, ages ten to thirteen. DOC huts operate on a first come, first served basis and officially this hut can accommodate twenty-two people. The hut warden is nowhere to be seen.

The evening blurs in a series of practicalities. Before we can all sit down to Tales from the Land of Jonny Wilkinson and Harry Potter, the hut warden arrives and is a little startled. She is twenty-three-years old, arrived in New Zealand (from her native Canada) a week ago and has been in the job for three days. She immediately instils order in the bedding scrum and insists that the trampers get bunks. She stands up to the six-feet-plus male parents, who crowd round her talking about the first come, first served rule and insisting that they gave someone from DOC advanced notice. She is inexperienced, foreign, short, blonde, petite and absolutely in charge.

I keep my head down and chat to the lone female parent, who has the best washing-up view in the world: from the sink we watch the sun set over Mount Taranaki, another of New Zealand's volcanoes and a whitened pimple some 140 kilometres away on the west coast of the North Island. New Zealand was the first sovereign state in the world to give women the vote, so I trust that tomorrow morning one of the male parents will be doing the washing-up. Tonight, there's already enough controversy in the hut, so I make no comment. From the other side of the hut, the deep, pink light of the sun flushes the valley along which I hope to walk tomorrow and makes me stare all over again at the remarkable Ngauruhoe.

One of the evening duties is signing the intentions book. The purpose of these books, which are in every DOC hut, is to provide basic information to assist anyone who is following on behind looking for your body. In addition to the basic practical information required (name, number in party, planned route and destination, date due out etc.) the two final fields for entry are 'Main Activity on This Trip' and 'Comments'. Previous signatories have scribbled a mixture of amusing, earnest and inspired remarks. Some of the entries have even avoided mentioning Mordor. Nevertheless, Frodo and Sam somehow arrive here afresh every day. If Gandalf had read this book to find out how their quest was progressing, he would have thought they were caught in an evil time warp.

My Comment comes easily ('The 30 children were a surprise!'), but I have to wonder about my Main Activity. What am I doing here, exactly? Trying to get as far away from mobile phone reception as I can? Trying to get fit again after two years feeling tired? Fulfilling a life-long ambition to become a hobbit? Or just the usual: trying to work out what to do next, now that I'm in my thirties, man-less and, for all that I care about it, career-less? No. This is too dull and too long to write in the space provided. In the end I write what I ought to be doing: 'stopping thinking'.

Torches and candles provide the only light after sunset. Leaving the table, I take my plate to the sink but don't see the bench that has been moved since I sat down. I land heavily on my knees on the hard wooden floor, much to the amusement of the children. Deeply embarrassed, I jump up light-heartedly and move quickly to the sink, pretending that my knees aren't exploding in pain. No one could mistake me for an experienced tramper.

In the night the storms start. Before sleep has taken hold, a deafening crack signals the near loss of the hut roof and the wind whips on and on into the night, battering up loud protests from every surface. There's nothing we can do but lie in our sleeping bags waiting for it to be over (please, God, let it be over): if anyone were to venture outside, they would be swept down the valley in an instant.

Fifteen boys in the bottom bunks whisper furiously in accompaniment to the wind, toughing it out with bravado and small jokes. Just before dawn

I drift into a drowsy, noise-assisted half-sleep. I dream of crawling over mountain tops on my belly while the wind chases after my soul.

Day two: *The great migration*

'WILL you PLEASE SHUT UP!' hisses the German tramper in a whisper that is a yell. Her complaint is aimed at the boys, but it is she who wakes me. As sunlight floods the bunkroom it takes several minutes for me to register its meaning: there is sunlight; the storm has gone. While the children run around as if nothing ever happened, the adults stand at the hut door and gaze out in amazement at the valley: it is still there and it feels for all the world as if it could be a calm, sunny day.

The hut warden's quarters have also survived the night and the warden confirms that I can attempt the saddle. The weather should hold long enough for it to be safe. I'm allowed to go into the mountains.

I have much to learn before I master the tramper's art of the dawn getaway. My backpack is so tightly filled that I can't close the top unless everything goes into exactly the right place and in exactly the same order as it came out, only in reverse. I spent the 1980s wrestling Rubik's cube with about the same success. To make matters worse, I have diligently packed everything into waterproof bags. For an item to make it successfully into the pack, it must be united with its bag-mates, twisted into the bag, squeezed free from air and slotted into the appropriate place. I have to keep reopening plastic bags to remind myself what's inside.

It's past 8.00 am by the time I finally walk out of earshot of the classroom – only to reach the main path and discover that I'm joining a state highway. The Tongariro Crossing transport companies have seen the sudden shift in the weather and have laid on all the buses to the Crossing. Today is the first day in at least three when the official transport has been running. I can expect something very different from the solitude of yesterday.

The fresh faces and tiny daysacks of the day trippers prove that I spent all of yesterday afternoon getting to a hut that is only a thirty-minute walk away from a car park. Maybe they have had the better idea: after four hours' walking and a dramatic, sleep-deprived night, I have barely even started the track. On the bright side, however, most of the buses arrive before 7.30 am, so I am joining the stragglers. If I maintain a reasonably slow pace (tough, but I think I can manage it), I should be able to enjoy the relative peace and quiet of the rearguard in the march.

The sun rises from behind the Mangatepopo saddle, which is the day's main grunt. We are chasing the shade along the centre of the valley and can already sense the wave of heat that will strike when the sun sweeps over the saddle. Ngauruhoe is looking entrancing. The strips of snow in its vertical folds are glinting their last in the sun and the colours of the rock underneath are beginning to show through, with streaks of red in between grey scree.

As I walk I try to resolve a cultural dilemma between Maori and Pakeha traditions – Pakeha being the Maori term for European settlers. My Pakeha past says 'see mountain, must climb it' and so I'm rather tempted to take the side route that I'll find later on today, to the top of Mount Ngauruhoe. It isn't strictly a path – just a route for sliding and scrambling over loose scree, which even from here looks as if a badly timed sneeze could set off a huge slip. Plus, climbers are advised not to go over into the lip of the volcano because of the noxious gases emitted, even on an average, inactive day. The traditional Maori approach, however, is to respect mountains by not trampling all over them. Ngatoro-i-rangi had priest-like status – and look what happened even to him. Local Maori strove to avoid even their gaze trespassing on these mountains, never mind their feet. Given the dominance of the mountains on the skyline of this part of the North Island, managing not to look at them at all would be a remarkable achievement. The regular cloud cover must have helped no end.

Near the foot of Mount Ngauruhoe is a short side track to Soda Springs – an indulgent break after merely an hour, but a good excuse to evade some extremely chatty day trippers. These springs seem to have been misnamed. As far as I remember from my admittedly unsuccessful study of chemistry, soda is used to make soap. Sulphur, on the other hand, is used to make foul smells and I mutter that someone might like to think of changing the name of these springs, before beating a hasty retreat back to the main track.

This is where the real test begins, as I begin the infamous climb up my now favourite mountain. Not that I can see it properly any more. All I can see as I look up are false summits in a bumpy wall of rock and soil. I try to plot the shortest, least painful routes from me to the next visual edge. Curse my heavy pack next to all these light daysacks; curse all those heavy carrots and apples I felt I couldn't do without.

Different speed lanes open as hundreds of people scramble up the enormous rockery. It seems that people behave in much the same way on a mountain as they do everywhere else. There's a fair amount of overtaking, undertaking and cutting up going on. The competitive sorts are straining along in focused silence (and I would normally number myself amongst the competitive sorts, but I have a tendency to pretend I'm not in a competition at all when I'm so hopelessly off the pace). Unbelievably, some people are even checking out members of the opposite sex. Many are succeeding in looking cool as they stand and swig from water bottles, hand on hips, tanned limbs on display. I am not one of them.

There's some awkwardness about the greetings protocol. Should you say hello to everyone who passes through your sweat zone? At what point must you think of some polite conversation if you're climbing next to someone at roughly the same pace? Is it just terribly British me who's using up energy worrying about these social dilemmas?

A decent camaraderie builds up between those of us who are now regularly being overtaken. It's not easy to step aside to let someone pass, especially when on all fours, but I'm doing my best and I'm probably doubling my distance as a result. Fortunately, the views behind are spectacular, so regular stops to stand up straight and stare behind seem perfectly excusable. Mangatepopo Hut is now a tiny dot at the far end of the valley.

To my horror, a large number of much tinier dots is now starting to tackle the first section of the climb. The school party has changed its plans (they were only going to walk to Soda Springs and back) and my little friends are following me at an alarmingly quick pace. I marvel at the hardiness of the natives. Thirty young children and their guardians think nothing of scrambling several hundred metres up a mountain for a morning lesson. So this is how they breed Kiwis.

The tough part of the climb should last about forty-five minutes, but when I finally totter over the last little summit, I have been straining uphill for over seventy-five minutes and I can't understand how there are still people streaming up to the saddle behind me when, surely, everyone in New Zealand has overtaken me this morning. I'm not sure whether to be pleased that the worst of the day's climbs is over, or worried that I'm only officially one hour and forty-five minutes into a day's tramping that could take six hours or more.

Not that this matters next to the views all around. As I stand on the side of Mount Ngauruhoe, its barnacle top is the entire 180 degree view facing south. Back to the west the Mangatepopo valley is shimmering in the heat and Mount Taranaki – now about 143 kilometres away – is a white pimple smudged behind ozone. To the north is one side of Mount Tongariro, the summit of which is yet another ethically contentious side trip further along the track. Finally, to the east is the next part of the Crossing, along the flat bed of the South Crater. It is now strikingly obvious that I need not have worried about the cultural etiquette of climbing to the summit of Mount Ngauruhoe. I am clearly not up to the job, unless I want to risk having to pass the remaining craters, lakes and peaks of the day in darkness.

Decision made, I wander to the rim of the South Crater just as the children come running up behind me, fresh as daisies, and start a snowball fight. By the time I've answered yet more of their questions, the flow of people up and over the saddle has dried up in the heat. The children turn to go back down the way they came and any one else who's still trying to come up will have to navigate past this waterfall of small limbs.

If you read more than one collection of Maori history and legends, you soon discover that there is rarely just one version of events. This is partly because Maori traditionally retell their histories and legends orally and within their own tribes. The need to write everything down in one received version is the urge of the Pakeha. In the retellings down the generations, certain bits may be omitted, embellished or deliberately adapted to convey whatever message is important to the teller in his time (what history isn't?). Add to this the variation made possible through translations into English and you can merrily abandon any attempt to find 'the truth'. The only alternative seems to be to go with whichever version you like the best. Henceforth, therefore, I shall be thinking of Ngauruhoe as the wild hair of little Hoe.

However, one important set of events on which authors seem agreed is how Tongariro National Park came into existence. The Park today encompasses some 79,598 hectares of land, but its core is the original gift of 2,630 hectares by the impressively named and titled Te Heuheu Tukino IV (Horonuku), paramount chief of Ngati Tuwharetoa. (This is perhaps good enough reason in itself not to have to write things down a lot.)

The gift was made on 23 September 1887, after many years of rival tribes and Europeans claiming and disputing rights of ownership over the land. Maori had no concept of permanent, private ownership of land, but had a very firm concept of the tapu (sacredness) of Mounts Tongariro, Ngauruhoe and Ruapehu. Faced with seeing the mountains sold off piecemeal to the highest Pakeha bidder and thereby also seeing his tribe lose its honour, Te Heuheu Tukino IV gifted the whole area to the Crown and to the people of New Zealand. The scheme seems to have worked at the time and the area became New Zealand's first National Park in 1894. It's anyone's guess, though, as to what Te Heuheu Tukino IV would make of today's day trippers, trampers and skiers.

I gaze out onto South Crater and ponder the unimaginative names given by Pakeha to the landscape. Today I shall pass through or round the South Crater, the Central Crater, the North Crater and the rebelliously titled Red Crater, which presumably only escaped being called East Crater by the teeth of its rim. Oh, and next to the North Crater, I shall find the Blue Lake, presumably so named because water quite often looks blue. I venture to suggest that Pakeha naming conventions leave a little to be desired.

Maori names are far more interesting. Pukekaikiore means 'the hill to eat rats', which apparently refers to the defeat of one tribe by another (the members of the defeated tribe being the 'rats'). Ruapehu means a reverberating sound like that beaten on a gong to alert warriors that a village is about to be attacked, while Tongariro means 'to be carried away by a south wind', which is a fair description of what happens to hundreds of visitors here every summer.

At the entrance to the South Crater I find the German tramper at the end of a break. I try to explain how dull I think the name is compared with the vast, colourful crater before us. She looks at me strangely, but then seems to understand my point and offers an alternative.

'Maybe it could be called Egg Crater. It is an oval shape and the earth is browny yellow, like an egg.'

She contemplates her own suggestion and then adds, 'Although there would need to be a very big bird to lay an egg like this.'

She's not wrong: it looks like miles from one end of the crater to the other.

'How about Tequila Sunrise Crater?' I suggest. 'It could be the top of an enormous glass. The snow and ice streaking down into the crater from the walls could be frosting around the rim of the glass. The poles that mark the track are tiny cocktail sticks. The orangey-yellow earth is the drink. A cocktail fit for the gods.'

She motors off unimpressed. I plod onwards after waiting for a few more stragglers to pass me by. I am finally alone again in this captivating place. Not only this, but the South Crater is as gloriously flat as the previous section was steep, so I can now gape continuously at the 360-degree views as I walk, without falling over. Reaching the far side, it's time to start going up again. Backward glances now reveal a slight dip in the lip of Mount Ngauruhoe on this side, where the snow has almost entirely melted to reveal deep red rock. It is like looking quite literally at the heart of the mountain. Stopping to turn and look behind me now has nothing to do with letting my pounding heart slow; if anything, my heart quickens when I pause to look back.

Mount Ngauruhoe routinely emits little puffs of ash and gas, but hasn't erupted since 1975. Up until then it had erupted about every nine years, which makes you wonder – particularly when you're standing right beside it – whether it's overdue for something explosive.

It's difficult to know what's going on in this enormous subterranean hotpot. In the wider thermal zone there are geysers and hot springs whose activity has been significantly altered by the presence of geothermal power stations. Ngauruhoe might not have to erupt to release some of its frustrations: the 1995 eruption of Mount Ruapehu blew off quite a bit of steam just a few miles away. When you have absolutely no idea what's going on beneath your feet, however, some colourful thoughts can enter your head.

The ascent out of South Crater requires some hasty grabbing onto nearby rocks. The snow underfoot has iced over during the night – and a strong, bitter wind is further encouraging me to slip backwards. After a few precariously balanced adjustments, I'm muffled in all the layers shed earlier in the day plus everything else I've got for keeping ears and fingers warm. I have to move fast to keep my blood circulating and I have to move slowly to keep my blood from slipping, along with the rest of me, back to the bottom of the crater.

The wind gains force as I gain height. For added challenge, the track now also narrows and becomes still steeper, until I feel like I am stamping to get some traction up a slide for very tall children. This would be a time when I wouldn't mind other people around me. Maddeningly, the hordes have now disappeared (were they a hallucination or have they been swept away?). Scanning the horizon, I gain some comfort when I spot two other souls a little way ahead. After watching their progress for a few seconds, however, it seems more likely that I'll have to rescue them than the other way round.

Somehow (and very slowly) I haul myself up to the top of the ridge. This is what those weather warnings were about. I am standing on a narrow ridge at 1,886 metres with a gale force wind whipping down the wing. I am, of course, not actually standing at all. Neither is the wind a constant strength, but a series of tackles, the timing and force of which are too unpredictable for me to dare evolving into bipedal form. Early Maori tradition dictated that no normal man should enter this mountainous region because the mountain spirits would destroy him. I'm beginning to see the sense in that.

In a bizarre echo of last night's dream, I crawl over the very top of the ridge on my stomach. Thank goodness for all those heavy carrots and apples in my backpack weighing me down; thank goodness I'm not just carrying a daysack. And then I get a glimpse of the deep gash in the earth into which the wind is trying to sweep me – and it is the most beautiful sight I think I've ever seen.

To the right of this dangerously exposed ridge, the slit in the earth falls away to a depth far below the line of visibility, even after I crawl to the edge of the gash on my belly, trying simultaneously to flatten myself against the ground and yet peer up and over into the void. The earth here has been ripped apart and the rock on the far side of the gash is deep, glowing, bloody red. There are veins of brown and dark grey, like on a good slab of raw meat (no supermarket cut). The side of the slit has wavy contours to show that this was no straight knife wound, but a great tear. I lie there for a few minutes just trying to take in something for which my guidebook has left me utterly unprepared.

I wriggle back onto the path as a bearded man staggers over the ridge. We shout greetings and he takes a photo for me. Neither of us is able to stand up for the occasion and I can barely open my eyes against the gale of grit, but we manage one quick shutter release before he totters off down the other side and I attempt to apply a fresh layer of suncream. This is a facial scrub of which the most sadistic Turkish bath scrubbers would be proud. Suncream mingles with sand and grit in my eyes, ears, nose and mouth. You can't get much closer to a mountain than eating it.

Descending is utterly different. Strong sunlight has melted all snow and ice on this side, leaving a bed of deep, soft grey sand and scree underfoot. Those still confident in their thigh muscles bounce down this steep strip. Those who appreciate the size of the drops on both sides proceed with more care. One lady I see descends very, very slowly on her bottom. A few cocky teenagers scramble over the ridge and then foot-ski down, filling the boots of anyone slower than them with a thick spray of grey sand.

Halfway through the descent I sit down and burrow my heels into the loose scree in front of me to stop myself slipping forwards and down. Time for some lunch and for some fresh gaping – this time on another world of craters and lakes. I'm happy to exchange greetings with passing walkers, but it feels good not to have to talk any more than this. It feels good to sit on my own, alone and small in this strange world. To know that I only have to get up when I want to; that I can sit here for as long as I like.

By my feet, but a couple of hundred metres below, lie the Emerald Lakes. Each of these ponds is a different size and shape and has its own shade of blue. The name is more imaginative than some, but Sapphire Lakes might be more accurate.

Past these lakes lies another vast bowl of a crater. This one has a raised black stain across one side of it, where lava from one of the many eruptions ended its run. There's another little climb out of this crater, but this climb is easy. I'm now angling my pack expertly into the wind, parrying and feinting like I know what I'm doing. Still like a small child in a big playground, I can't stop twirling round to catch the sensational views on offer from every single degree of the 360. It makes for a walking style odder than that of hip-gyrating Olympic walkers.

I twirl along the rim separating the Central Crater and the vast Blue Lake, which looks so calm in all the postcards, but it could be surfed in this wind. I'm nearly at the end of the longest, hardest day of the tramp. There are another two full days yet to come and there's still the small matter of that weather front – but I'm beginning to feel that I might make it all the way.

Another one-and-a-half hours of walking finally brings Ketetahi Hut within flopping distance. Its veranda marks the end of day two of the Tongariro Northern Circuit but there is still a steady stream of people soldiering on along the track. For the day tripper, it's still about another two hours' walk from here to the nearest car park.

I've been to the Ketetahi car park at pick-up time and it's not a pretty sight. Hundreds of people slump in a state of shock and exhaustion, wondering how the New Zealand tourist industry can describe the Tongariro Crossing as a one-day walk. They've just had the hardest day of their trip to New Zealand and are deeply glad to be at the finish. A sturdy minority, who bounded over the track, refuse to admit to being tired. However, by pick-up time, they have been waiting in a car park for hours and they are cold and bored. Ask any of these people it if was worth it, though, and they look up with shining eyes and sigh an emphatic 'Yes'.

As I start to tend to blisters on the hut veranda, it's like sitting on the Champs Elysées – by which I really only mean that it's easy to believe that if you sit here long enough, then everyone you know will eventually pass by. All other aspects – the haute couture, the urban sophistication, the *parfum de* body, the general tending to blisters – make it easy to tell the two apart. It's as if the local volcanoes have decided to give noxious gases and lava a miss this year and are leaking people instead. People are the new hot rock.

Three of those who now arrive are the lean, tall guys I saw on the track. I noticed them because when I stepped to one side of a narrow piece of track to let them pass they said nothing at all. There was no 'thank you' or acknowledgement, despite the steep drop I'd just braved for them. They didn't even look at me. Then, about ten minutes later, they had stopped to attend to something and it was my turn to pass, but they made no attempt to return the favour and I chose to grate myself on the rock wall at the side of the path rather than confront them.

As they sit on my veranda I curiously listen in to their conversation to see if I can work out where they're from. I can't – this is a language I've never heard before. So I ask them. After they have had some sport with this strange woman, making me try to guess their origins (and I am very polite as I do so, despite a strong urge not to be) they concede an answer: they are Israeli.

I have never met any Israelis before, not that these ones have been a wonderful advertisement for their homeland so far. Having engaged them in conversation, however, they are open and humorous and soon have me attempting to pronounce the one sound that they say exists only in Israeli and Dutch. From their renditions, it sounds like the noise you might make if you had something stuck at the back of your nose and wanted to snort-suck it into your mouth. Presumably other cultures managed to develop the art of nose-blowing as a working alternative to this nasal skill, but it proves remarkably fun to 'cjjcjhhh' with them all over the veranda.

In the general scrum of bodies I make sure I spread my possessions over a free bunk and try to assess the size of tonight's party. I'm in luck. Nine Kiwi students and five Australians are my only hut-mates in a now spacious twenty-two-bunk hut.

'G'day. Are you all on your own?' an Aussie asks.

'Yes. Good job too, considering how slow I am. Wouldn't want to hold anyone up.'

'Ah – we send Adam on ahead with most of the gear.' He indicates the one in their party who is the youngest by about twenty years. 'As you can see, the rest of us fall into the "older and bolder" category.'

'Are you walking the Northern Circuit? Only, I don't think I've seen you all day.'

'Yeah we are – but we're doing it backwards. DOC told us that there's a couple o' parties o' school kids roaming around some o' the huts. Said that if we went anticlockwise we'd miss 'em.' He sees my face and laughs. 'I take it you didn't!'

The Kiwis join in. 'Hey, how are you? Are you on your own?'

My pack is noticeably smaller than everyone else's, even though nine of them are only staying out on the track for one night. Rather than worrying about what vital equipment I may have omitted to bring, I can't help but feel a little bit pleased with myself for packing so efficiently. As I unpack, however, I realise that there was one thing that wasn't weighing me down on today's climb after all. I have left the stolen saucepan at Mangatepopo Hut.

Day three: Down the dragon's tail

The dawn views from Ketetahi Hut veranda are even more impressive than the sunsets. Lakes tend to pull a layer of mist and cloud over themselves at night and this hut stands high above two large ones: Rotoaira in the foreground and the much vaster Lake Taupo on the horizon. 'Roto' means 'lake' in Maori and Rotoaira could indeed be the Lake of Air, with its thick fluffy cloud blanket hiding its waters. Lake Taupo doesn't have a 'roto' in its name, no doubt because it's not a lake, but another volcano.

The first hour of today's route retraces the tussock-tickled sides of Mount Tongariro back to the Blue Lake. What comes down must apparently go up again, but this time I have the entire track to myself. The Aussies left an hour before me (I must work on this morning thing) and it will be a few more hours yet before the tourist army marches over the lip of the Red Crater and into view.

In a one finger salute to meteorologists everywhere, the sun is rising into a cloudless sky for the second day in a row and there isn't so much as a sniff of wind, so I don't have to worry about the safety of the Aussie pensioners making their way up and over the exposed lip of the Red Crater. From the ridge between the Blue Lake and the Central Crater it is possible to see its raised gash, with Mount Ngauruhoe behind it and Mount Ruapehu behind that, all in a line. It's an impressive front row, though none of them looks to be spoiling for a fight this morning. If anything were to be belched out today, it feels as if I might be the only person in the world to witness it.

Just before the Emerald Lakes an urban signpost rises incongruously from the ground to mark the junction between one dusty track and another. Both tracks are indistinguishable from the dusty sand and rock of the crater floor through which they pass. The signpost announces that Waihohonu Hut is a mere four-and-a-half hours away.

Here begins a grand descent to the desert floor. The track doesn't climb this high again, so I indulge in half an hour of just sitting quietly amongst this elevated beauty. Keeping still, it is possible to hear the multitude of tiny crinkles, splinterings and shufflings of last night's frost and ice being charmed by the morning sun. The lake in front of me looks utterly tranquil, but is draining away at incredible speed as a roaring waterfall that I will see from the next section of the track. Beyond the lake are unobstructed views of the desert-like floor of the wide valley below, across which the track travels for most of the rest of the day. The flat valley floor is littered with rocks that look, from up here, like tiny cubes of bacon on a predominantly cheesy pizza. In the ozone haze it is difficult to see where the valley ends and I realise that this day's long haul is only just beginning.

The Whanganui Maori call these central volcanoes of the North Island the Mountain Clan. They are personified in legends and are the ancestors of the tribe. They are, however, not all well behaved. An oft-repeated legend tells that Mount Taranaki fell in love with Mount Pihanga, who was promised to Mount Tongariro. (Versions differ as to whether Tongariro and Pihanga were already married or not, whether Pihanga returned Taranaki's affections and, if so, whether they consummated their attraction. I get distracted by thoughts of what two large volcanoes consummating might look like. However, the point on which to focus is that there was a love triangle involving at least two hot-headed mountains.)

Tongariro and Taranaki fought a great battle, which Taranaki lost. Distraught, Taranaki fled south-west, carving out the path of the Whanganui River – the route covered so quickly by those cattle in the February floods. When Taranaki reached the sea he was guided north-west to his current resting place, on the western flank of the North Island. Maori legend maintains that one day Taranaki will return to the Mountain Clan.

There is scientific evidence that may support this idea. In the Taranaki region the centre of volcanic activity has been slowly moving in a south-easterly direction. This is the reason, for example, why Mount Taranaki has a parasitic cone (Fantham's Peak) on its south-eastern flank. The movement is, however, *extremely* slow: Fantham's Peak may be no younger than 20,000 years. Which means that it vastly pre-dates the arrival of Maori in New Zealand. Is the legend a lucky guess? Or did human beings spend a long time developing a scientific method of study that has simply confirmed what local tribes knew anyway?

The Whanganui Maori are strongly connected to their Mountain Clan because these mountains provide the headwaters for the Whanganui River, which has immense spiritual and practical significance to the tribes and sub-tribes who live along its length. The river is their life force and is also at the heart of one of the biggest ongoing disputes between Maori tribes and the Crown. If all goes according to plan, I shall be discovering the source of the dispute for myself when I'm canoeing down the Whanganui River, and doing all I can to encourage this life force to like me.

But I mustn't canoe before I can walk. And I don't want to upset the Mountain Clan. I've seen footage of what happens when they're provoked. Up close, I don't want to see them angry. Or, for that matter, consummating.

Walking down to the desert floor feels like picking my way very carefully down the haunches of an outsized dragon. The shape of this enormous fold of rock is accurate down to the final curl of the tail. The rocks and stones on the surface look like weathered scars on the pitted hide. If I needed anything else to remind me just how small and insignificant I am on Earth, then slip-stumbling down this dragon's tail is it.

Once on the valley floor, a new game begins. Its working title is 'The World's Slowest Slalom' and it involves making your way to a slim wooden pole, passing to one side of it, finding the quickest route to the next pole, and so on. At walking speed you really wouldn't think this difficult, but the poles are spaced such that I keep losing concentration between them. I find myself regularly looking round and realising that I've wandered off at an unhelpful tangent to the line between the nearest two poles. Sometimes I have to stop and spend a couple of minutes trying to spot where the next pole is, even though they're no more than about forty metres apart.

Only the poles mark the track here. On the ground are loose stones, coverings of delicate lichens busily clinging on to life, and hardly any footprints. There are also great monoliths of rock rearing up from nowhere, presumably having been spat forcibly from a volcano at some point over the last few thousand years. It looks as if there have been several eagerly contested spitting and belching competitions.

Many of the chunks of rock rear up to four or five times my height and many more times my girth. They squat inconspicuously in pools of flat sand, like giant termite mounds or oversized grave markers. How impressive it is to be able to hurl one of these babies the 800 or so metres from even the nearest vent. I once tried to launch a ball of spittle from a railway bridge onto the tracks below. I ended up with a wet shoe.

I take a seat on the desert floor for a chocolate break, facing back towards Mount Ngauruhoe, having spent a good few minutes trying to find a spot where my bottom won't crush the life from some delicate lichen. In between me and the mountain are great folds of rock layered one in front of another. It looks like a children's theatre, the type fashioned from cardboard boxes by inventive mothers. Slits are cut in the sides of the box, through which the puppeteer pulls and pushes two-dimensional bits of scenery. Layering these strips of scenery behind each other gives the scene a three-dimensional feel.

Looking towards Mount Ngauruhoe, tall ridges of solidified lava seem as thin as those bits of paper scenery, and I am a child glued to the show. Life is playing out its scenes here; it's just that my human eyes work on too short a time frame to see what's happening.

If this were a desert in the land of Oz (New Zealand's nearest neighbour – a mere 1,600 or so kilometres away), there would be no end of things crawling around here that could kill a tramper at the merest flick of a tentacle or a tongue. Australia boasts a daunting array of deadly snakes, spiders, lizards, crocodiles, fish ... and so on. In the whole of New Zealand, however, there is just one native spider that can seriously harm human beings. (One type of spider, that is, not some orphaned arachnid living out the remainder of its days alone in a cave somewhere.) This is the katipo spider, a close relative of the North American black widow and the Australian redback. It is a testament to the toughness of this little family of killers that they alone manage to maintain a hold amongst New Zealand's otherwise friendly fauna.

Before I leave New Zealand, I shall have discovered that there are plenty of creatures here that can and will harm human beings after all (and particularly those who insist on wandering around in the bush for days on end). For now, though, I sit on the desert floor deliriously unconcerned about the local fauna and what it might make of – or from – me.

A dot appears on the horizon and becomes a four-legged creature heading towards me. It is moving so quickly that I'm surprised there isn't a dust cloud hanging behind it. When it passes beside me, my greeting is acknowledged by a cursory 'Hi' before the man powers away in a blur of professional walking sticks and legs. I bite off another bit of chocolate and stare at the show a little longer.

The wooden poles keep appearing and disappearing and appearing again. Deep grooves have been worn into them by the wind whipping grains of sand along the desert floor. They look as though they were erected decades ago and have been abandoned to the elements. Eventually they will wear right through and become puddles of wood dust on a bed of rock dust.

Although the Tongariro Crossing is the most popular day walk in New Zealand, the rest of the Tongariro Northern Circuit is somewhat underpopulated. About 6,000 people complete the whole of the Tongariro Northern Circuit each year. This is an average of just fifty people per day on the Circuit, even assuming that it's only passable for four months of the year. Spread out over forty-nine kilometres, that's an average of just over one person per kilometre of track – or, as I like to think of it, me and my pack in our kilometre of space.

After a couple of hours in the wilderness, Oturere Hut emerges from behind a rock. Handwritten notices warn trampers that levels in the rainwater tanks are dangerously low and that we should make every effort to conserve water, which seems only fitting in this desert terrain.

After Oturere Hut the track traverses ruched earth, similar to the folds and furrows of day one, but taller and steeper. I try to let the stunning views of yet another face of Mount Ngauruhoe distract me from the searing pain of blisters being rubbed raw for the second time. The familiar rhythm of up, down, up, down is soon so painful that I am adjusting my boot and pack straps at every peak and trough just to bring the pain level down from searing to intense.

Mentally, the day is remarkably soothing. Away from the social hubbub of the Tongariro Crossing, the size and stillness of this landscape has an odd effect on time and my thoughts. I think about past relationships and why they ended, and about work and why my ambition has fizzled up. I think about these things for what feels like ages, but a glance at my watch tells me that just ten minutes have passed. It has taken just ten minutes to analyse the major themes in my life, to think through the decisions I've made, to come to terms with my biggest failings and to feel at peace with all of this. My head is clear and my limbs maintain the steady rhythm of the track.

My next glance at my watch shows that more than an hour has fled. For the last hour I have not thought a single thought or felt a single emotion. I have just been tramping.

Another human being finally appears, clumping along the top of a ridge. He is a Dutchman attempting to walk the whole Circuit anticlockwise in just two days, with a pack bigger than mine and two more of those fine stick-legs. He blurs away after getting my estimate of the distance to Oturere Hut (I can't really remember any more, it already seems like days ago) and I am left to reflect on just how paltry my efforts are in comparison with the truly masochistic.

Another half an hour of pain later, a wood appears from nowhere. Inside are a few ghost trees, where old man's beard lichen has taken over and drips from each twig, looking like the ghostly vapour that routinely flaps around the limbs of the faking baddy in Scooby Doo cartoons before his evil plan and unconvincing costume are uncovered. Old man's beard lichen apparently coexists with its host rather than killing it. Looking at the drowned victims in this wood it's hard to be convinced of this.

Red in the face and sweaty, I suddenly realise why this is called tramping. After three days of exercise and nothing more than a quick splash of soap and water on my face at either end of the day, I'm beginning to look and smell like a tramp. And it is just as I tune in to the full nose-crinkling horror of my body aromas that a perfect Adonis climbs sure-footedly up the hill and comes to rest by my side. He is tall, dark and handsome. Moreover, he is going my way.

He is another Dutchman walking the Circuit in two days, which means that he last saw a shower just yesterday. We complete the final twenty minutes to Waihohonu Hut together, with me walking much more quickly than I would otherwise have done – not to match his longer stride, but to prevent him from inhaling my sweaty scent.

At the hut I gleefully discover a triple bunk and climb stiffly up to claim the penthouse suite that nobody else wants anyway.

'Oh, thank God you're not Israelis,' mutters a well-spoken English girl after the introductions are made. It's just Europeans tonight. 'Have any of you come across any Israelis?'

The others hesitate.

'I met three Israelis yesterday,' I answer. 'They were the first I've met.'

'You do know about Israelis, don't you?' she asks, all Miss Marple-ish, before proceeding immediately to the answer. 'They all have to do military service. For two years, after they leave university. Then they all go travelling for a year. They all do the same trip around the world. They all come to New Zealand and they all go tramping believing that they can do anything because they've been in the Israeli Army. They are often poorly prepared and don't realise how quickly the weather can change here. DOC staff are constantly advising them not to go out ill-equipped, but they go anyway.

Lots of them have to be rescued. Not that they pay for the cost of the rescue operations.'

Hmm. Going against DOC advice. Not taking the right equipment. Even if everything this girl says is true, I'm not sure I can offer a sympathetic 'tut'. I haven't yet been reckless, but I am suddenly aware that I could be doing much better.

Day four: The long way home

In the morning we are short of water – not because we've partied away the limited supply, but because the temperature dropped so low overnight that the water in the main tank has frozen. Having managed to descend from the rafters without injury, I impetuously ask the Adonis if he'd like to have a celebratory dinner with me tonight. I don't often ask men out, not least because in all three previous instances I was turned down with varying degrees of graciousness. But, to my delighted surprise, the Dutch hunk thinks my proposal a great idea; I've got a date. Perhaps I would have had more success in previous approaches if I'd been wearing the fragrance of four-day-old sweat. Wearing my pheromones on my sleeve, as it were.

The first side trip on today's route is to the Ohinepango Springs. Walking up the side of the clear and deep Ohinepango stream, it's hard not to expect the springs to be a forceful head of water. Where the track ends, however, it's only just possible to see fresh water bubbling up underneath overhangs of rock and young beech forest. The side trip takes just an hour, but the terrain is so mystical under early morning fog that by the time I step back onto the main track all thoughts of other human beings have once more gone from my head.

Whakapapa Village is still five-and-a-half hours away. DOC signs use estimated walking times, not distances, as their base currency, which seems sensible given that many of the people who tramp these tracks won't spend much time calculating their average speed over fluctuating gradients and given that DOC is basically trying to stop people dying in the bush. However, the effect these signs have on people is fascinating to behold. A typical hut conversation goes something like this, 'That section between Ketetahi and Oturere was supposed to take three or four hours. I did it in two and a half today.'

'I did it in two.'

'We did it in under three, but we took at least an hour for lunch.'

Trampers even use the Comments section in the intentions books in the huts to brag about their pace to people they'll never meet. It's as if, having come all the way to some of the most spectacular scenery in the world, the only acceptable thing to do is to walk past it faster than everyone else there, or die in the attempt. Even this morning, my Dutch Adonis, the English couple and a pair of Belgians talked about how quickly they were all intending to get back to Whakapapa Village. I kept very quiet. I'm slow. I know I'm slow. But here's the thing: sometimes I'm slow *on purpose*. I walk slowly. I enjoy walking slowly. I even come to a complete stop just to admire views. Somebody arrest me.

The second side trip of the day, to the Old Waihohonu Hut, brings home just how easy it is these days to potter around these majestic mountains. The Old Waihohonu Hut was built in 1903–04 and was reached, after a gruelling journey lasting several days, by horse-drawn coaches and on foot. People (hardy people, that is) came here to do some proper walking. Or, in the case of William Mead and Bernard Drake in 1913, to walk up Mount Ruapehu, tie little more than planks of wood to their feet and invent recreational skiing in New Zealand. Skiing without ski lifts, of course, is just a lot more uphill walking.

It's not as if the hut would have provided much in the way of luxurious shelter between these treks. The old hut has corrugated iron walls (in a double layer with some pumice in between for insulation) and is divided into two rooms, one of which has an open fireplace. You could sleep six people in each room with a modest degree of comfort, assuming no one had brought much of anything with them – an unlikely scenario given that they'd be carrying a few weeks' worth of gear.

When the hut was being used by both men and women, the women got to sleep in the room without the fire. Instead of facilities for cooking and keeping warm, they were treated to a bunkroom luxury all of their own: a mirror. Now, the last thing I want to see at the end of a long day walking in the mountains is exactly what I look like. Given a choice between a fire and a mirror, the mirror would lose. Given a choice between nothing and a mirror, the mirror would lose.

Surviving photographs show both male and female 'holidaymakers' attired in full Edwardian finery: layers of skirts and, hidden beneath them, corsets for the women; shirts, cravats and undoubtedly their own weird undergarments for the men. Standing in the now empty hut, I try to imagine the characters that stayed here and the emotions that must have been played out within these corrugated surrounds.

Compared with the prototype version, modern huts are the height of luxury. They are wooden, in keeping with the alpine feel, and the bunks have covered foam mattresses. They have sinks (indoors *and* outdoors), tables, benches, gas cookers and gas heaters – and access to everything is on a first come, first served basis, regardless of gender. Gas is supplied only during the summer, though: if you're wimp enough to need a gas heater in temperatures of minus five onwards then don't be on this track in winter.

The most agreeable surprise I've had about hut facilities (apart from the fact that they don't include mirrors) concerns the toilet arrangements. Cubicles are located at a discreet distance from the huts themselves. They have doors with locks. They have proper toilet seats over the inevitable buried vat holding the smelly stuff. And I can't help but wonder what proportion of the hut fees goes to the kind people who empty them out.

Now that I'm only about five hours away from base, I finally believe I'm going to make it. I'm rather proud of the way my body is standing up to the test, but mostly I have the fickleness of high pressure systems to thank for my progress. I'm here by the good grace of the weather. I'm not surprised, therefore, when the low pressure system finally sweeps over my head and starts to discharge its responsibilities. I can't work up much concern about the plummeting temperature or the driving sleet because the only energy I have left for worrying is wholly occupied with my poor feet. I clearly have no idea how to deal with blisters. I've pretty much left them to it and the fellows have been throwing such a party in my shoes that they are now hungover and in pain. I have developed so many new layers of skin over my heels that it's remarkable my boots still fit – and, of course, it feels very much as if they don't.

This doesn't stop me from turning off on the longest and hardest side trip of the day, to the Tama Lakes. The Tama Lakes are what makes the Northern Circuit the complete trip for all students of geography. By this point, the young geographer has been through a major volcanic zone caused by tectonic plate subduction and littered with the full range of volcanic accessories (craters, hot springs, magma pipes, mineral lakes, lava flows etc.). He has enjoyed a meteorological short cut or two through all the types of weather his syllabus contains. He has learned of different types of land use by human settlements, without having to delve too far into the tiresome world of historians. He has seen such a range of brightly coloured rocks that he almost understands why people choose geology instead. And now, at the Tama Lakes, he can study up close some magnificent products of the process that has kept many a geographer going through an otherwise difficult examination: glaciation.

What would the world have looked like before glaciers? It seems that every mountain, hill, valley, stone, pebble and outcrop of rock big enough to bully sand has at some point or other been irrevocably gouged, scraped, deposited, cracked, crushed or otherwise meddled with by a glacier. There are currently eight named glaciers still reshaping Mount Ruapehu. In this landscape, however, the violent and fiery work of tectonic plate-rubbing tends to distract attention from the more ponderous power of merely very cold water.

The walk up to look out over the Lower Tama Lake is an easy ten-minute matter. The path from there to the Upper Tama Lake is forty-five minutes of steep scrambling, but as I reach the top the clouds clear and I am confronted by views on all sides that rival those on the Crossing. It's like taking a spectacular, remote spot in the Welsh hills and then adding an outsized volcano at either end of the horizon.

I bow my head, first to Ngauruhoe and then to Ruapehu. As far as I'm aware, I'm not following Maori protocol. It just feels right. Then, having checked to make sure that there's no one else in sight, I stand on this peak between volcanoes and burst into whoops and yells and other very loud noises, waving my arms and skipping up and down for accompaniment. I've tramped my way up and down more than forty kilometres of track and this is my last serious hill before a mere couple of hours' trot back to buildings and paved roads and lots of other people and a small shop that now seems like a well-stocked supermarket. If I had just successfully completed the first slide down Mount Ruapehu with planks of wood strapped to my feet I couldn't feel more jubilant.

The final five kilometres are long ones. They leave me wondering whether I really will be able to tackle many more of these Great Walks. I will make it back to Whakapapa Village tonight, but I won't be a pretty sight. I've had a Great Walk, but now I'm fit only for a Great Collapse.

To occupy my feverish mind, I compose a theme song. Cunningly (or so my addled brain thinks), I employ the Kiwi pronunciation of 'sweaty', which rhymes perfectly with the British pronunciation of 'pretty':

I feel sweaty
And so smelly
I feel sweaty and smelly today
That I pity
Anyone who were to pass my way

I am dirty
And quite dampened
I have cramp and
Blisters on my feet
And I pity
Anyone whom I should chance to meet

Who's that slumping girl in the mirror there?
Who can this disgusting girl be?
Such a reddened face
Such an ugly look
Such a sweaty mess
Such a tired me

My brain is so numb it considers these lyrics hilarious. In the middle of my twenty-ninth attempt to find a decent last verse, I cross the end of the track. However, I must keep going in order to report my continued survival at the DOC office.

I reach the DOC office seconds before it closes for the day. There has been no ribbon at the finish line and none of my familiar green and yellow friends are behind the counter, so there isn't even any weather banter to be had. Out of habit I check the weather forecast for the next two days. Then I limp off to dinner.

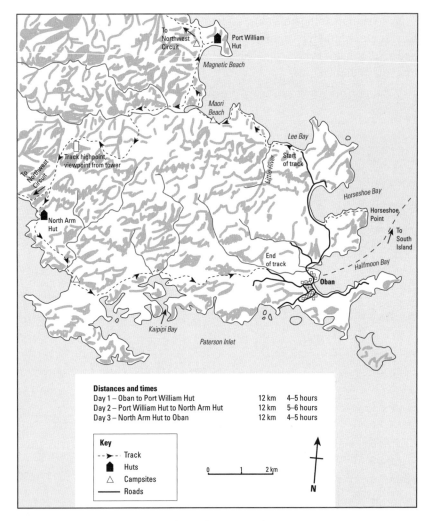

The Rakiura Track

3
The last place to survive: The Rakiura Track

New Zealand mostly comprises two large islands. There are also many smaller islands flying the New Zealand flag, some of which are so far south that it's far too cold there to do anything so frivolous as to erect a flagpole. However, a mere thirty kilometres or so off the southern tip of the South Island lies the third largest island of New Zealand. Stewart Island is the preserve of dense forest that remains almost entirely undisturbed by the usual inclinations of mankind to log, burn, clear or otherwise maim and destroy. Stewart Island is also the home of the Rakiura Track.

Getting to Stewart Island involves first finding a small town called Bluff on the remote, southern tip of the South Island, and then catching a ferry across a stretch of water that has inspired the tiny Stewart Island tourist industry to print onto T-shirts the words, 'I survived the Foveaux Strait'. These days, there is also an airborne alternative to arriving on the island, but given that a standard in-flight safety demonstration lasts longer than the flight time, I opt for the greater excitement of an hour spent pitching around in the waves.

Just getting to Bluff is part of the transition to small island life. En route from much larger Invercargill I help the driver load up the little minibus with the week's newspapers and mail and then deliver these packages to various houses along the roadside. The final batch of news is loaded onto the small ferry with me. However, the ferry isn't as quiet as I had expected. A party of seventeen American students is also travelling to Stewart Island this morning. They are overexcited and loud and determined to engage everyone in conversation. A girl of no more than eighteen, sporting Pippi Longstocking braids and an election-winning smile, approaches me to tell me about their plans.

'Hey there! How's it going?!'

'Fine, thanks. How are you?'

'Oh we're great. Just great! We haven't been to Stewart Island before. We're doing a semester in Dunedin and this is our big Easter Break adventure.'

She proceeds to tell me a lot more about her group than I could possibly need to know. My required role in the exchange is to listen, smile and nod, throwing in an occasional 'Wow' or 'That's great'. If anyone were ever to create any Mr Men or Little Misses for the over twelves, this girl would be the perfect model for Little Miss Youthful Exuberance. I envy her her bounce, not to mention the perfect symmetry of her plaits.

She mentions that her party is going to be walking the Rakiura Track, starting out today. I had been deliberating whether to begin today or wait until tomorrow. Now I know I'll wait. I can relax for the day and run the risk of meeting an even larger group tomorrow.

After a while, Little Miss YE (and I am embarrassed to admit that I can't remember her real name) suddenly enquires about me. I am slightly knocked off balance by this, but what has grabbed her attention about me is revealed in her first question, 'Are you on your own?'

'Yes.'

She looks shocked. 'But don't you get lonely? I get lonely even when I'm with other people. I'm no good on my own at all.'

'I haven't been lonely yet. I quite like it so far.'

'But what will you do on Stewart Island?'

'I've come to walk the Rakiura Track too. Although I probably won't set out until tomorrow, so I'm afraid I'll miss you guys by a day.'

'You're going to walk the track?! On your own?!! For three days? Jeez – I could never do that.'

I couldn't walk with sixteen others. For years now, I have had so much conversation and company – at work, at home, on trains, on buses, in bars, shops and even libraries – that solitude and silence are strange luxuries. Dinner with the Dutchman was lovely, but I'm glad it was just that. He has gone north and I have come south. We will email each other, but that's enough. I'm not looking to walk with anyone else.

I try to suggest to Little Miss YE that she might be amazed at what she can do on her own. I try to explain how wonderful it feels to be alone with just your own thoughts and Mother Nature. Somehow, though, I can't satisfactorily convey the serenity of solo tramping while I am bobbing up and down and shouting over the combined din of engine, wind and excited young Americans. She takes her leave of me, off to continue 'working the boat'. I resume staring at the small island across the waves. She thinks I am insane.

Maybe I am part nut, but I like the fact that you can only see signs of human life when you get right up close to this island. From across the waves, it is the forest canopy alone that is visible, barring the occasional rock that has so far escaped vegetation.

Take an enormous land mass, let a chunk of it split off from the rest before mammals have managed to crawl into existence, let that chunk be divided by the sea into smaller bits and then just leave one of the smallest of these bits alone for millions and millions of years. That's Stewart Island. That is also why the forests of Stewart Island are rather special and why some eighty-five per cent of Stewart Island is now National Park. As I squint at the island through the raindrops just starting to lash the boat, I can only assume that the remaining fifteen per cent is simply wilderness.

People came into this wilderness a few hundred years ago. They came here to kill seals and whales and seabirds. They felled timber and battled to survive on the island. In 1872, the government of New Zealand even sponsored people from the Shetland Islands to settle here. Nothing really worked.

The small township of Oban is where the ferry docks and is the hub of Halfmoon Bay, the only remaining focus of human habitation on the island. The free map of the township handed out at the Visitor Centre is not quite on a scale of 1:1, but it does identify and individually name some sixty buildings, which encompasses almost every building in Oban. More than two-thirds are marked as places to stay because the locals welcome visitors into their homes. These B&Bs are obvious on the map, with names like Albert's Place, Skip's Place, Joy's Place and Jones's Halfmoon Haven. For no good reason that I can report, I find it disconcertingly difficult to follow this map. The distances are so small that in the time I take to look at the map I've already walked past my destination. Perhaps Little Miss YE is actually Little Miss Wiser Than Me and I really shouldn't be allowed out on my own after all.

At the hostel (after walking twice the required distance) a man called Peter is full of interesting stories about the island.

'There have been tensions between some of the locals and DOC,' he whispers, dramatically.

The bulk of the island was only designated a National Park in 2002, bringing more trampers and greater DOC presence to Stewart Island. However, there are some unclear boundaries between the National Park and private land, with certain sections of the Rakiura Track only being available for use through the permission of local landowners. Moreover, the Rakiura Track was here long before it was a Great Walk – and its status as a Great Walk is controversial for some. Nevertheless, I can't quite tell whether Peter's tales of personality clashes are genuine, or a little over-embellished for the visitor.

His finale is a story about the police presence on the island. Today the lone ranger comes on rotation from the 'mainland', but until a few years ago the island had its own live-in policeman.

'One policeman had a large family. The local crime wave was no more than a gentle ripple, so the family used one of the cells as a child's bedroom and another for storing the family liquor. When a cell was finally needed to house a villain, the poor policeman forgot that his liquor would be company for the crook, who proved unable to walk in a straight line in the morning.'

Day one: Into the forest

Unlike the merry villain, I am walking quite competently when I set off early the next day. The first wave of blisters has retreated and I'm ready to go over the top again.

The official start of the Rakiura Track is about five kilometres north of Oban, but I'm going to walk all the way out from the door of my hostel and back again. Not only that, but I plan to encompass a few side trips on the first day as well, because otherwise, frankly, the Rakiura Track looks a little wimpy after the Tongariro Northern Circuit. Even if I walk out from Oban and back again, I will only cover thirty-six kilometres in three days. I can expect to be walking for just four or five hours on days one and three, with a heady six hours to cover on day two. I can't quite walk the track in two days, but I can get prematurely cocky about this being a three-day stroll in a park.

Given the size of Oban, it doesn't take very long to leave it behind and find myself literally out on the open road. A few cars trundle past and I smile and wave to the driver in each one, turning to greet the ones that approach from behind me. The smiling and waving happens instinctively: it's just the kind of thing you do here. It is also enthusiastically returned by all, which only serves to make me even more smiley and wavy. Little Miss YE watch out.

The first side trip of the day takes me up along the northern arch of Halfmoon Bay to a place called Moturau Moana. Even in my supremely smiley and wavy state, I am underwhelmed by the small garden in the middle of nowhere, which has as its main attraction a couple of lawns and a few labels with names of trees attached to sticks in the ground. Unless the sticks have been mischievously placed near the wrong trees (and, as far as I can tell, they haven't), there doesn't seem to be much of interest in this garden, particularly when compared with the forest all around it. Perhaps I am missing the point. Perhaps it is remarkable that somebody managed to clear two small sections of the forest here down to neat grassy lawns and then continue to hold back the green invaders at the borders. One of the reasons why Stewart Island wasn't used as a location for any of the *Lord of the Rings* films could be that no cameraman would be able to squeeze himself, his kit and even a hobbit-sized actor between one tree and the next.

Back on the road I soon reach the south end of Horseshoe Bay, which, apparently, might actually be Halfmoon Bay. Confused? Well, the story goes that the names of these two bays were originally the other way around, but that an admiralty cartographer got the names muddled up, thereby giving the stamp of officialdom to the wrong names. Some say that Horseshoe Bay (as it is now named) is clearly the shape of a half-moon, and vice versa. I stare at the outlines of Halfmoon Bay and Horseshoe Bay on the map, trying to reach my own conclusion on the matter. It finally occurs to me that the shape of a horseshoe is similar to that of a half-moon and that this might be just a good story dreamed up by the locals to puzzle the silly tourists.

The second side trip from the road runs along the southern edge of Horseshoe Bay and out to Horseshoe Point. It takes about half an hour to reach the Point itself, along a track that effortlessly combines bog, puddle and mud into this season's look. Horseshoe Point is apparently a great place from which to observe the Foveaux Strait, which suggests there might be more traffic than just the little ferry coming and going every day (when the waves permit). I scan the stretch of water but fail to see a single fishing boat, New Zealand Navy vessel, French nuclear warship or even tourist charter craft. Instead there are large groups of sea birds doing a considerable amount of coming and going all over the place out there: shags, cape pigeons, albatross and muttonbirds – the latter being a particular favourite on Maori menus.

New Zealand was once a haven for birds of all kinds because there were no mammalian predators here for millions of years (although how we know these kinds of things never ceases to amaze me). Of the three main islands, Stewart Island has escaped with the least interference from mammals and is therefore known for its bird life – and even more for its land-based avians than for the tasty ones endlessly skimming its borders. One of the more exciting aspects of tramping in Stewart Island forest is that this probably represents my best chance of ever seeing a kiwi in the wild.

Amongst the many bird species that have been wiped out or endangered by the unfashionably late arrival of mammals in these parts, the kiwi seems particularly tragic. This is partly because it is the unofficial national emblem of New Zealand and partly because it is a rather fascinating, unassuming bird that just wants to go about its business of poking holes in the ground, but keeps having its eggs and its offspring slavered over by creatures that couldn't be more alien to them if they'd suddenly stepped off a spaceship and declared the Earth to be theirs.

Having watched a kiwi rooting around its enclosure in a Rotorua museum, I am keen to sight one of these entrancing upside-down-pear-shaped birds in its natural environment.

Most other creatures I know of have a centre of gravity that positions the head somewhere at the top of the body. The centre of gravity for a kiwi, however, seems to be focused on keeping its huge round body balanced over its two short legs, with the head hanging down near the ground. If a kiwi were knocked backwards onto its bottom, I suspect it would take some furious and skilful rocking for it to get back on its feet. The kiwi is perhaps the creature best prepared for nuclear Armageddon: with its enormous bottom, its head hanging down by its knees and its extremely long beak, this endangered and fascinating bird will, when the time comes, have no problem in kissing its own bottom goodbye.

The morning ferry from Bluff bobs its way into sight and my spirits flop with the thought that it might hold another huge group of visitors about to chase me along the track. I splosh back to the road as quickly as I can, so that I can at least retain my head start.

It's difficult to stride out quickly along Horseshoe Bay, with its tiny boats bobbing up and down, its smooth crescent of sand (is this a moon I see?) and its gentle slush of waves relaxing me. The mood is broken, however, by the march of feet behind me, faint at first but quickly getting louder. I walk towards the waves to let them pass, but one of the foot soldiers chases after me. Could I take a photo of their group please? Youthful Americans, although fortunately only five this time. Yes, I'll see them at Port William Hut tonight. Looking forward to it.

On the road over the peninsula between Horseshoe Bay and Lee Bay – where the Rakiura Track officially begins – a couple of strange sights flip my thoughts away from American gangs and back to the wonders of small island life. The first is a telephone pinned to a post at the side of the road, in amongst the forest and at about my head height. The telephone is black and of a vintage that I've only previously seen in museums. It looks well maintained and for all the world like a working public telephone, minus the tedious modern accoutrements that demand cash or card or some other form of payment. I resist the urge to pick up the handset and see if anyone's there, partly because I wouldn't know what to say and partly because the liquor in the police cell has long since been consumed. It would be amusing, though, if the phone were suddenly to ring out before a tramper had noticed it amongst the foliage. Forget the Halfmoon versus Horseshoe debate – if I were a local I would spend many an hour rigging up a hiding place to watch the effect of just one such telephone call.

A little further along the road lies something rather more obvious and even more bizarre. Standing on a pole is a house that is either a very large doll's house or a very, very small real house. Like a doll's house the cross section is open to view. Each room inside is filled with furniture, linen and accessories that are home-made and skilfully so. There is no hint as to whom it belongs or why it is there. I can only assume that there's a real house set back behind the foliage here, in which the creator of the mini-house lives. I don't know how long you have to live on the island to start doing things like this, but it's almost worth staying to find out.

Already more than two hours into the day's walking I reach the official start of the Rakiura Track, where a large sculpture celebrates the main Maori legend regarding the creation of New Zealand. The legend runs that the South Island of New Zealand is a canoe that was used by the half-god Maui for fishing. The enormous fish that Maui pulled from the sea is the North Island, and the anchor stone of the canoe is Stewart Island. The original Maori name for Stewart Island is therefore Te Punga o Te Waka o Maui, which roughly translates as 'The Anchor Stone of Maui's Canoe'. Unsurprisingly, though, there are at least two other Maori names for the island. The first is Motunui, or 'large island'. The second is Rakiura, or 'the land of glowing skies' (no volcano references, I'm pleased to hear, just great sunsets and the occasional sighting of the aurora australis, or Southern Lights). For good measure, there's another possible explanation behind the Maori name for the island: Rakiura could be the abbreviated version of Te Rakiura a Te Rakitamau, or the 'great blush of Rakitamau', in reference to the latter's embarrassment when refused the hand in marriage of not one, but two daughters of an island chief.

Using the canoe story, the sculpture at the start of the track is of three links in an enormous chain pointing towards the South Island. The links at either end disappear into the ground, as if this is just the tiny visible part of a giant chain linking the islands. Trampers walk through the middle link to start the track. It's quite convincing. However, it also bears a feature that the sculptor did not intend: at the top of the middle link is a bullet mark where a local took out his (or her) frustration on the sculpture. The bullet hole is quite small. However, word spreads quickly in these parts, so I suspect that most people who pass through here know to look for it and to give a fleeting nod to the thought that there are just some things that a mere visitor will never know.

An estimated 2,300 people now walk the Rakiura Track each year. I don't know whether the marksman objected to the influx of a greater number of people to the island, the interference of DOC, the protection of so much of the island with National Park status or all or none of these developments. The locals I have talked to so far all seem generally in favour of the tourists, who must surely take over at times. Neither do the locals just tolerate tourists for the money they leave here. The role of the tourist on Stewart Island is also to provide new information from, and another perspective on, the world. As one man put it, when he stopped for a chat whilst walking his dog the previous evening, 'In a place like this, you pretty much know everyone's views on everything. We have tourists to stay at our place because we need the conversation.'

Making my way along the well-graded start of the track, I also ponder the fact that Kiwis seem, so far, to be a friendly and welcoming bunch. There's no reason to believe that the marksman could be hiding in the dense bush on either side of the track, ready to take potshots at the invaders.

A small explosion on my left suddenly sends the trees and bushes into violent rearrangement and something comes hurtling towards me at a pace with which I'm not comfortable. Before my eyes can focus on what and where it is, my ears are telling me that it's not some lone sniper, but a helicopter – and perhaps the escalation of protest from lone shots aimed at impenetrable metal sculptures in the middle of the night to the adoption of full Vietcong tactics. A second or two (and about twenty heartbeats) later, I catch sight of the protestor. I'm embarrassed to discover that it is a pigeon.

To be more precise, it is a New Zealand pigeon (or kereru), the average size of which is far, far bigger than anything that has ever targeted Trafalgar Square. I've never been a huge fan of pigeons in the UK, even if I disregard the quantities of guano they unleash over everything. I have a theory that all pigeons actually have white feathers, but that they choose to live in the muckiest, most polluted places and are therefore always covered in a layer of fumes and grime. It is this filthy appearance I dislike most and now this wood pigeon adds its own considerable weight to my argument. It flashes sleek purples and greens at me as its long wings beat holes in the air, trying to generate enough lift to keep its huge body airborne. Size is something I hadn't fully factored into my theory but, comparing this specimen with its London cousins, it seems that smoking really does stunt your growth. As it wheels away, I estimate I'd have difficulty fitting the body of this bird into my backpack, such is its girth. On further reflection with a slower heart rate, it might not have been quite that big. However, I fervently hope that neither I nor the local pigeons will be surprising each other again.

A calmer twenty minutes' walk brings me to a wooden bridge over Little River. Just before the bridge a DOC sign reads:

> **Warning** – This water is not safe to drink.
> Treated sewage is discharged into this river upstream.
> Trampers are advised not to drink this water.

As I cross the bridge I peer down into the water, which is golden brown in the sun and looking distinctly like *un*treated liquid sewage. After the clear, crystal blue of Tongariro streams and lakes, this is an unwelcome return to pollution, although even I am surprised at the openness with which the brown is on display. With an inward sigh I keep going towards a place called Peter's Point. (Peter was apparently a man who came out to live here to try to grow strawberries. Legend, alas, does not divulge why Peter wanted to grow strawberries or why Peter wanted to grow strawberries here. Legend does, however, reveal that he ended up manufacturing lime – to sweeten a soil otherwise inhospitable to strawberries – and then selling the lime to other farmers on the island and on the South Island. If at first you don't succeed, something else will turn up.)

Seeing no sign of any strawberries or anything other than forest, I start the trifling descent to Maori Beach. Rakiura National Park is not known for its hills. The highest point on the island is optimistically called Mount Anglem, which stands at a mere 980 metres and isn't even on the route of the Rakiura Track. This is another reason why I'm confident that I'll reach the end of this Great Walk, perhaps even with some energy left.

At one end of Maori Beach is another delightful little brown stream to cross. I dutifully look around for the sign warning me not to drink the water, but I can't see one. Neither can I see a footbridge. I scrabble a little way upstream on rocks underneath forest overhang and still can't see a bridge. The stream is a mini-estuary and the tide is coming in, swelling its size and not doing much to remove the brown stains. Feeling as if I'm taking another step towards becoming a proper Outdoors Person, I swing my boots round my neck (taking care not to kick myself in the chin) and wade across the stream. I had been looking forward to wading through swirling waters at some point on my adventures. I just hadn't pictured the scene with excrement.

Maori Beach is a delight. I can't see any remnants of the attempts at human settlement here (a sawmill, a school and a few dwellings were here as recently as the 1920s). However, it is hard to miss the hundreds of pointers to the far more successful non-human settlements. The creamy sand is generously sprinkled with shells from a broad menu of potential seafood meals – and not just appetisers, judging by the size of many of them. There is a particularly excellent range of large helter-skelter shells, perfectly preserved in a spectrum of colours that I'm surprised to find exists outside of those make-up counters that gather near the doors of big department stores.

Being until recently a mostly Indoors Person, I don't know the names for the crunchy little houses around my feet. Consultation with the trusty guidebook reveals a list that sounds as scary in English as in Latin: large ostrich foot, knobbed whelk, southern volute, Cooks' turban, pink barnacle, oyster and various bivalves. I immediately start calculations to determine the number of shells I can allow myself to take away with me, alongside a clean environmental conscience. It's a National Park and if everyone took a load of shells ... but they come from a regenerating source ... After a ridiculously long internal debate, I walk past the most exquisite shells I have ever seen and stuff my itchy hands into my pockets.

The entertainment here doesn't stop at the abandoned armour of spineless beings. I take a seat on a sand dune to watch the energetic performance of the waves at the furthest, north-west end of the beach. Even as an Indoors Person I know that waves crest and break in fairly rhythmic and regular fashion. I know that on some beaches the combined effects of terrain, wind and tides produces really big, foamy waves on which brave people try to dance with the aid of plastic slabs. I know that the sizes, strengths and angles of waves vary and yet I am still chuckling aloud at the behaviour of a twenty-metre stretch of water here. Each wave rears up like a python being charmed out of its basket – by a particularly speedy tune that has just shocked it out of a sneaky nap. Each wave then hangs in the air for a second or two before flopping down, seemingly exhausted from the effort and unable to create much splash for running up the beach. There's none of the usual crest and break routine going on here, just an awful lot of watery attempts to stand up. Every twentieth wave or so, a Herculean effort is made and a ridge of water suspends itself at an impossible height before the inevitable belly flop to the floor. Watching this, it is easy to understand how many people (not all of them Maori) believe that spirits live in this land.

At the far end of Maori Beach is another deep brown stream to cross and I'm surprised there's not more of a stink. This time, however, there is a swing bridge that would grace an Indiana Jones action scene. Narrow and constructed entirely from wire and steel rope, it sports a sign warning that the maximum load is one person (what about my heavy backpack?) and has, right in the centre, a boot-shaped hole that has been mended with chicken wire. It has a bounce in it that could send me for an unpleasant swim if I don't maintain just the right combination of balance and forward propulsion.

Then the world changes. Dense forest canopy obscures the grey afternoon light and the track is a series of sloppy, muddy pools suspended between tree roots. I schloop in and out of mud and realise that I have lingered too long on funny wave beach. Tonight's hut may only be a couple of kilometres away, but this is not terrain that lends itself to meeting or beating track time estimates. This is terrain that lends itself to sucking boots off feet and twisting ankles.

It soon gets darker, though I can't tell whether this is because of thickening vegetation, darkening clouds or fading daylight. I'm heading for another beach, after a tricky climb up and down a small headland, but the tide is now high and I've missed the opportunity to escape from the darkening cover onto sand. Instead I have to take a tortuous route above the shoreline, where I become convinced that the sun has set. All the mud has confused me. I've been battling through it in a separate time zone. A four-hour walk has turned into a six-hour wade through mud.

I slip badly whilst trying to negotiate a downward flight of wooden stairs.

Each of the steps is a deep trough of runny mud, with the exposed wooden lip of the trough providing the only solid footing. Solid, but not firm, because the wood has no wire overcoat here and, like everything else around, is sodden. One foot slips on the wet wood and I find myself doing the splits at an interesting downward angle, with the weight of my pack not helping matters and planks of wood poking into places they shouldn't. Pains shoot through a few taut muscles and squished joints as I search for a way to lever myself upright. Quickly.

Unfortunately, the only solid things near me are tree trunks that are just out of reach. I have to jiggle and slide around in the mud until I'm at an angle that I think I recognise as upright again. I didn't know I could still do the splits. Apparently I can't, although a whole new career in mud wrestling may be opening up before me.

The brief triumph of having manoeuvred myself back into a standing position quickly sinks under a new wave of realism. I'm miles away from anywhere, it really is getting dark, bits of me now hurt and I haven't seen anyone for hours. Even if a huge group of people was just around the corner, no one would hear my SOS whistle blasts over the crash of the waves. If I slip, fall and can't right myself again, I'll be spending the night bent into the position in which I land. For a couple of seconds I can't decide whether to continue, to make the most of the remaining light, or to take a break for the benefit of knees now trembling (not yet from fear but through the physical effort of negotiating body and pack downhill over mud-soaked tree roots). It starts to rain.

Pressing on, I miss my footing another couple of times, but with less crunching consequences. As if my brain weren't fully occupied with the effort required to maintain my balance, I now start to worry about my stove. I checked it before I set out, but it's new, I've never used one before and I've only brought one gas canister with me. I ponder how I'll try to make pasta absorb cold water if I can't get the stove to work. It's not designed to be used in wind or rain, so it won't work well if I have to set up an impromptu camp in a pool of mud.

Just as I am making nice, sensible plans to address my most doom-laden scenarios, and without any warning, I step out on a grassy clearing and find Port William Hut. Inside are eight Kiwi lads who are a fair way through two large chilly bins of beer (how did they get those out here?). 'Chilly bins' is the Kiwi term for enormous coolers, which are normally far too large and heavy to be seen in DOC huts. Also in the hut are a Kiwi family of five, the Americans, three Brits, a few other Europeans, and a vile, pervasive stench of sweat and mould. Retreating quickly to a bench outside the bunkroom, two ladies take me under their equally muddy wings.

'Hi. How are you?'

'Um … Tired. Muddy. And – without wishing to be rude – not at all looking forward to sleeping in that bunkroom tonight. Otherwise, I'm good.'

They laugh. 'Ah yes. That's why we're sitting here. Teenage boys, you know. The sap is certainly rising.'

We introduce ourselves. They are Sarah and Gill and are both that wonderful age in women that can be anything from thirty to sixty. Sarah is blonde, bubbly and possibly even shorter than me. Gill is tall with long, dark hair and something of the Amazon about her.

'Tell us, did you see many birds today?' Sarah asks. 'Only we were rather looking forward to all the bird life and we've hardly seen any. We saw a whitetail deer on the first part of the track, but hardly any birds.'

They are from the South Island and were expecting to be overwhelmed by a cacophony of songs from the treetops, such is the power of Stewart Island's reputation. Now they come to mention it, I'm not sure that I've seen or heard much bird activity today and we are soon engrossed in a discussion about the impact of introduced predators and DOC's use of something called 1080.

To give it its full title (but only once, because it's a mouthful), 1080 is shorthand for sodium monofluoroacetate and the impact of a mouthful of this stuff is the subject of many a fireside debate in New Zealand. DOC drops 1080 poison into the country's various parks and forests in an effort to staunch the flow of pests – particularly possums.

Possums were introduced into this bird sanctuary by … yes, you've guessed it: us Brits (via Australia, but even so, I don't think we can deny the link). Don't be fooled by any Aussie views on their protected possums: each year in New Zealand, an estimated seventy million possums munch their way through about seven million tonnes of valuable new tree growth, kiwi chicks, kiwi eggs and lots of other bits of plants and birds that DOC is desperately trying to protect. DOC sends small armies into the bush to hunt them down, but even if every living Kiwi were to take up arms against the possums, they would be outnumbered by almost eighteen to one.

In New Zealand, the possum is not protected. In New Zealand, children are raised to bash and kill any possum they see and visitors are reminded that, in this country, drivers swerve to *hit* possums. The use of 1080 poison seems to be the only thing that DOC can do on the scale required, but then poisons don't discriminate in what they kill – and if a bird eats an animal that ate some 1080 …

Gill concludes the discussion with her own view. '1080 kills. It's as simple as that. It kills birds as much as it kills their predators. There must be a better way.'

All this talk of poisoning reminds me of a certain other environmental issue that seems to plague only Stewart Island and to be politely omitted from conversations: the deeply brown water. Sarah and Gill are friendly, practical sorts, so I take a deep breath of the stink-free air outside the hut and, as it were, wade in.

'Did you notice the DOC sign just before Little River today?'

Sarah is clearly as sensitive as I have been to the issue. 'I know! Not really what you expect to find on a Great Walk. Lucky we hadn't run out of water.'

So far the subject seems acceptable. I plough on.

'What really surprised me was the colour of the water. I'm no expert on sewage, treated or otherwise, but I didn't expect the whole river to be quite so brown. And that wasn't even the worst of it. Did you notice that the next two streams – the ones either side of Maori Beach – were thick with the stuff too? And there weren't any signs up there.'

The reaction from Sarah and Gill to this bond-forming tramper's indignation is not all I had expected it to be. Sarah bursts out laughing so loudly and quickly that a snort explodes and catches the attention of our teenage hut-mates, beers in hand, at the other end of the porch. Gill rocks silently for a couple of seconds and then peals in waves of giggles over the top, so that all in the vicinity are now wondering what could be so funny. Under their attention I want to act like the great wit who has just cracked a corking joke, only I can't pull this off because I don't have the faintest idea what the joke is.

Sarah recovers first. 'Do you mean to say you thought all that brown was … well … excrement?!' She stifles another snort while Gill wipes the tears from her eyes.

'Um. Well. Yes, actually. I'm guessing now it isn't.'

'No! It's tannins from all the leaves. The brown tannins stain the water, from dead leaves on the ground.'

Gill is now looking thoughtful. 'But there was that sign at Little River. It never occurred to me that it might be something other than leaves in the water. And I guess the water is an unusually dark brown here.'

They both consider for a brief moment the thought that has incensed me all afternoon.

'No. Can't be,' decides Sarah.

'Yes. Definitely just the leaves,' concludes Gill.

I am obviously delighted with the news that this wonderful (if dark, muddy and a bit scary) forest is not carrying highways of human effluent. I am less delighted with what now appears to be my intense stupidity. I mean, on reflection, how much poo did I think a few hundred inhabitants and tourists might produce daily? There is nonetheless good reason to be thankful even for this: Sarah and Gill are now firm friends and under their supervision my stove is soon working. Dinner is on its way.

One of the notices inside the hut lists the appropriate points of etiquette for hut usage. I am a little surprised by the third point, which reads:

> **Firearms:** Before entering the hut, remove ammunition and bolts from firearms so they cannot be fired accidentally.

There is no qualification to this statement, no preliminary 'If carrying a firearm …' or 'For hut users with firearms …' There is simply an assumption that the people who come here are packing something a little more deadly than a sleeping bag, spare clothes and trampers' rations. Trying to be subtle, I sneak a look round the hut, taking in the belongings in sight and the faces of my hut-mates. I can't see any firearms, but there are an awful lot of corners not illuminated by candle or torch. I wonder whether I should be worried about teenage boys and chilly bins of beer.

Under cover of darkness the hut warden finally appears and shyly makes his way round the room to check hut passes. He is not an effusive conversationalist, but I discover that this is his holiday. Every year he takes a couple of weeks off work (in the South Island) and comes to Port William Hut where he spends his days diving for oysters in the sea and hunting deer, or anything else that might pass his way on the land. I immediately like him, but as soon as he's quietly made his way round the room he disappears back into the night. So that's at least one person here with a firearm.

Day two: Under the boardwalk

By morning I still haven't acclimatised to odour of teenage boy but I have managed a decent night of hut sleep. Whilst trying to separate my belongings from the strewn jumbles, I wonder whether I should wander onto the headland the other side of the hut to check out the Poti Repo nature walk.

The nature walk was supposed to be my third and final side trip of yesterday, but by the time I'd arrived at the hut I'd had no energy, daylight or enthusiasm left for walking any further than the long-drop toilet at the edge of the clearing. The name Poti Repo translates as 'Corner of Swamp' and, having been walking through the soggy centre of swampland all day yesterday, it had taken a nanosecond to decide that I could give the corner a miss, figuring that with the light of a new day I might feel different.

It is not to be. The walk back out from Port William Hut (the first forty-five minutes of today's six-hour route) traces back along the last forty-five minutes of yesterday's route – those forty-five minutes that stretched out into what felt more like two hours of gloom and mud and dark thoughts. After breakfast, however, the tide is low enough for the walk to be conducted in a civilised manner along the beach. Leave much later and I'll have to venture back along the sloppy, splits-inducing high-tide route. I'm more than prepared to miss out on the nature walk in order to avoid having to go back into that section of forest.

The beach on which Port William Hut lies is marvellously titled Magnetic Beach. Gold was discovered here in 1866, although luckily for the island's forests, there wasn't much of it and the prospectors left again fairly quickly. Looking back along the sand towards the hut, I catch a final glimpse of the hut warden (or, to be more precise, his flippers) disappearing into the cold sea. A lone prospector, albeit not for gold. Unless he wasn't letting on.

The sand on Magnetic Beach is dark, almost grey, but heavily tattooed with flecks of gold. The gold speckles tumble around in the wave run-off and sparkle convincingly. It's as if an ocean-going tanker from the same stock as the Exxon Valdez has run aground, but carrying gold glitter instead of oil. If Dame Edna Everage ever wanted to take a beach holiday without going incognito as a man, then this would be the place for her.

After the haven of glittering sand and bare rock that is Magnetic Beach comes the return to the swamp. Let's talk about mud – safe in the knowledge that it's far more comfortable to talk about it than to wade through it. The mud is of our own making. Strip away foliage and roots and the rain has nothing to cling to but the restless earth. Add a few thousand trampers into the mix and you have the perfect recipe for slop; slop that has been freshly turned for me by the seventeen pairs of youthful American walking boots that passed through here yesterday.

It is clear that many, many people have tried to avoid the deepest, runniest mud by walking at the sides of the track ('side-swiping' as Sarah and Gill call it). This has resulted in the enlargement of the track in many places from a three-feet-wide strip of quick-mud to a winding highway of sog. Whole sections stretch out to a few metres in width and with no firm ground in sight. When you stand at the start of one of these sections it is hard to determine which boggy pool covers ground firm enough to hold the weight of you and your pack, and which boggy pool will swallow you whole.

Further concentration is required when dealing with the ups and downs – and what Stewart Island lacks in magnificent mountain backdrops, it more than makes up for in not having any land that is actually flat. Mud of varying depths nestles between tree roots to be scrambled around, with intense concentration required for upward scrambles and even more focus for the downward plunges. As I stumble and splatter over the worst of these I see my dream of a new career in mud wrestling fading away from me; I'm barely winning the battle against just the mud.

One of the features of a Great Walk in New Zealand is that it has to be reasonably accessible to all. What stops the Rakiura Track from being an inaccessible, inhospitable trawl through mud along its entire length is the marvellous boardwalk. My sincere congratulations and thanks go to the men and women who laid and who maintain the miles of boardwalk on this route. Boardwalk that is suspended above the quagmire and adorned with wire to prevent boot-on-wet-wood slippage (which is funnier but more painful than slipping on mud). Boardwalk that is as soggy as everything else around it and yet somehow not rotten. Boardwalk that protects life at ground level from feet, and vice versa. Boardwalk that only occasionally succumbs to the mud beneath, where it lies drowning – and making you unsure whether you'll see your leg again if you try to use it as a stepping stone.

Many of the ups and downs on the route have been boardwalked into suspended staircases, making the speed of ascents and descents dependent on fitness rather than mud-manoeuvring skills. Today is a bizarre mix of army training assault course (the type where new recruits crawl face down through mud) and advanced step aerobics class.

There are two longer tramping tracks on Stewart Island and neither has such luxuries as boardwalk. The North-West Circuit covers some 125 kilometres and takes between eight and twelve days to complete. The Southern Circuit covers about fifty-six kilometres and requires at least four days. Hut talk on Stewart Island tells of those who attempt these two more serious tramping tracks and disappear up to groin height in unavoidable mud.

The views that accompany the mud and boardwalk on the Rakiura Track are of forest, forest and more forest. To be more precise, this is podocarp forest – podocarp being a term used, but not explained, in almost every New Zealand guidebook. It sounds suitably primordial and mysterious, but it just refers to a particular family of Latin names for trees.

Almost every National Park in New Zealand boasts its share of podocarp forest. Unlike most other forests here, however, there are no beech trees in Stewart Island forest. The trees that dominate (with exotic names like rimu, kamahi, miro, rata and manuka) specialise in producing trillions (or so it looks) of tiny, short, thin leaves that flop down on great drooping branches towards the earth, or stretch up and out beyond sight, depending on the modus operandi of the species. The ground is covered in layers of mosses, lichens, ferns and rotting bits of things, which apparently leach very dark brown tannins into passing streams. No two trees or clumps of moss are the same and it often seems as if there is at least as much rotting as growing going on. Here, where death is such a vibrant part of life and where the air is the most oxygenated rush I may ever inhale, I feel utterly at peace – even when trying to work a boot out from underneath the foot or so of mud where it is currently stuck.

There are no little side trips on today's route. It's hard enough to maintain just one track through all these roots and streams and deceptive hills. Everyone who is walking the whole track is therefore following exactly the same route. We all set off within an hour of each other this morning, with everyone taking advantage of the exposed beach to avoid the first section of mud. As always, not everyone at the hut is doing the same thing (the teenage boys just seem to be living there with their beer) and there are approximately fifteen of us aiming for North Arm Hut tonight.

As we wind our way through mud and over boardwalk, it feels like a game of two-kilometres-an-hour tag: you climb over a piece of tree to find a couple of fellow trampers finishing a break, whereupon you get out your chocolate bar and, after a friendly chat, they head off to catch up with the group ahead of them. No one is charging along today. Mud is a great leveller.

For parts of the day I walk with Sarah and Gill, happy to relinquish the joy of being alone with my own thoughts – and pace – in return for the hilarity that seems to surround them. Gill is purposefully striding through the epicentre of every pool of mud and swamp. She bought new knee-high gaiters for this trip and is determined to give them a thorough trial; the gleam in her eye brightens every time her load-bearing leg plunges down to knee level. Sarah, on the other hand, spends several minutes hovering at the edge of each new tricky patch, assessing and reassessing the route of least wetness. It seems that not every Kiwi is outrageously hardy in the wilderness, after all.

We debate 'Straight Through versus Side-Swiping' for a good kilometre or so. All aspects are considered: preservation of the environment, preservation of self, speed, ease, efficiency and entertainment value. In the end, the hard evidence cannot be ignored: Gill not only travels at twice the speed of her side-swiping sidekick, but somehow has less mud clinging to her when she gets there. I try to follow in her footsteps, only to experience the first of many of the day's mud-over-the-top-of-the-boots incidents. (I'm not wearing anything so useful as gaiters.)

Spending time waiting for Sarah to complete side-swiping manoeuvres also provides plenty of opportunity to appreciate the sensation of mud oozing through socks and between toes. Is this the beginning of the end of evolution: trampers, one by one, disappearing slowly into the primordial sludge whence we allegedly crawled all those years ago?

The guidebooks find little to comment on with regard to the six hours between Port William Hut and North Arm Hut. Mud, boardwalk and forest: all contemptuously dismissed as 'boring' by a German chap who overtakes me halfway through the day. I would politely venture to suggest (and I would have done so to my German friend if he hadn't immediately motored away from me) that for those who know how to look, forests are full of interesting things at every turn. There are lots and lots of turns on the Rakiura Track, no two of which are the same. As GK Chesterton once put it, 'Is ditchwater dull? Naturalists with microscopes have told me that it teems with quiet fun.'

For those who require something else to feed their thoughts, a viewpoint is positioned about an hour before North Arm Hut. The viewpoint is the highest point on the track and I am expecting it to be a hill with a small clearing in the endless canopy of trees, through which we'll finally get to see out of the forest. When we get there, however, there is no clearing in the trees. Instead, someone has gone to the trouble of squeezing a high wooden platform into the small space between trees. Trampers climb up a metal staircase – which is so steep and narrow it's more like a ladder – and pop out just above the tips of the neighbouring branches. Someone hauled all this wood and metal out here so that the Rakiura Track could boast of one viewpoint, without losing a single tree. It's a pretty good spot, too, if you're not the one carrying the wood and metal about.

The viewpoint principally looks out over Paterson Inlet: a bite-sized chunk taken from the island by goodness knows what geological messing about. Of Stewart Island's 750 kilometres of coastline, Paterson Inlet takes up more than 160. This is the bite size of something with a substantial jaw span.

In the centre of the watery gap lies Ulva Island, one of New Zealand's growing number of island sanctuaries where DOC and other conservation bodies are trying to help some of the remaining birds from endangered native species, first, just to survive and second, to get jiggy. It must be an entertaining kind of life to spend your days promoting avian copulation: matchmaking here, assisting fertilisation there.

Perched on top of the viewpoint and trying not to think about how to get a kiwi turned on, it is obvious that we've been crawling around a miniscule part of Stewart Island's acres and acres of forest. As far as the eye can see is forest and sea. After climbing back down the ladder–stairs, there is once again just forest.

North Arm Hut is set back on another small beach following a three-kilometre descent from the viewpoint on calf-wrenching stepped boardwalk. It is as lovely as the last hut was not. To preserve its loveliness, every mud-drenched outer garment has to be carefully stripped off prior to entry.

The evening is full of high tales from other tracks. The Americans and I swap notes on wind velocities in Tongariro National Park and I'm amused to hear that not only did they, like me, crawl on their bellies over the lip of the Red Crater, but that during a couple of particularly strong gusts the boys actually sat on the two girls to prevent them from being blown over the edge. Such gallantry.

Hours into the stories and long after a pitch black night has set in, the hut door swings open and in walk two girls of no more than twenty-five, accompanied by a blast of freezing night air that fails to take the edge off a distinctly tramp-ish stench.

'Oh – hi,' stutters the first girl on seeing several faces turn her way.

'Hi!' greet the Americans. 'You're not walking the Rakiura Track, are you?'

'No.' Both girls are now inside and realise after a few seconds that something more is expected from them. They add an explanation:

'We set out to walk the North-West Circuit and while we were on it we met some hunters. They were going onto the Southern Circuit and they gave us food, so we went with them. We're now on our way back to Oban.'

I begin to realise what this means. 'You've done the North-West Circuit, which is ten days minimum – and then straight onto the Southern Circuit …'

They fill in the blank. 'We've been out for twenty-one days. I think … Yeah. About twenty-one.'

No wonder they're a bit dazed around company – and no wonder even my untrained nose could smell them coming. They are Clare, from Canada, and Anja, from Holland; they met on another track, got on well and thought they'd give the infamous North-West Circuit a go together.

I'd met another pair like this one back on the ferry from Bluff. It's the mud: a hardened minority of trampers hear how difficult and wild the North-West Circuit is and they team up to help each other through it. They emerge after many days in the bush, encrusted with mud and not quite sure how to deal with the real world that is the small, isolated, island township of Oban.

During the night I have to brave the wind and rain-lashed path to the toilets and immediately hit a problem: I can't pick out my own dear boots from the line-up of mud-encased footwear on the porch. It takes ten minutes of bladder-bursting insole examination under torchlight to pick out the footwear that I have worn every day for the last ... well, for long enough to be thinking of them as my own dear boots. This is upsetting.

Day three: Back to reality

The final four or five hours of the Rakiura Track are remarkably similar to the previous ten hours or so, in that they feature a familiar blend of forest, mud and boardwalk. An added diversion are the mudflats by which the track now passes, allowing you to dash out from under an endless expanse of leaves to admire an almost endless expanse of sand-based mud (a different variety of mud entirely).

Despite the lower altitudes today (down from the heady heights of 300 metres or so) the temperature has plummeted. At Kaipipi Bay I stare at a dwelling embedded in the forest on the other side of an inlet but can't work out if anyone survives there. The wind whips across the sea as if a fleet of invisible helicopters is taking off. It starts to rain again.

Eventually the track turns to primitive road. The old Kaipipi Road was once the busiest, best-kept road on the island and is now part stream, part mud pool, part solid ground. The solid bits are dispersed randomly amongst the rest and anyone not adopting Gill's patented Straight Through walking style here would be meandering like a drunkard across twice the required distance. It will not be until my next track that I master the true art of Straight Through tramping, though, so I look a little tipsy until I am finally stamping down Main Road, leaving boot-outlined clumps of mud along the final three-quarters of an hour of tarmac to the pub in Oban.

No kiwis have been sighted, but at least the heavy rain holds off until Sarah, Gill and I are enjoying a drink with what feels like the entire population of Stewart Island.

'You must take our addresses,' insists Sarah. 'Come and stay if you're nearby.'

They give me their contact details and I look down at the two-line addresses.

'Don't you have postcodes?' I ask.

'Postcodes?' Gill asks.

'Oh yes – postcodes,' Sarah says, looking thoughtful. 'I think I've got one somewhere, but I never use it. No one does. There's no need.'

I look down at their addresses. It must be nice to live in a country that doesn't need postcodes.

In the Oban pub, the locals know all the locals and the trampers know all the trampers. Nobody here needs a postcode but everyone here needs decent boots. Most of the locals are distinguishable from visiting trampers by their calf-high white gumboots. If Stewart Island ever became the world's tiniest independent nation, it wouldn't have far to look for a national emblem – and, as the rain lashes down outside, really, what else would you possibly wear out here?

Of course, what I don't realise is that this isn't really heavy rain. Not yet. Not until I enter Fiordland and attempt the most famous tramping track in the world: the Milford Track.

4
The really famous one:
The Milford Track

The Milford Track is one of the most famous walks in the world. There are a number of reasons for this: the track lies in the middle of a UNESCO World Heritage area; the landscape is stunning by most people's standards; the track has been in recreational use for more than 115 years; and it used to be the route to riches for anyone mining greenstone. Above all else, however, the marketing for this track has been exceptional. Long before Gandalf came to roam across this corner of the world, the Milford Track had the kind of publicity with which other tracks couldn't (or, at least, didn't) compete.

Much of this publicity stemmed from an article about the track by an Englishwoman, Blanche Baughan, that appeared in *The London Spectator* in 1908. The editor changed the title of the article (as editors are wont to do) to make it more eye-catching. The new title became the epithet for the track itself: 'The Finest Walk in the World'.

This much most travel guides and advertisements for the track divulge.

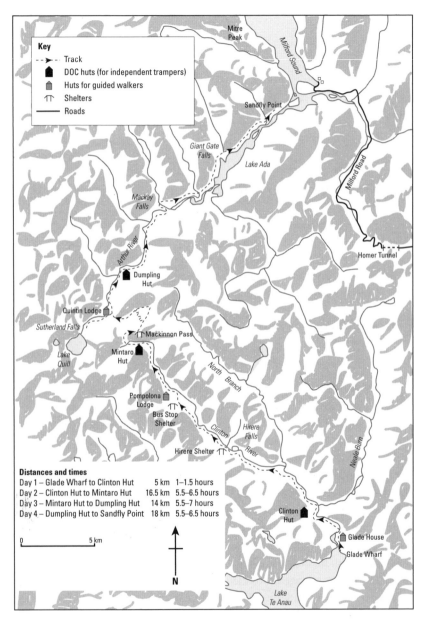

Key
- - ->- Track
- ■ DOC huts (for independent trampers)
- ⬠ Huts for guided walkers
- ⊤⊤ Shelters
- —— Roads

Mitre Peak

Milford Sound

Sandfly Point

Giant Gate Falls

Lake Ada

Milford Road

Mackay Falls

Homer Tunnel

Arthur River

Dumpling Hut

Quintin Lodge

Sutherland Falls

Mackinnon Pass

Lake Quill

Mintaro Hut

North Branch

Pompolona Lodge

Bus Stop Shelter

Clinton River

Hirere Falls

Neale Burn

Hirere Shelter

Distances and times
Day 1 – Glade Wharf to Clinton Hut   5 km   1–1.5 hours
Day 2 – Clinton Hut to Mintaro Hut   16.5 km   5.5–6.5 hours
Day 3 – Mintaro Hut to Dumpling Hut   14 km   5.5–7 hours
Day 4 – Dumpling Hut to Sandfly Point   18 km   5.5–6.5 hours

0   5 km

Clinton Hut

Glade House

Glade Wharf

Lake Te Anau

N

The Milford Track

However, they don't mention any of the fascinating details of Blanche Baughan's life, such as how this Englishwoman came to be tramping the Milford Track at the turn of the twentieth century. It seems that Blanche Baughan was free to travel alone to the other side of the world (long before twenty-four hour flights existed) and to go tramping because she refused to marry. Moreover, recent biographical material explains that her reason for refusing was that she was afraid she may have inherited a psychiatric illness. Apparently her mother murdered her husband (i.e. Blanche's father) when Blanche was ten years old – and Blanche's grandfather on her mother's side had also been convicted of murder. Blanche's mother became a psychiatric invalid, with Blanche her nurse.

Miss Baughan, it seems, would have been worth meeting. She travelled widely, both before and after moving to New Zealand in 1900 following her mother's death. As well as being a tramper, she was a poet, writer, teacher, nurse, prison reform campaigner, amateur botanist, early social worker, local councillor and even considered herself to be a mystic. Yet one of her most famous legacies is an article about the Milford Track that few of its trampers will now read. 'The Finest Walk in the World'? Or just a notable walk? Over the next four days I hope to find out whether the Milford Track's epithet is deserved, or whether it is just the work of an unconventional woman, a hyperbolic editor and almost a century of slick publicity.

The first problem for any tramper attempting to view the alleged beauty of the Milford Track is that there is a very real chance that they won't see much of it at all.

To say that Fiordland is known for its high rainfall is like saying that the English football team loses the occasional match on penalties, or that Shakespeare is known for writing a couple of decent plays. Most regions of the world measure annual rainfall in millimetres or inches; Fiordland rainfall is measured in metres – seven to ten of them each year. Neither is this restricted to any particular season (one joke runs that the rainy season here is from April to March). More than 200 days in any Fiordland year feature rain.

Some Kiwis say that it's the large mass of hot air blowing over from Australia that's the problem, but I don't think this has yet been proven scientifically. If we believe our geography textbooks, rain results when moisture-laden air blows in from the sea, rises over the land and rapidly cools at higher altitudes. Now, there's an awful lot of sea to the south and west of Fiordland, from which air has oodles of time and space to pick up moisture. Here lie the Tasman Sea, non-stop to Australia some 1,600 kilometres away, and the Southern Ocean, non-stop to Antarctica some 3,000 kilometres away. Fiordland is the first bit of New Zealand to meet the wet air. It is also a land of mountains, many of which rise to more than 1,500 metres above sea level. If wet air wanted to rise quickly and cool rapidly, it never had it so good. Thus, on any one day in the mountains of Fiordland there's a good chance that you will encounter rain heavy enough to block your view of pretty much everything else. Spend four consecutive days out there and you improve your chances no end.

DOC does all it can to manage expectations about Fiordland weather. Trampers are cheerfully told (and told again, just in case) that they can expect to get thoroughly wet on Fiordland tracks. I particularly like the wording in the Milford Track Independent Tramping Guide:

> Walkers can expect ...
> – To walk through flood water up to a metre deep after or during heavy rain
> – To cross unbridged streams
> – To get wet and muddy boots – it's part of the Milford Track experience.

It stops just short of adding a cheery exclamation mark at the end, but leaves me in no doubt that it's going to be wet out there. I am also told (and in bold) that it is not possible to dry clothes in the huts. So – it's not just going to be wet, but miserable too.

Two further aspects of the 'Milford Track experience' round off perfectly this picture of sopping discomfort for the independent tramper. The first is that it's almost impossible to choose when to walk the track based on short-term weather forecasts. Due to the popularity of this track, most of the places for a season are reserved in July and August of the preceding year, under a booking and scheduling system that makes German train timetabling under the Third Reich look sloppy and inefficient. The track is officially 'open' from late October to late April each year (all down to weather again). A maximum of forty independent trampers may start the track on each day

Tongariro Northern Circuit, Day 2. The view from the ground while crawling along the lip of the Red Crater on my stomach.

Tongariro Northern Circuit, Day 2. Several hundred people exit stage left, too small to be seen other than by the dusty trail they leave.

Tongariro Northern Circuit, Day 3. The Red Crater, Mount Ngauruhoe and, in the distance, Mount Ruapehu, silent beneath the splinterings and shufflings of frost and ice in morning sunlight.

Tongariro Northern Circuit, Day 4. Like taking a spectacular, remote spot in the Welsh hills and adding an outsized volcano to the horizon.

Rakiura Track, Day 2. An overnight stop for Stewart Island trampers and holiday home to a temporary hut warden unafraid of solitude.

Rakiura Track, Day 2. Some generally sound advice.

Milford Track, Day 1. The unmistakable sign of a different species of tramper.

No stopping until the 'Safe Area' sign is reached, but the 'Safe Area' sign appears more than a day later.

Milford Track, Day 2. Fiordland moss and lichen glow so vibrantly that dawn seems to come as much from the ground as from the sky.

Milford Track, Day 2. A four-metre high memorial standing on a mountain pass at an altitude of around 1,100 metres is still dwarfed by the surrounding peaks. Unlike the nearby Mackinnon Pass Hut, this memorial has never been swept off the Pass by the wind.

Milford Track, Day 4. The view from within God's laundry.

Kepler Track, Day 1. An untypical promise on an otherwise typical DOC sign. Local definitions of 'fit' and 'good weather' may differ from visitors' hopes.

The Kepler Challenge and Luxmore Grunt. A welcome sight, sadly unavailable to the average tramper on the Kepler Track.

Kepler Track, Day 2. A long drop toilet, in more ways than one.

Routeburn Track, Day 1. Some of the easiest muscles to strain on this track are in the neck.

Kepler Track, Day 4. Fiordland has more types of moss than the untrained eye can appreciate. This variety could almost be mistaken for the feathers of the kakapo, New Zealand's rare flightless parrot.

Routeburn Track, Day 1. A rare moment: alone on Key Summit – and temporarily exposed without backpack, hat or sunglasses.

Routeburn Track, Day 2. The most beautiful company with whom it has ever been my privilege to breakfast.

during this season. Everyone must start and finish at the same place. Everyone must take four days to walk the 53.5 kilometres. Everyone must stay in the pre-designated huts en route, in the pre-designated order. Trampers thus have to book their places long before anyone gets wind (as it were) of Hurricane Bruce or Edna or whoever, which could be setting off with them and adding extra challenge to the four days that they are required to stay out there.

The second interesting aspect of the impending drenching is that there are two sets of people who start the track every day – and the experience (of wetness and everything else) will be entirely different for the two species. I belong to Species Number Two. We are Freedom Trampers, or Independent Trampers. Being called a Freedom Tramper makes me feel like I should be endlessly blowing on my emergency whistle and waving a heavy banner (and possibly getting shot at as well), so I prefer to think of us as Independent Trampers. Members of Species Number One are the Guided Walkers. I accord them the honour of being Number One Species not through any acknowledgement of the principles of a class-based society (they're generally richer), but simply because historically they came first. Oh, and everything possible is done for them to ensure that they get far less wet and uncomfortable than the Independent Trampers.

Day one: An unusual start

Day one dawns in a remarkably sunny and cheerful way. This is not to say very much because I am starting out from Te Anau, a town that sits on the leeward side of all those air-cooling mountains. Te Anau sees barely more than a metre of rain a year.

Unlike both of my previous tracks I can't just walk out from the nearest township to the start of this track. A large chunk of today will be taken up with just getting to the start, using specially scheduled transport. I can't help but feel that this is cheating. Surely the point of these walks is to sling your backpack over your shoulder (or, as quite often in my case, reverse into it from a seated position) and head for the hills, looking like a proper Outdoors Person? Instead, a minibus will take me twenty-seven kilometres to Te Anau Downs and a ferry will take me the remaining thirty kilometres to Glade Wharf. I will travel further by bus and ferry today than I will walk over the following three days. I will also be accompanied by many others. As the minibus crunches off, I don't feel like a tramper. I feel like a tourist.

The journey to the start of the track travels almost the entire length of Lake Te Anau, which is one of many lakes in Fiordland (it's that rain again) but is also the largest expanse of water in the South Island and the second largest in the country (dear old volcanic Lake Taupo being the prize winner). The lake is tall and thin with three long, straggly arms reaching out west into the folds of mountains that separate the lake from the sea. I'm not surprised by the bland names given to these three enormous lightning flashes of water: South Fiord, Middle Fiord and North Fiord. The Middle Fiord forks at its end and the two tips are equally blessed with the names North West Arm and South West Arm. I may never need to ask for a spade while I am in New Zealand, but if I do, I shall most definitely know what to call it.

After a moment's reflection, however, I am surprised and confused by the titles South Fiord, Middle Fiord and North Fiord. After poring over my map I am even more puzzled. It appears that the only three named fiords in the whole of Fiordland (a not insubstantial 1.2 million hectares) are the three arms of this lake, which, from dimly remembered geography lessons, are not actually fiords. They are arms of a lake.

Discussion with fellow passengers ensues as we test our understanding of geographical terminology. On the map, the coast of Fiordland has sixteen sounds (many of which have arms) and a fair spattering of bays, inlets, coves and passages. We agree that a sound is normally a short-ish stretch of water separating two larger areas of sea or two pieces of land, usually an island from a mainland. In New Zealand these tend to be called straits instead, but that's for another day. We also agree that a fiord is a glacier-carved inlet in which the sea is surrounded by mountains, usually of the tall and sheer variety. Not that this helps: we appear to have agreed that Fiordland is full of things that ought to be called fiords but aren't, along with a few things that shouldn't be called fiords, but are.

Motoring up Lake Te Anau past its fiords (or arms, or whatever), the captain suddenly swerves the boat to the right, taking us onto a direct collision course with a tiny island. Just before we hit the rocky shore, he cuts the engines and invites us all to look for the small wooden cross that stands in a clearing on this island. The cross was erected in memory of Quintin Mackinnon, a European explorer intimately connected with Fiordland and the Milford Track: he discovered the crucial pass through the mountains, he cut half the track, he lived on it and he ran the first guided walking tours along it (which I suspect were a little less luxurious back then). Quintin disappeared when his boat, the *Juliet*, was wrecked on Lake Te Anau during a storm. It is generally believed that he drowned.

To satisfy my own curiosity about another possible cause of death, I check the information in my guidebook. This tells me that Quintin went missing in 1892, which was sixteen years before Miss Baughan's article appeared in *The London Spectator*. It seems reasonably safe to conclude that Miss Baughan didn't have anything to do with Quintin's death.

The sun is squintingly strong as our boat comes to rest at the northern end of the lake, next to the tiny platform that is Glade Wharf. The captain makes his final announcement over the tannoy, 'Well, here you go ladies and gentlemen. Now, if the Guided Walkers would let the Freedom Walkers disembark first please, because they have further to walk than you today to get to their first hut. Thank you all for travelling with us today – and good luck.'

A Yorkshire accent pipes up next to me. 'Ah, they just want to get rid of the riff-raff as soon as they can.'

A number of us laugh because it could be true. The Guided Walkers and Independent Trampers share the boat transport at both ends of the track, but otherwise are efficiently and deliberately segregated.

When the Independent Trampers boarded the ferry we were asked to leave our backpacks on a platform at the rear, where we threw them in a pile. As I disembark I see four rows of Milford Track Guided Walks backpacks, neatly packed and stacked. They are all the same design and colour. Each one sports the MTGW logo and a three digit number. Come in, number 372. Your time is up.

I am the first off the boat and immediately head for what looks like the track. From the wharf point, however, there are three tracks leading off in different directions. The track that leads north-west (the direction I was expecting to take) can't be The Track because it's as wide as a road. However, the two track-sized tracks both lead off in the wrong direction.

On the wharf an impressive amount of strap-adjusting and stretching is going on and nobody else looks like setting off immediately. I stand there feeling like a supreme fool, but knowing that I'd look even more of a fool if

I set off on the wrong path. I am saved by two uniformed guides who come shooting off the boat and virtually run off down the road-sized track. I follow on behind them and am soon inhaling their cigarette smoke.

The unsealed road winds along by the side of the Clinton River and underneath some impressive peaks. It also lies under a canopy of trees that prevents both species of tramper from seeing much else until we emerge, after a mere ten minutes or so, at a building that would not look out of place in a Swiss ski resort.

Glade House has posh windows (double-glazed, I swear), an already smoking chimney, the scent of juicy kitchen smells and the general air of being a jolly nice place to spend a night. Rumour has it that Glade House even has a piano lounge. It is the first 'hut' for the Guided Walkers and only this wealthier species of walker may cross its threshold. We Independent Trampers must pass by and cross the swingy wooden footbridge to the Other Side.

The track (now appropriately track sized) continues to wind along the bank of the Clinton River under the canopy of beech trees. At regular intervals narrow side tracks lead off to the river, worn away by tens of thousands of walkers pottering over to get a glimpse of the river and the valley sides. With thirty-nine people close on my tail I duck off onto one of these side tracks and pop out onto a rocky beach on a bend in the river.

The sun is shining, the valley sides are steep and a South Island robin hops over to keep me company. Far be it from me to give him any food, but he continues to hop around me as if he's trying to ask me something and I just can't work out what it is. South Island robins have a creamy white chest on an otherwise charcoal coloured body and are slightly bigger than the red-breasted Christmas card type (although the difference isn't quite as striking as with the pigeons). This will sound a bit weird, but the best feature of the South Island robin is its eyes, which look kind and intelligent. Not that I make a habit of staring deeply into birds' eyes (it being very difficult, for one thing, when they have them on either side of their heads), but this one keeps looking at me intently through one eye and then turning his head and doing the same with the other eye – as if the eyes-on-the-side-of-the-head thing were an evolutionary error.

Still not sure what the little chap is trying to convey, I turn my attention to an enormous tree stump that is lying at rather an odd angle on the rocks, with a circle of roots still attached. Even dead and stripped of its branches this tree looks much bigger than the ones on the banks. It seems odd that it would have grown to such a height out here in the middle of the rocky riverbed. It dawns on me (more slowly than frankly it should) that this tree did not grow here at all. Although the river is now a fairly docile torrent, there will be days out here – many days – when none of these rocks are visible and when trees are swept down the mountainsides and along the rivers. This one was just so big that it didn't make it all the way to the lake in pieces.

The frustrating thing about the walk to the first hut is that it takes only about an hour. To stretch it out to something more deserving of a calorie-packed dinner, I follow the short, boardwalked side track round a wetland area. From the protective boardwalk it is possible to see in one sweep all three layers of habitat that exist here: wetland, beech forest and barren mountain tops. The mosses and other spongy plants on the ground are in the most fabulous oranges, yellows and brilliant greens – the kind of Day-Glo colours that people wore a lot as socks and wristbands in the 1980s. Please say it wasn't just me.

Even with much dawdling and attempted bird communing I reach Clinton Hut long before I'm ready to stop walking. Judging by the feverish activity in the kitchen, I also reach the hut long after everyone else.

The kitchen is a separate structure on this site, with row upon row of gas cookers, tables, benches and polypropylened limbs in action. I am intrigued to find out what has brought all these people to the Milford Track. What kind of people brave the high fees (even for Independent Trampers) and the threat of at least one drenching – *and* are sufficiently organised to book themselves on to a track up to nine months in advance? My own levels of organisation haven't gone anywhere near this far: I booked my place after a late cancellation ten days ago. Ah, the benefits of travelling alone.

We are an interesting collection of people, we forty, and not quite what I was expecting. The age range is considerable. There is a Kiwi family of four in which the two boys are under ten years old. There are two parties of friends in their fifties and sixties, faces and backpacks crumpled but still up to the job. Amongst those in between are a middle-aged Kiwi couple, the male half of which keeps calling me Shazza and slapping me on the back, for reasons I can't fathom, and a sprinkling of Europeans, with the four Brits the biggest and loudest contingent.

More than two-thirds of the Independent Trampers are Kiwis. During idle chat over boiling pots of carbohydrates, they each confess in turn that they've always wanted to walk the Milford Track and have finally decided to do so. It seems that the most famous track in a country full of tracks is as much of a draw for the locals as it is for the tourists.

Clinton Hut is more like a small village than the self-contained huts on other tracks. There is a central square of decking, which I christen 'the Village Brown'. On to the Brown face two bunkroom blocks and the large kitchen-dining room, while, from the open side of the Brown, a path leads the short distance to the ablutions block. In the bunkrooms are bunk beds and oodles of space for hanging and scattering belongings. The kitchen-dining block is as large as any school canteen and – a wonder to behold – it has electric lights; powered by solar energy and therefore subject to strict curfews, but still … electric lights.

The *pièce de résistance*, however, is the ablutions block. This is a separate building housing rows of toilet cubicles and sinks. Until now the only DOC toilets I've seen are the outsized, telephone-booth type of boxes that encase a toilet seat over a composting hole. Even from the outside, it is clear that Milford Track toilets are something special. These are toilets that flush! Toilet paper is provided! Sadly, the treats don't stop there: with a deep sigh of disappointment I notice that a small mirror has been placed on the wall above each sink.

Back in the canteen the air is steaming up nicely when the hut warden arrives for the Milford Track Hut Warden Talk. More formal than on the other tracks (and making the room feel even more like a school canteen), the speech covers all the main items and a few new ones as well. Everyone must clean up after themselves and take all their rubbish with them. No one must feed the keas – the strong, cheeky and destructively inquisitive alpine parrots. No one must encourage the keas in any way – they are fully capable of ripping open backpacks and stealing vital equipment without encouragement. Water should be filtered, chemically treated or boiled for at least three minutes before being drunk (this being the official DOC stance, although the other wardens I've met so far have freely admitted that they personally don't bother). Oh – and it looks like there's some rain heading for our valley, which might be with us by tomorrow evening. He'll let us know in the morning.

A very entertaining couple of hours follow, in which we four Brits commence the bonding process by mercilessly making fun of each other. Ian and Matt were students together (in Sheffield) and Matt now works in Melbourne, so they are tramping in New Zealand as a holiday together. Ian is everything you'd expect from a Yorkshireman who regularly yomps around his county. Matt, frankly, is not – but neither does he seem to care. Dominic, meanwhile, is several years younger than us, being the wrong side of twenty-five. He is much taller than us and has black, curly hair in Einstein style, thereby adding a further six inches to his height. He is from the Home Counties and is bumming around New Zealand waiting for the ski season to start. Mercifully, he also has a sense of humour and isn't lacking in self-confidence, because he is obviously going to be the butt of the jokes for the next three days.

Dom and I conduct a disyllabic argument about the name of a travellers' card game.

'Arsehole.'

'Shithead.'

'Arsehole!'

'Shithead!'

This continues until we realise that these are, in fact, two entirely different card games and settle down to play them both. I may not be the most sociable walker in the world, but it looks like the Milford Track evenings will be fun.

Day two: Rain? What rain?

In the morning, the boys wish me 'Good afternoon' as they set off smugly together before I've even broken into my morning recipe of muesli presoaked in a pot of yoghurt (no cooking, no washing up). The hut warden has been and gone and rain is still forecast. He has advised us to try to go up Mackinnon Pass today, if we can, because we may still get some views from the Pass before the cloud comes in. This would be an additional three to four hours of walking after the scheduled six hours for today. We'll see.

The advantage of being a late breakfaster is that I have the whole track to myself when I set off. Inside the green underworld, this is a real treat. On every surface – vertical, horizontal and everything in-between – lies a liberal coating of moss and lichen. It glows, as if the dawn is coming from the earth as much as from the sky. Old man's beard drops from every fork of every twig. It looks as though Jack Frost has discarded the brilliant white look and gone crazy with a new line in vibrant greens. Marvellous tendrils hang from every twig, branch and trunk in never-landing drips and impolitely pointed fingers.

As if the visual magic weren't enough, there is a scent to the air that is completely new to me. It is beyond pleasant: it is intoxicating and addictive. It blends ozone and forest and river. If I stayed here forever, I'd never get another cold.

The track continues upstream with more side routes worn down to the riverside. Taking another of these little detours, I trip over a tree root and almost fall down the two-metre drop into the river. I curse myself for not concentrating. All I'm thinking about is how to avoid the eighty or so other walkers on this section of the track today. I'm learning that I enjoy company in the huts, but need to be alone when I'm walking. There are just too many beautiful things to take in to be distracted by conversation or someone else's rhythm.

The Milford Track is not for the lover of solitude. It proves impossible to maintain a position behind the other Independent Trampers and in front of the Guided Walkers. I catch up with the tail-enders from my price bracket and we laugh as we endlessly overtake and are overtaken, depending on who's stopped to look at what and for how long. It is impossible not to keep stopping and gaping at nature's idiosyncrasies.

I diligently try to follow my progress on the map. On the reverse of the map are a number of warnings about what happens to sections of this track after heavy rain, but so far the ground is dry and the sun is out. I look for Hirere Falls and find a line – a trickle – from tip to toe of the 1,800-plus metres of rock opposite. Fifteen minutes later I round a corner and see a DOC sign labelled Hirere Falls and pointing off at another sliver of silver suspended on a completely different part of the rock wall opposite. Orienteering skills are not required on this track, which is just as well given the current standard of mine.

In addition to signposts are other little touches to remind the tramper that they are on the tramping equivalent of a motorway: mileposts; shelters for rainy days; and toilets. The toilets are of the big green telephone box variety (nature calling …), but this is more than I've seen elsewhere between huts. It is a reminder that lots and lots of people walk the Milford Track, many of whom have never have done anything like this before. They may not have not read Kathleen Meyer's practical guide, *How To Shit In The Woods*. They may not know how, where and with what equipment to answer the call of nature responsibly in her own backyard. I don't know how often these toilets are emptied (and I don't want to ask). From the outside they look little bigger than a telephone box, but from the inside there's a whole other ecosystem there.

For most of day two the track runs slightly but continuously uphill and pops out from under its forest camouflage with growing enthusiasm. When it does, there are views down other mountain-hemmed valleys, up the sides of our own or along its remaining length to the high point on the track, the Mackinnon Pass. The valley floor is only a few hundred metres wide, but about four kilometres separates the two lines of peaks 2,000 metres up.

The track also passes through a swamp that would grace any ghoulish movie. Formed when the vegetation slipped off the mountain sides and trapped some of the river water on the valley floor, the swamp puts on an excellent show of blackened tree stumps looming up from eerily calm water. Fresh water in Fiordland is supposed to be always rushing about somewhere; it's not supposed to be suspended in silence and stillness.

It is remarkable that plants manage to cling to these mountain sides. There are healthy numbers of beech trees at the lowest altitudes, but still no end of shrubs and ferns in sight as you crick your neck back. There's an awful lot of clinging going on up there.

The section of track from not far after Clinton Hut to Quintin Lodge (a few hours into tomorrow's route) is prime avalanche territory. Fifty-six mapped avalanche paths cross the Milford Track in this zone. That's fifty-six *mapped* paths. If an avalanche started somewhere up there, I wouldn't even know about it from down here until it fell on me. Whether or not it's on a mapped route probably wouldn't be the first thought to enter my head.

The thoughts that do enter my head while I'm walking are a real mixed bag: whether the benefits of retrieving chocolate and water from the pack will exceed the effort involved; why I'm becoming more and more fond of being on my own; whether a good photograph of moss is a contradiction in terms; whether I should pursue a new career as a hut warden; and how useful it has proved to have dragged my attention away from the deodorant problems of my school geography teacher and instead listened to what he had to say about glaciation.

I'm embroiled in some of the meatier issues when there is a sudden flash of brown movement on the ground ahead. Oh my goodness – it's a chicken-sized brown bird with no wings. It's a kiwi! I stay absolutely still while it moves its bottom around a bit and disappears off into a wooden shelter at the side of the track. I creep forward as if I'm trying to moonwalk in reverse and it pops its head out of its hiding place and potters over.

It is not a kiwi. This is a weka – another species from New Zealand's excellent line in flightless birds. It looks not unlike a brown mallard, not least because ducks have an odd way of walking too – except with a duck you sense that if it trips up it will be able to steady itself with its wings. Miss Pecky here walks up to me, potters round me a few times and then meanders off again. Three Independent Trampers appear and I excitedly tell them of the weka, show them where she went, relate how friendly she is and wait with them for her next appearance, which spectacularly fails to take place.

Not long after meeting Miss Pecky, and whilst about to cross one of the day's many half-dry stream beds, I chance upon an intriguing DOC sign. 'No Stopping', it tells me: I am about to enter an area with a high avalanche risk; I must not stop in this area; I must not stop until I reach the end of this area. There's no indication from any of the literature I'm carrying as to where this zone of terror may end. I sit down, inches before the sign. I eat a lot of chocolate. Then I get up and I don't stop until I'm throwing all my things onto the bunk that the boys have reserved for me at Mintaro Hut.

The clouds are descending and it's 3.30 pm by the time I reach the hut. Decision time: do I attempt another three or four hours of climbing up and down Mackinnon Pass to see whatever views may be left under the clouds? Or do I wait until tomorrow and hope it's not too cloudy then? The majority of people are bunkering down for the night as I set off up the hard bit of the Milford Track. Released from my freeriding pack-mate, I bound up the ascent. Only after half an hour do I wonder whether I should have abandoned all my belongings so merrily. A torch might have been useful, for example. And maybe that whistle.

There's nothing for it but to make sure that I get back before it gets too dark. I knock off the ascent in under an hour, but then become hopelessly engrossed in the views. From up here the view reaches back along today's valley and out along tomorrow's, with an extra mountain towering above on both flanks; a stunned waterfall, frozen over rock and air; a few tarns doing their best not to be blown dry; and, this evening, a rather large bird of prey hovering under the belly of the darkening clouds, putting me on the evening menu.

The descent does scare me – and rightly so given my foolishness. Back in the hut, though, Dom has another matter of grave concern: the Milford Track Olympics. Buoyed up with youthful testosterone, Dom has christened the four of us 'Team GB'. (Actually, I suspect it's just the three of them, but they're polite enough not to say so.) Despite the huge numbers of other walkers, there's only one other team as far as Dom is concerned: 'Team Israel'. Team Israel comprises one person, who is the fittest amongst us forty. He's the fittest person I've ever met. He set off last this morning, got to the hut before me and was up and down Mackinnon Pass before the rest of us had dropped our packs.

Talk of competitive tactics swiftly deteriorates into less mentally challenging card games and on to an early night. We are shattered. Heads hit improvised pillows as forty people simultaneously pass out.

A few seconds later, rain starts to whip against the hut. With it comes a thunderous explosion that jolts me awake. After a second roar I jam my earplugs so far down into my ears that it hurts, but makes no difference. A sequence of frequent snorts punctuates the irregular howls. Great: not one, but two industrial snorers lying right next to me.

After half an hour of repositioning, cramming ever more things into my ears and failed attempts to visualise myself into a quiet haven of rest, I am all out of ideas. I climb out of my sleeping bag, roll it up and tiptoe out of the bunkroom, smiling humourlessly at my need to make as little noise as possible. In the kitchen I pull three wooden benches together, rue the lack of industrialised uniformity in these parts (all the benches are different heights) and make my second assault on sleep. Odd noises in the kitchen sound as if they're being made by invading kea or possums, but the only thing that will make me move again tonight is if something bites me.

Day three: The real Milford experience

By morning, remarkably little has changed: I still haven't fallen asleep and the rain is just as heavy. The downpour has been continuous – and I know because I listened to all of it above the snoring. It requires no effort to be last to leave today; effort is required to get going at all. I am, in any case, never the very last to leave: Team Israel is always the actual last to leave; I am just the last of the confirmed non-bionic trampers.

The re-ascent of Mackinnon Pass takes far longer under the weight of backpack and rain. The ascent comprises a thought-numbing series of rocky switchbacks – those low-incline, zigzaggy attempts to make climbing something steep feel like walking on a treadmill set to the beginners' incline. I'm not a huge fan of switchbacks: if there's a lot of up to be walked, I'd rather go straight up.

Not much of the Milford Track survives unchanged from one year to another. A couple of switchbacks have already been washed away this season and DOC staff have shaped a series of impromptu steps into the mountainside. The improvised track is nearly vertical, so a long, thick rope has been secured at the top somewhere and trailed down through the mud. With my pack on and with heavy rain washing the steps into mud slips, I haul myself up using the soggy rope.

As I totter up the final couple of zigzags, battening down all my hatches against the rain and wind, one of the Milford Track Guided Walk guides motors past me. She too is carrying a full backpack. She is also carrying several thermos flasks, wearing shorts and moving at twice my speed. This girl is hardy.

The mystery of the thermos flasks is solved at the Mackinnon Memorial. As the Guided Walkers tumble up onto the flat top of the Pass, they are greeted with steaming mugs of hot chocolate, tea and coffee. The Memorial is a twenty-minute walk away from the Pass shelter, where they can expect more comprehensive treats.

The Mackinnon Memorial marks the top of the hard climb, but not the highest point on the Pass. I potter over to read the inscription, partly to mask how out of breath I am. The inscription is of the standard type: factual and informative to a point. The most interesting part, however, is the information omitted.

The first and most glaring omission is that the memorial is dedicated to only one of the two people who discovered this pass. It was discovered in 1888 by Quintin Mackinnon and Ernest Mitchell. There had been a race to find a pass. The government wanted to find a way to get more tourists to Milford Sound and began to fund work on the track. At least two teams tried to find a pass through the mountains. Another team (Thomas Mackenzie and W.S. Pillans) didn't find a way through, but two mountains near the track seem to have been named after them. Our friends Quintin and Ernest did find their way through, but Ernest seems to have been almost entirely forgotten. I cannot find a single mountain, lake, river, hut or even waterfall in this area named after him. When it comes to publicity, it really does pay to disappear in mysterious circumstances.

The second omission is less obvious, but is the reason I propose another – and entirely different – reason for renaming the Mackinnon Memorial. After Quintin's mysterious – and presumed – death, the Gaelic Society of New Zealand and the Otago Rugby Football Union thought it would be a nice idea to erect a memorial to him, in honour of all he did for the Milford Track. It seemed obvious that Quintin's crowning achievement was the discovery of the pass and so it seemed logical to erect a memorial there. Now, from whichever side you approach it, the pass is a good seven to nine hours' walk away from the nearest boat ride to the nearest settlement. Neither does the pass experience the kind of weather that is conducive to building projects. When a Dunedin stonemason called James Robertson was asked to build the memorial, he spotted these little hurdles and refused the commission. He was already sixty-seven years old and wasn't sure he'd physically be up to the job. The Gaelic Society was apparently insistent: he, like Quintin, was Scottish; he was the best stonemason in the country; and the memorial must be erected. Robertson relented. He then spent four months living in a hut at the bottom of the pass, going up and down the mountain side, toiling away in wind and rain and probably a lot worse, at an altitude of 1,100 metres. In April 1915 he finished the memorial. And three months later he died. And *that* is why I like to think of this pillar of stones and mortar as the Robertson Memorial.

The Kiwi family from our group is standing further on from the memorial at the point where the path edges close to the drop into the next valley (a twelve-second drop, apparently, although if anyone were to jump off now, the wind would deposit them back up here before they'd got to four). The two little boys are holding Dad's hands as he points out the views he saw when he first came up here thirty years ago. In front of them is a thick wall of cloud. They don't look as if they're standing on the edge of a cliff. The boys are numbly and dutifully staring at the wall of cloud while Dad talks. If they had booked to walk the track just one day earlier, they would have seen both valleys from here.

Once we've all had enough of loitering around the memorial watching hot drinks being served to the Guided Walkers, we troop onwards to the Pass Hut, heads down, hoods up, everything hunched. The Pass Hut is the only hut that accommodates both species of walker here – albeit in separate rooms. The Guided Walkers get more than half the space and, when Dom and I cheekily try to sneak in to their room, we find the door firmly locked. Like Bisto Kids, we stand with noses pressed to the scent coming from the room next door.

The public 'half' of the shelter is like a steam room, although at a temperature twenty degrees lower than that might imply. As we peel off the layers of dripping 'waterproof' gear, a thick fog of steam rises, the likes of which I have never seen before. When I wave my arms I can write letters in the air. Each of us has a thick, white 'Ready Brek glow' around our edges and the more people arrive, the more the clouds keep rolling in – until there's as little visibility inside as out.

Through the mist we make cheery comments and someone stations herself by the single gas hob we're allowed in our room, boiling water and doling it out to anyone in need. It's difficult to know what to do for the best: do I stay here until I've had a good snack and a hot drink, even though I'm chilling and beginning to realise just how wet I am? Or, do I press on to the allegedly worst part of the track (no – the uphill bit wasn't it) and let adrenalin do the rest?

'Can't buy the views, can they?' chuckles one of the Kiwi contingent with a nod towards the Guided Walkers' enclave.

'Weather not included!' chortles another, as an amused debate opens up on the merits of Guided Walking versus Independent Tramping.

'I hear they pay up to $2,000 for this experience!'

'It's a range. It depends on what they opt for – the king-sized suite or a shared room. That kind of thing. They certainly don't pay any less than $1,500. Some might even pay more than $2,000.'

'What do we pay in total, when you add all the transport in?'

'About $260.'

'Well, in that case, they're more than welcome to their hot chocolate!'

'But they get one night more than we do and they get to stay in the Mitre Peak Lodge on their final night. It's usually reserved exclusively for them.'

'They get an extra night on the track? Is that a bonus, in weather like this?'

It's all downhill from the Pass Hut, but that phrase will never have a darker meaning. The descent from Mackinnon Pass is so steep that my ears pop several times. There is still no visibility beyond the next five metres. In my head I picture all the sights I saw from the top of the pass yesterday. It's difficult and spooky to imagine the frozen waterfall and jagged peaks rearing invisibly beside me. This must be how those who believe in God feel: an immense presence that is by your side and yet invisible.

The only other connection with life inside the cloud is through sound. Most sounds are of water in various modes of travel: pattering down onto rocks and leaves; gathering and swirling into streams along the track; gushing down in waterfalls; and thickening the sweeps of the wind. There is an occasional, but loud and alarming, crack and 'wumph' of rock falling from somewhere above me. The first time I hear this noise I think it's the crack of a large fork of lightning, but then the tumbling of rocks gives it away. Three loud, splintering rockfalls take place somewhere nearby during the first two hours of knee-flexing alone.

Apparently, if an avalanche is headed your way and you can't get out of its path, you're supposed to fling yourself up against the nearest big rock or tree. This is partly for shelter from the debris and partly because there is a very, very small chance that a really, really big object will hold its own in the crush. It presumably doesn't help if you can see neither the avalanches nor the nearest big objects.

Of course, if there were a very high risk of rockfall on to the track or of flash floods sweeping away track and trampers, the hut warden would not have let us set out this morning. Then again, maybe she would. Nature is wild here and everyone rightly assumes that everyone else knows that. It is obvious. It's marvellous, actually, just to be let loose into the possibilities of danger, without having to sign any silly legal waivers or have the world made falsely safe. Such joys have been lost in my homeland, which has merrily followed the American-laid Path of Greatest Legal Redress. In New Zealand, you just get on with it. And if you're knocked on the head by an avalanche, then everyone else will get on with it on your behalf. Heck, if you disappear in more mysterious circumstances here, you might even have something named after you.

DOC signs appear and disappear through the whiteness: Sutherland Falls are apparently over there somewhere; this way for the detour during avalanche season (remind me – when isn't it avalanche season here?). The world is very tiny and slippy. Under the treeline the rocky track gets slimier and slippier. By the time I reach Quintin Lodge, every muscle and ligament in my knees has been tested and retested as if it had just taken part in the annual maintenance check for Air Force One.

Much as we'd like to, we Independent Trampers don't get to stay in Quintin Lodge. Not for us are the cheery dinner smells or the roaring fire, although the Guided Walks outfit does allow us a small, cold room in which to dump our packs if we care to take the side trip to Sutherland Falls. Something in me has snapped into place over the last few hours (fortunately not any bones or tendons, although they've been doing their bit too). It no longer matters that I am soaked through, tired and uncomfortable. I will be walking the extra hour and a half to see Sutherland Falls up close. There is no other way to see them today.

The boys are already on their way back.

'How are you doing?' asks Matt from the pool of mud with which he is engaged.

'Oh, you know,' I grin.

'Well, you've got another thirty minutes still to go, but it's well worth it,' he adds.

Dom is also enthused. 'It's brilliant! But you have to go in it. If you go over the river, you can then edge round and behind the waterfall. Me and Matt went in.'

'You will get very wet, though,' adds Ian.

Very wet? Do I look dry?

At the Falls I find a couple of neat middle-aged Japanese ladies wearing tennis pumps and clutching umbrellas. These are Guided Walkers who have been to the Lodge, changed into dry clothes and popped out for a quick look at the waterfall before dinner. I squelch on and start my assault on the river, much to their grave consternation. Thankfully for all of us they are beyond earshot when I unintentionally sit down in the middle of the river. This makes progress easier because I'm no longer looking for the path of least water (why was I before?) and I am soon standing up to my knees in the stuff, gazing at thousands of cubic tons of it hurtling off the rock above my head. The noise makes me physically wince and more than covers the shrieks of excitement that nobody who stands here would be able to suppress.

The water plummets 580 metres over three tiers. These are amongst the highest falls in New Zealand – a country that specialises in big mountains and high rainfall. They are named after yet another Scottish explorer. Donald Sutherland arrived in Milford Sound in 1878 (with the whalers and sealers, I'm afraid) and stayed there for more than forty years. Legend relates that in 1880, Donald set off up the Arthur Valley with a chap called John Mackay. They discovered a pretty impressive waterfall and tossed a coin to determine which of their names it should bear. (I'm going to try not to bemoan here the way that explorers named everything after themselves. I'll do it later instead.) Thus, at the toss of a coin, Mackay Falls were named. Several days later, however, they discovered the three-tiered wonder underneath which I'm standing and it duly became Sutherland Falls. The smugness with which Sutherland allegedly greeted this twist of fate may go part-way to explaining why he was 'the hermit of Milford Sound'.

Having emerged from underneath the hermit's falls, I discover that Ian was right: I wasn't wet before. *Now* I'm wet. I need to keep moving and the final three kilometres pass by as quickly as knee joints and water will permit. A long section of this track was washed into the river by previous rain and the detour looks like it's losing the battle as well. It's now so dark with rain that the nightlife is coming out: a morepork blinks from its low-hanging branch at this scurrying sponge, before sweeping away down the valley.

By the time I squelch up the steps of Dumpling Hut, I feel that to be squished quickly by an avalanche now would be a blessing. I have no energy, no hope, no adrenalin and no sense of humour left to deal with what I'm about to find out.

The food in the top of my pack is wet. The clothes underneath the food are wet. The sleeping sheet and sleeping bag underneath the clothes are wet. Inside the waterproof pack cover, inside the pack, inside the several bin bags with which I've lined the pack and inside the three other bags in which my sleeping bag was wrapped – there is a puddle.

I'm one of the last to arrive and the back of the kitchen has been turned into such a Chinese laundry that I can only assume there's a lit fire somewhere in the middle of it. To my eternal gratitude, as soon as a few of the others find out what's happened to my sleeping bag, they move themselves and their dripping clothes back from the heat and tell me to take the space right in the middle. Pity has won out over the first-come, first-served system and I am enormously grateful.

'Hiya!' bounces Matt, as I slump over to the boys.

Ian is in cheery mood too. 'Catch up, girl. We've been here for ages. Where've you been?'

'Getting wet.'

Ian bustles on. 'You'd best get your stove going if you're going to have dinner and boil tomorrow's water before the lights go out.'

I look up, slowly. 'Tomorrow's water will come straight from the tap. Like today's did. And yesterday's.'

Ian goes pop-eyed: 'You mean you haven't been boiling your water?'

'Well, none of the hut wardens bother, so I figured I wouldn't waste the gas.'

'We wondered about that too.' Ian and Matt exchange knowing looks. 'The hut wardens on the Kepler Track said they just drink the water, but the wardens here do say to boil it.'

Dom looks up. 'Those aren't your normal clothes are they? What – did you bring a special outfit for the final night?'

I take a deep breath. I let it out again, very slowly. 'Gentlemen. I am wet. I am cold. I am miserable. I have had no sleep. I have walked for eight hours in the rain. I am sitting here shivering in my thermal underwear because everything I own is either wet or sopping. This includes my sleeping bag. I am not happy and I'm very sorry, but I have completely and utterly lost my sense of humour.'

For a moment, they think this is another one of my jokes and sit diligently waiting for the punchline. When they realise it's not coming, they offer hot water, a sympathetic change of subject and a game of cards. I am quite pathetically grateful.

Two hours later, wrapped in Matt's emergency foil blanket and a now merely dampened sleeping bag, I lie down by the fire and begin another long night of listening to rain.

Day four: Trench foot

As day four leaks into existence, I still haven't slept. I'm beginning to think it might be the tannins in the distinctly yellow water. The others step over me and by 7.00 am more than half of them have left. They seem very concerned about whether the track has washed away and whether they'll make it to the end in time to catch the boat, which leaves at 2.15 pm and 3.15 pm. I'm more concerned about whether I'll ever find all the articles of my clothing that are scattered around the hut failing to dry.

Team Israel is also breakfasting lazily. He'll only need about three hours to walk out; he'll probably only need a couple if we're swimming. I feel a bit sorry for him: if we didn't all have to follow the regimented four-day schedule for this track, he'd have walked the whole route in a day and a half.

The hut warden breezes in. 'Good morning!' he calls, in that bright, breezy way these wardens have when the weather is truly awful. Any minute now he'll flick a casual glance skywards and announce 'Nah – that's not rain'.

Team Israel has been following the events of the night. 'Is the path clear, then?'

'Yeah, it's OK. I've radioed down the track and it's open. Shouldn't give you any problems. It's an easy walk out. You two have got the right idea to wait around here for a bit. Well, there is one part ... But, no ... shouldn't be a problem.'

I'm not quite happy to leave it there. 'Er ... Do you want to tell us about it anyway?'

'Oh, it's just a section where the track was washed away a few weeks ago.

You have to go up and over the slip. You'll definitely get your feet wet today after all the rain, but it's clearly marked. Maybe just allow a bit of extra time for it. Did anyone's things get wet yesterday?'

Team Israel nods at me. 'Yes – her sleeping bag and clothes.'

The warden bursts out laughing. He laughs heartily for more than a minute and then tells me I should have used a DOC Pack Liner. Just as soon as I've had some sleep, I look forward to having a laugh myself.

After more than forty hours of heavy rain, Fiordland style, the Arthur Valley displays everything for which the Milford Track is famous. High valley walls are streaked with lines of water, like extremely fatty rashers of bacon. On their way to the ground, the silver threads appear and disappear between low-lying horizontal trails of vapour.

The sky above is thick and white and the valley floor is filled with clouds that have been drained by their forty-hour shift. They have flopped down exhausted into the valley that has one of the highest average annual rainfall figures in Fiordland. The white clouds folded into the mountains make it look as if the whole forest is smoking.

The condition of the track along this valley varies. The first part winds along by the riverbed in a flat and welcoming fashion. It then disappears under several thousand tons of valley-side. This is another of those slips in which Fiordland specialises. The term 'slip' euphemises what happens here. A 'slip' is a small thing, a slight thing. A slip on a banana skin is funny, not fatal. A ladies' slip is subtle, not seen. A slip in which all those tons of rock and vegetation plummet 1,500 metres is an entirely different proposition. These walls of granite, gneiss and schist up to 2,000 metres high are sometimes no stronger than the walls of a sandcastle that crumble as advancing waves wash into them. Perhaps only in New Zealand would such an event be given such a small, practical name. Elsewhere it might be called a landslide, a major rockfall or the work of some pretty angry gods.

Maori legend concerning the creation of Fiordland does indeed feature the actions of a pretty hefty god. It also involves a slightly different version of the creation of the South Island. In this version, the South Island was still a canoe, but not under the control of the mischievous half-god Maui. This time four gods were using the canoe to explore the seas when the canoe sank and turned to stone. The west side settled much higher than the eastern side and so the four brothers rushed to the western side, where they also turned to stone. They became Aoraki (or Mount Cook, the highest mountain in New Zealand) and its three neighbouring peaks.

The gods decided that this mountainous land must be sculpted to be fit for human habitation. Fiordland was the hardest part to sculpt, but the god Tu Te Rakiwhanoa set to work with an enormous adze. He carved the fiords, starting in the south and working his way north. The northern fiords were therefore carved with greater finesse and the height of the mountains around the fiords increases from south to north. The northernmost fiord, Milford Sound, is the most exquisitely carved and has the highest walls. Milford Sound is the destination for all those who walk the Milford Track.

It sometimes seems as if Tu Te Rakiwhanoa hasn't finished his work and is still hacking bits off the mountain sides. Where the 'slip' covers the track, there's no alternative but to go up and over. Previous pairs of boots have helped DOC staff to cut a makeshift path over the debris. The snag is that a good path for feet is also a good path for water. To climb up the side of the slip this morning is to climb up a waterfall. To clamber down the other side of the slip this morning is to clamber down another waterfall and into a fast-flowing stream, more than two feet deep. With dense forest canopy still all around, there is no alternative to wading through cold, quick water – other than losing your balance and sitting down in it instead.

By this point, wading through water up to my armpits would not make me wetter. Then the path leaps over the river by means of a swing bridge and a new set of hazards is revealed. Much of this section of the track was cut by blasting a line through the walls of rock on the northern side of the river. The ankle-twisting angles of splintered rock also sport coverings of algae and moss to help bring you to your knees.

I don't want to miss anything, so, despite the discomfort, I take the side track to Bell Rock and Mackay Falls. Bell Rock is an oddity in a world of marvels. On the outside, it is shaped like – well, like a very large rock. Crawling underneath, however, you find a bell-shaped hollow where there should be more rock. The scientific explanation is that this rock used to be somewhere else and facing in a different direction, which allowed water to wear away its insides. It was then moved to its current location in one of those little slips that happen here. If Bell Rock were to be dislodged from its current resting place while someone was checking out its innards, it would be some days before that person could be freed. This is despite the rock being in one of the more accessible parts of one of the busiest tracks in New Zealand. It's all relative.

One part of my brain is delighting in the wildness of the landscape and goggling at each new waterfall. The other part is performing a constant discomfort assessment, the focus of which is my feet. I'm giving serious thought to a condition called trench foot, so named because it was suffered by soldiers in the trenches in the First World War. These soldiers spent days and months standing in the mud and water at the bottom of the trenches. The skin on their feet became flaccid, flaky, and – in the worst cases – mouldy. It is what you'd expect to happen if you stayed in the bath for a week, and it is thoroughly unpleasant. After just two days of marching in soggy socks and boots, I'm beginning to wonder how long it takes before trench foot sets in.

The Arthur Valley today is like God's laundry. Clouds hang low, drained white from their exertions and looking like the white cotton cycle has finished and all the sheets have been hung up to air. I seem stuck in the rinse cycle. I've never known what 'rinse hold' means, but those words certainly sound appropriate for this rain without end.

The hardy female Guided Walkers' guide overtakes me for the third day in a row. For the third time, we say a cheery hello and for the third time, I watch her naked legs power away from me. I try once again to work out her secret. This is Straight Through Tramping of a whole new calibre. Gill's patented Straight Through Walking on the Rakiura Track was a way of walking through mud and water as if you don't mind that it's there. This guide's Straight Through Tramping is a way of walking through mud and water as if it's just not there at all. She puts a foot down as if it has only pushed through air to reach the ground, rather than through the foot or so of water on the track. She pushes off from the ground as if it's solid underfoot, rather than a squelch of mud.

After the guide's long limbs have disappeared, I attempt Straight Through Tramping. I plot a direct line from A to B and move up a gear. Splosh, splosh, schloop, glump. It's quite exhilarating. It's so exhilarating that I am soon walking not just directly along the centre of the track, but deliberately heading for the bits that look the wettest or the deepest or the trickiest. It's not quite like being a child, because I know that I'm the one who will have to clean and dry my own kit at the end of all this, but I hadn't expected today to hold quite such a ridiculous amount of fun.

I am thus powering along when I round a corner and almost fall over the guide. She is bent over, picking things up from the ground. She shows me what she has found: several used tea bags and a couple of batteries. I offer to take them in my rubbish bag, which is hanging on the outside of my pack. I am a little shocked by the rubbish.

'Do you see much rubbish on this track?'

'You do sometimes. It depends, but you won't have seen much on this track because we guides and the DOC staff pick up everything we see. People can be thoughtless sometimes.'

'Do you think it's done deliberately, or just dropped through carelessness?'

'Oh, I like to think it's carelessness. You'd have to be pretty dumb to be in a place like this and deliberately drop litter. Same result, though. And seeing batteries makes me really mad.'

Having safely stashed our poisonous cargo, we power away again and she has soon disappeared. A few minutes later, I arrive at a wooden shelter and rediscover about half of my group. All of the 'older and bolder' Independent Trampers are here, with camping stoves out, brewing tea and a hot lunch.

'Shazza!' booms the chief snorer, and slaps me on the shoulder because my pack my back covered. They are in good spirits, although they've already been out in the rain for a couple of hours longer than me. This thought makes me realise that I must be travelling at quite some speed today. I check my watch: just after 1.00 pm. DOC timings allow an hour and a half between here and Sandfly Point, which is the end of the track. If I keep going, I might just make it to the first boat. This has two points of appeal: I will get to dryness an hour earlier than I thought; and I'll get to show the boys just how fast this member of Team GB can walk when she wants to. I hadn't even got up when they left this morning. They said their goodbyes laughing at my soggy gear and thinking they wouldn't see me again.

I push on, not understanding why I am suddenly and for the first time so far ahead of track time estimates. I am surprised to discover that I am humming. My conscious mind has been bypassed and something else has been conducting my vocal chords. Now conscious of it, I carry on the tune until I work out what it is. I am humming the April Showers song from the film *Bambi*. It takes a further few seconds before I realise that it is indeed April and that the downpour has slowed to a shower. Drip, drip, drop, little April showers, indeed. I don't know whether it's the air, the sleep deprivation or the continuous walking that has done it. If it's the walking, then I can look forward to more of this because I intend to carry on with this tramping lark. I am wet, cold and exhausted, but I am hooked – and I hope that there is more to discover about my subconscious than a propensity for strangely appropriate Disney songs.

The last few kilometres of the Milford Track are road-sized again. Attempts were made to cut a road along this valley, but this is all that is left. I find another shelter, inside which are huddled more of the Independent Trampers. As I approach I see one of the younger Kiwis outside the shelter and ask him if he knows how much further it is.

'You've made it. This is Sandfly Point.'

'No.' I check my watch, disbelievingly. It is only 1.45pm. 'Really?'

'No – only joking. It's about another half an hour.'

'Right. See you there!' I say, striding ahead.

He calls out 'Hold on! I was joking. The second time, that is. This really is the end of the track.'

I look up and there it is: the signpost for Sandfly Point. Old walking boots are tied to it, some of which look in better condition than my own right now. Blow me. I can actually walk quite fast when I want to.

The natural phenomenon at the end of the Milford Track is the reason this track exists and is the tourist's Mecca of the South Island: Milford Sound. Until 1954, the track was the only available overland route for travellers to see Milford Sound, and Milford Sound was worth the effort.

Before the tourists, Maori walked through the mountains of Fiordland to reach the pounamu in Milford Sound. Pounamu was used for making jewellery and the blades of adzes, which were used for carving and cutting wood and were therefore crucial for both spiritual and practical reasons. The Pakeha name given to pounamu was greenstone, for reasons that don't need explaining. It was (and is) found only in New Zealand – and only in a handful of places here. A pendant made from pounamu is still highly prized today, albeit mainly for the tourist trade.

For Maori, Milford Sound was a special place for more than just its pounamu. Tu Te Rakiwhanoa apparently did too much of a good job in creating this Sound. When the other gods saw Milford Sound, they were afraid that every human being would want to live here. To stop this from happening the Goddess of the Underworld, Hine-nui-te-po, sent sandflies to live in Milford Sound and all along the valleys of Fiordland. No sand required. Where there is water and a little bit of light and warmth, the sandfly flourishes. One advantage of walking the track in the rain and cold, therefore, is that you only get wet and cold, you aren't also bitten. At least, not quite so much.

Sandflies are small – almost small enough to crawl through the pores of a waterproof jacket. They are also vicious in pursuit of the right type of blood. They land on any available piece of skin. Their bites can stay red and itch maddeningly for days afterwards.

A sandfly bite is a psychological blow as well as a physical one. This is because it is the female sandflies that do the bloodsucking and they use the blood to aid reproduction. In other words, to accompany your unsightly itchy bite mark, you have the knowledge that you've just helped to produce more of the critters. I have no first-hand experience of this double whammy: sandflies don't seem to like me. Maybe I have bad blood, or bad skin (is eczema finally useful for something?), but I am apparently unappetising to the sandfly.

The boys quickly recover from their shock at seeing me arrive twenty minutes before the first boat leaves and admit to being impressed by my progress. Sandfly Point does not disappoint. Dom sits at the back of the boat with his hood tightly drawn and his gloved hands clamped over the remaining bits of exposed face flesh, while sandflies try to burrow their way in for lunch. He sees nothing of Mitre Peak, the most famous of Milford Sound's peaks, which rises more than 1,690 metres, almost vertically, from the water. But then, neither do the rest of us: the Sound is cloaked in cloud and we can't see up past a couple of hundred metres above the boat. I'm not sure I mind. Mist hangs on the water and our boat feels tiny in this watery space. Its engine makes the only noise, whereas on a sunny day, we would be competing with kayakers, diving boats and other charter craft.

Milford Sound is no longer accessible only via the Milford Track. Between 1935 and 1954 big-thinking Kiwis somehow built a road to Milford Sound.

Its construction is a story in itself, full of tricky engineering and the deaths of brave men. Its legacy is a goldmine of tourists by the coach load. Numerous cruises run every day, postcards abound and an underwater observatory has been built, because everything about Milford Sound is remarkable, even the bits you can't see. All the rain here washes a layer of tannin-stained fresh water onto the salt water in the Sound. The depth of this dark fresh water varies, but it is enough to maintain a dark salt-water environment that is otherwise only found at depths too great for human interaction. People come here to stare at black coral and strange deep-sea creatures. People come here to gaze up at Mitre Peak and take endless postcard photographs. People come here to kayak and dive. People come here sometimes just to say they came here.

Ian, Matt, Dom and I squelch past the shiny desks of the cruise operators in the airport-like entrance hall. Neatly dressed Japanese tourists stare at us in shock and give us a wide berth. Clothes that were merely wet on the track are now uncomfortable in conditioned air. The boys are thrown out of the men's toilets for trying to change into their dry clothes. A guard takes up position at the door to stop them trying again.

'Are you going to go on one of the cruises now that you've got a couple of hours to spare?' Matt asks me. He and Ian are booked in at the Milford backpackers tonight, so they're off to get dry and will try a cruise tomorrow.

'I'm not sure. I feel a bit, kind of … not here. Does that sound silly?'

'No. We know exactly what you mean.'

We continue to stand there, wet and mute. Living here, Donald Sutherland saw no other human beings for two years. This is a place famous for its sounds of silence. Today, most people who come here go through this lobby, get onto a boat and motor out onto the Sound. If they're lucky, at some point the captain will cut the engines for everyone to hear the silence. How else can it be done for the volume of people who now visit?

As we say our goodbyes I decide that we trampers are important to this tourist world after all – and not just because of the money we pay to walk the track. Standing in our little puddle, we are a reminder of how people used to get to Milford Sound. We are a throwback to a previous age. And if nothing else, we must be making all these nice people feel very good about their own choice of transport to Milford Sound. There are worse things I could have done today.

When Blanche Baughan walked the Milford Track, she would have stayed overnight here before turning round and walking all the way back again. If good weather was promised for the next two days, many of us would want to do the same. But we can't. We're at the end of the conveyor belt.

When Blanche Baughan walked the Milford Track, far fewer people were doing so. There was no road to Milford Sound and few boats arrived from the sea, so the Sound itself was the preserve of trampers. In its earlier state, almost inaccessible and more of a true wilderness, the Milford Track would probably have felt like The Finest Walk in the World. Today, it remains so for anyone who loves moss or lichen and for anyone who likes the sociable side of walking a track with up to eighty other people. Oh, and for anyone who loves just to get very, very wet.

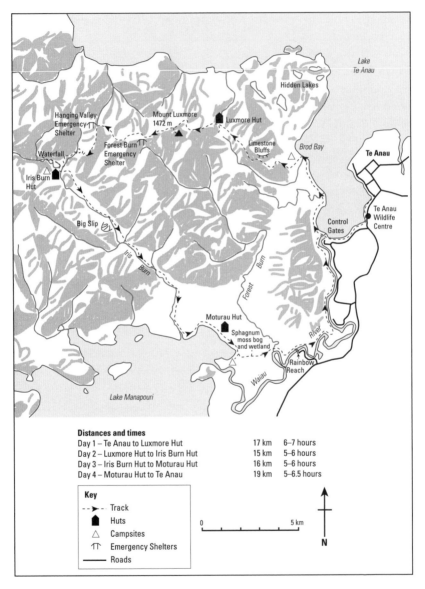

Distances and times

Day 1 – Te Anau to Luxmore Hut	17 km	6–7 hours
Day 2 – Luxmore Hut to Iris Burn Hut	15 km	5–6 hours
Day 3 – Iris Burn Hut to Moturau Hut	16 km	5–6 hours
Day 4 – Moturau Hut to Te Anau	19 km	5–6.5 hours

Key

- --->--- Track
- ⬛ Huts
- △ Campsites
- ⌒ Emergency Shelters
- — Roads

0   5 km

N

The Kepler Track

5
Deliberately painful: The Kepler Track

If I were to nominate my favourite early European explorer in New Zealand, it would be James McKerrow. Here at last is a man who named mountains after something other than himself, his explorer friends or his reigning monarch. (Unfortunately, McKerrow's name was, after all, given to a lake, a mount, a glacier and a mountain range, but it wasn't him that did this.) James McKerrow named the Kepler Mountains in honour of Johannes Kepler, the seventeenth-century Bavarian astronomer who was the first to suggest that the Earth and planets move round the sun in elliptical orbits. That is to say, he was the first to suggest this as far as records today are concerned.

Two hundred and fifty years after Johannes Kepler drew his squished circles, James McKerrow surveyed the mountains of Fiordland and broke with tradition by naming mountains after famous scientists. Now, I'm not suggesting that McKerrow was a conventionally exciting man by twenty-first century standards. A surveyor with a penchant for walking in mountains and an interest in dead scientists doesn't sound like the first person who might strip at a party. Still, I can't help liking a quiet revolutionary.

Day one: The grunt

The track named after the mountains named after the scientist starts at the opposite end of Lake Te Anau from the Milford Track. At this southern end of the lake lie the town of Te Anau, a diminutive statue of Quintin Mackinnon, a row of incongruous poplar trees, a few boats, a waterplane, a tribe of ducks with whose personalities I have become quite worryingly familiar, and the Te Anau Wildlife Centre.

The Wildlife Centre is one of my reasons for walking the five kilometres to the start of the track, rather than driving, like most people do. The Wildlife Centre houses, amongst other things, a bird so endangered that it can only be seen here or in one restricted and almost entirely inaccessible section of Fiordland mountains. I peer into the luscious enclosure of the takahe. One hobbles over and goes to sleep near my feet.

The takahe was designed by a small child with a pack of crayons. Its body is slightly too round, like most things drawn with thick pens by small, chubby hands. It has a short, fat beak, which was clearly designed in profile, looks like a Gallic nose and was coloured in using the strongest, brightest red in the box. Its body is deep blue, but so rotund that the blue crayon ran out part-way through colouring in and the bottle-green crayon was used to fill in along the top of its back.

Takahe don't fly (this is New Zealand, after all). Until 1948, it was thought that they no longer existed. Then a doctor called Geoffrey Orbell uncovered a population of 250–300 takahe in the Murchison Mountains on the southern shores of this lake. That's 250–300 birds in more than a million hectares of forested, mountainous terrain. It makes you wonder what else might be out there.

No more takahe, seems to be the answer. The remaining population fell to around 120 by 1981 but had recovered to 242 by 2002. This is in no small part due to the efforts of the conservation workers who now breed takahe in captivity and look after them in the wild. Imaginative use of glove puppets is one of the secrets of their success: chicks born in captivity are fed using takahe glove puppets and are taught about predators by a show in which a stuffed stoat beats up one of these glove puppets. Punch and Judy beware: Mother Takahe and Stinker 'The Evil' Stoat sounds far more entertaining.

As I peer at the sleeping takahe behind the wire, a stream of what seem to be baby takahe make a dash for freedom across the wide, unfenced, grassy area in which I'm standing. These are pukeko (swamp hens). They share the takahe's colours, but are sleeker, around a third of the size and far more common. The pukeko's designer had better pens and a working knowledge of aerodynamics. A pukeko in flight is not graceful, but neither is it impossible.

In looks, the takahe and pukeko reside on the same evolutionary highway. However, it's anyone's guess as to which is the less evolved. Instinct says that the streamlined pukeko is more advanced because it can fly, is much better at avoiding predators and has been so successful at breeding in New Zealand that it is often legal as stew. However, the pukeko has two features that make the portly takahe seem the height of nobility and sophistication. First, the pukeko has a small, bullseye marking of brilliant white in a place where this seems grossly impractical, suggesting that male pukeko need more than the usual assistance to perform evolution's most essential act successfully. Second, anyone watching a pukeko fly will not be thinking 'highly evolved'; its legs flail wildly and uncontrollably, as if in panic that they might be left behind.

Marking the start of the Kepler Track are the Control Gates, which I thought meant that ticketing on the Kepler Track is even more ruthless than for the Milford Track. I was wrong. The commodity being controlled here is water.

Around seventy per cent of New Zealand's electricity is generated by hydro schemes. This is, after all, a country not short of rainfall, lakes or steep drops. Most electricity is generated in the South Island but consumed in the North Island. However, Kiwi-style tension over such matters rarely rises above a pointed remark in a local newspaper and pales into insignificance compared with the fear of Kiwis on all islands that one day New Zealand might have nuclear power stations.

Nuclear energy is a sensitive subject in New Zealand. It is no coincidence that the *Rainbow Warrior* was at anchor in New Zealand waters when it was sunk by French spies trying to prevent further protests against nuclear testing in the Pacific. New Zealanders have never warmed to nuclear fission. In 1984 the New Zealand government told its American counterpart that it could not sail nuclear warships into New Zealand territory. The USA wailed. Its bath-time was being spoiled by Maui's fish. It suspended its obligations to New Zealand under the ANZUS defence pact, with knock-on effects on trade. Yet, despite the difficulties this has caused them, Kiwis have held their nerve. They don't like nuclear energy and they don't respond to being bullied.

For large chunks of the twentieth century, the casual observer could have been forgiven for thinking that Kiwis weren't fond of hydroelectricity schemes either. The Control Gates that mark the start and finish of the Kepler Track are part of the Manapouri hydroelectric power scheme and public opposition to this scheme is popularly known as the birth of environmentalism in New Zealand. To fully appreciate the scale of the issue, imagine a birth for which the gestation period lasted twenty years, the birthing pool measured 150 square kilometres, sixteen men were killed during the delivery and the midwife was a fresh-faced Labour government.

Could there ever be a single local issue in the UK for which just one petition to Parliament might be signed by ten per cent of the entire population? Or that might topple the Government? Even though the people directly affected numbered no more than about 2,000? Such was the scale of feeling generated by the Manapouri power scheme, even though it was located in the little-populated south-west corner of the South Island.

The basis of the scheme was simple and uncontroversial. An extremely large body of water (Lake Manapouri) sits 178 metres above sea level. The sea is not very far from its western tip. Dig a tunnel from the lake to the sea. Place a turbine in the tunnel. Run water from the lake down the tunnel and it will spin the turbine faster than you can count the dollars.

Now, the lake currently drains into a river at its south-eastern edge, so we'll have to stop that going on. Ooh, but there's another river on that side that we could divert into the lake to give us more water. Oo-ooh, and another river brings water into the lake from Lake Te Anau, so we could have more of that. We could dam all the rivers to control them. Hey, we could flood the Waiau River to join both lakes and make one big Super Lake! We could raise the natural water levels by up to thirty metres. Wouldn't that be something?

I picture the strategic engineers as a group of white, middle-aged men playing with a papier mâché model, plasticine and several beakers of water. This is partly because I've seen the public information film produced in the 1970s about the Manapouri power scheme. In this film a suited man with a pointy stick and an excess of facial hair explains, in an accent like the Queen's, how the scheme works to a group of well-groomed schoolchildren and mothers, who look dutifully impressed by how clever it all is. In front of them is a papier mâché model of southern Fiordland.

A watered-down (as it were) hydroelectric scheme survived the controversy. One of the greatest breakthroughs was the government's creation of a group called the Guardians of Lakes Manapouri, Monowai and Te Anau. No one had ever tried anything like this before. The Guardians were six individuals who had been prominent in the Save Manapouri movement; they weren't even an official body to start with. They only offered advice, but those who ran the power station listened to them. The Guardians were made – and still are – responsible for overseeing management of the lake levels. It's not an easy job, particularly given the size of the scheme and the levels of rainfall in these crinkles of the world. Still, what a wonderful job title and responsibility to have: Guardian of the Lakes. Worth getting up for in the morning.

I swing shut the people-gate on top of the Control Gates and enter the forest.

This forest provides amazing views. Here, some trees are like giant chicken feet, with three or four coarse, splayed 'toes' rising several metres from the ground before merging into one leg-like trunk. Others have trunks that grow vertically, then veer off parallel to the ground, before bending back to the vertical again. One looks like the neck of a diplodocus. Another has grown a full loop in its trunk. There is no clue as to the cause of this behaviour: the veering is in different directions and the trees that do it are dispersed between a normal-behaving majority. Otherwise, I could be forgiven for thinking that there is a nuclear power plant near here after all.

Other people appear at Brod Bay, which is almost two-and-a-half hours into my day, but is the drop-off point for water taxis that bring trampers over from Te Anau. Brod Bay is a small strip of coarse, grey sand. Here an uncharacteristic DOC signpost reads:

Luxmore Hut	← 4.30 hr
Iris Burn Hut	← 10 hr
Track times can be reduced by half	
for fit trampers in good weather.	

I picture the competitive tramper stopping at this sign, standing before it with a glint in his or her eye, slowly, confidently, raising a wrist to check the time and then powering away with every intention of getting to Luxmore Hut in two hours.

The sign does nothing for me. Despite my mad last-day dash on the Milford Track, I know I'll be doing well to be at Luxmore Hut in less than five hours. The Milford Track left me with a strained calf and an enormous sleep deficit. For two days afterwards, I felt shattered. I worried about glandular fever for the first time in ages. I wondered what I was thinking to take up tramping. And now, here I am – back on another track, hauling my pack up a punishing mountain, carrots and apples and all. I guess I really do have something to prove to myself.

The ascent of Mount Luxmore is a long – a very long – hard slog. The switchbacks are relentless. Trampers walk ten or twenty metres one way, then ten or twenty metres the other way, and always up. The switchbacks get steeper, too. They take on nasty little personalities of their own. They even have a special sticky clay-mud that glues boots to the ground.

To keep going, I mentally switch the effort between different parts of my body. First my thighs take the strain. Then my calves. Then my stomach and the balls of my feet. I once found myself in a yoga class balancing on my straightened right leg, with my left leg lifted parallel to the floor on my left side and my right hand touching the floor by my right foot, when the yoga teacher said, 'The brain of this posture is in the left elbow' (or somewhere like that). I thought I'd misheard at first, but when I dubiously focused all my thought on this unlikely body part, the posture suddenly became much, much easier to hold. Using the same principle now, I use different parts of me as the 'brain' of the climb. I give up when my little finger can stand the strain no more. I sit down, panting, and contemplate eating every carrot and apple in my pack.

The only way to decrease pack weight once you set off on any of these tracks is to eat the contents. One of the fundamental rules of tramping is 'pack it in, pack it out'. There are no rubbish bins on any of the tracks or in any of the huts. You can't throw rubbish surreptitiously into hut toilets because that breaks the pumps DOC use to empty them (and, goodness knows, you don't want to do that). You can occasionally throw rubbish onto a hut fire – but only if the rubbish will burn easily and the fire is a real one.

As I slog upwards, bent forwards under the weight of my pack, I become obsessed with the fact that someone did this deliberately. The Kepler Track is the only one of the Great Walks that was purpose-built. It was brought into existence in order to relieve overcrowding on the Milford and Routeburn Tracks, which essentially follow old Maori routes to the source of the valuable pounamu. Both of those tracks represent the least difficult routes through the mountains. After all, if you're heaving great lumps of dense rock around, you don't look for the most difficult mountains to climb.

The Kepler Track, on the other hand, has an entirely different *raison d'être*. It is a tramping challenge. It was designed by those sturdy, fit, bionic people who are DOC staff. It is therefore the hardest of the three Great Walks in Fiordland – and climbing Mount Luxmore is just the start of the pain.

As I finally ascend beyond the treeline, rain falls and cloud conceals everything. Exposed to the main Fiordland element, the track here is sticky, squelchy mud. I barely have enough control left over my leg muscles to stagger the remaining forty-five minutes to the hut.

The good news is that I have so far failed to develop any symptoms of giardia. For the tramper, drinking water infected with giardia is the equivalent of a small nip on the leg for Sigourney Weaver in *Alien*.

Giardia is an infection caused by microscopic parasites that can live in the intestines of people and animals. These parasites hitch rides in streams and rivers. They diligently travel for miles, searching out the mug, plate or mouth of the innocent tramper. Once swallowed, they make their home in the tramper's gut, which involves a great deal of what might sensitively be called redecorating. They like a particular range of vibrant colours. They are also minimalists: everything they find in their new home is quickly thrown out. Very quickly.

The bad news for me is that once a tramper has swallowed giardia cysts, it takes up to two weeks for them to settle in. If I did inadvertently take on some new tenants whilst on the Milford Track, they could start their home improvements in the next few days.

I don't want this to happen. Not only would it be painful and acutely embarrassing, but it would mean that Fiordland has been contaminated. These days, the spread of giardia in the world's waterways is largely down to human behaviour and I want the water here to be clean. I want to carry on drinking the water without boiling or filtering or fiddling with chemicals. I don't want to think that the presence of trampers is destroying the things we are here to enjoy.

When the rain sweeps me into Luxmore Hut I feel as if I've gone back to school. The canteen-common-room is full of excited chatter as fifty people take it in turns for dinner sittings. The bunk-bed dorms are equally busy.

The evening lesson is a nature walk led by the hut warden, one Peter Jackson. He shows us how to select a nice juicy tussock stem and nibble on the starch inside – an early survival trick for Maori and a contemporary survival trick for takahe. We learn that the plants at this altitude (1,100 metres) are riotously promiscuous. They don't wait for the right insect to bring the right pollen. Given limited options, the plants here mate with anything that comes along.

There is also an evening fieldtrip – to the Luxmore Caves. The track to the caves is a schoolboy's dream, being a trail of slippy mud several inches deep. Other than the presence of a short, wooden ladder at the entrance, the caves are exactly as they would have been when first discovered. Just a few metres inside, the darkness is breathtaking. Slivers of water run across the floor and every surface is wet to the touch. The rock contortions begin just above head height and descend irregularly as we progress into the mountain. Nothing on the lumpy floor or lumpier ceiling can be seen unless a torch is shining on it. Even in a group of seven, with seven torches, I am alarmed.

The caves supposedly extend one kilometre inside the mountain. We are not even one hundred metres down when we reach a hole at knee level, through which we must crawl to continue. Some are instantly on the floor and disappear while I cast my torch beam over the curious shapes just above our heads. There are short, swollen stalactites shaped like cows' udders. They hang from great waves of rock bulging up between deep crevices. The most amazing aspect is the pure whiteness all around. It is beautiful and enchanting and I can't wait to get out of there.

In the hut there are bodies and noise everywhere. All around trampers are observing the standard sequence of hut questions:
1 'Where are you from?'
2 'How long have you been in New Zealand?'
3 'Have you done any other tracks?'

To these might occasionally be added:

4   'What is your name?'

However, this is optional and frequently omitted.

On approaching me, fellow trampers add two preliminary questions:

0a 'Are you on your own?'

0b 'Don't you get lonely?'

People seem amazed that I am tramping alone (if anyone can be alone when sharing a hut with up to fifty people). I am amazed at their amazement. Solo trampers may be in the minority, but we're hardly an endangered species. Every time someone asks if I am alone, I can think of nothing more to say than 'yes'. It seems such an absurd question. It becomes more absurd when they say I'm very brave to be alone. So far I have been too polite to say what I really think: that tramping with someone else is the brave thing to do.

Day two: Don't look down

Day two of the Kepler Track is the one that really matters if you like views. This morning, as the sun filters through a light rain, fifty people *um* and *ah* over the best time to set out. The hut warden has written up the early morning forecast and it promises a typically tricky Fiordland day: 'rain and cloud clearing'. Leaving as late as possible promises the best chance to see the famous views. How fortunate that I'm still incapable of leaving early.

Tramping is as precariously dependent on the weather as my previous existence was not. From air-conditioned offices I could spot a change in season, but not the subtleties in between. Now I am absorbed by the weather – not least because I am frequently absorbing the weather. It determines where and when I go, what I wear, how comprehensively I wrap my belongings, what I see, how comfortable I am and, above all, how safe I am.

DOC carefully monitors the weather conditions on the Kepler Track and has to close it several times a year – and that's just during the open season from October to April. The track was closed only a couple of weeks ago with thick snow over the tops. Most of the day before us is spent at altitudes above 1,200 metres. This is the dangerous day.

We look like refugees as we make our way ever further up Mount Luxmore, winding in and out of its folds, moving slowly round and up. We are fifty people carrying their belongings on their backs and trudging slowly but steadily through the wind and rain, underneath a succession of rainbows, towards the promised views. It is exceedingly strange to share such an experience with so many other people and not know the names of most of them.

Collectively we are the best equipped bunch of refugees I've ever seen. Endless adjustments are made to clothing, packs and equipment in response to shifting conditions. Now it's raining – now it's sunny. Now there's a biting wind whipping into ears from one side – now from the other. Now I'm climbing and very sweaty – now I've been standing waiting for the clouds to reveal the view and I'm losing the feeling in my fingers.

The views are worth the many hours of tramping uphill. On the right-hand side of the track the scree slope of the mountain falls away towards the lake, now more than 1,000 metres below. To the left the mountain rises still further. On the ground are orange, grey, red and black rocks and stones. Someone must have let that child with the crayons loose up here as well.

Mount Luxmore is one head within quite a crowd. The track is in the middle of those 1.2 million hectares of Fiordland and in most directions are jagged peaks as far as the eye can see. Unfortunately, today that's only for a couple of kilometres. On a clear day, there are mountains to the horizon on most sides.

Having come this far I force my thighs on up along the side track to the top of Mount Luxmore. Twenty minutes further on, I stand holding onto the wooden trig point in the wind, watching as occasional patches of clear sky blow past and reveal tantalising portions of the view. I wait here stubbornly for an hour and a quarter, which is the time it takes for every piece of the view to be revealed.

The flat plain on the other side of Lake Te Anau is almost all farmed land, but the animals that graze here are not just some of the famous 47 million sheep of New Zealand, or even the slightly less famous 5 million cattle. In this corner of New Zealand the fields are full of deer – and how they got here is quite a story.

Deer are not native to New Zealand. The only native land mammals are three species of bat, one of which is now extinct. There are no prizes for guessing the origin of the first deer in New Zealand: England (1851).

However, the English weren't the only ones to blame: Theodore Roosevelt sent over a number of wapiti (the largest member of the deer family) in 1905, in return for a selection box of New Zealand's whacky native birds.

A display in the Auckland Museum shows non-native creatures in New Zealand, with one of each type stuffed, mounted and looking guilty. For each species there is a note describing who introduced it. The ancestors of the Maori have a respectable score of two, being the Pacific dog and the Pacific rat. The Europeans have a score of which any rugby team and many cricket teams would be proud.

There are two things about this display that I love. The first is that it gives precise dates of arrival for each type of animal, sometimes down to the day. This is not the type of information that many people in my homeland would know – much less display prominently in the national museum. The second is that it gives the reason for each introduction. Some are standard excuses: animals brought for food, recreational hunting, or those that arrived accidentally, such as ships' rats. Some are worryingly stupid reasons – stoats, for example, being introduced to try to control the numbers of rabbits, which had in turn been introduced for hunting and to make European settlers feel at home. Finally, some are downright whacky – hedgehogs, for example, being introduced in 1870 'for sentimental reasons'.

I understand why early European settlers wanted tangible reminders of a home they expected never to see again. What I don't understand is – why rabbits? And hedgehogs? It's a fascinating insight into the minds of early European settlers in New Zealand. And not a line of enquiry I intend to pursue any further.

Meanwhile, like the majority of New Zealand's imported mammals, deer thrived. They munched their way through forest, including the million or so hectares of forest in Fiordland. By the 1930s the New Zealand Government was paying hunters to shoot deer – and this is where the fun started.

The initial objective was to kill as many deer as possible in the shortest time. A small army of competitive males took to the bush, using guns, knives and survival skills to hunt their prey for weeks at a time. The competition was against the deer, the elements and each other.

Helicopters and 'home-made devices' were added to their arsenals, and in the 1970s things became crazier still. The new objective was to take the deer alive – and anyone who's ever seen the Fiordland landscape will appreciate just how difficult this would have been. Or maybe not. Maybe you have to have tried shooting a net-gun from a small, swinging helicopter, jumping out of said helicopter whilst still in flight, wrestling with a panicked, wild deer, flying through high, narrow fiords with a full cargo of deer swinging in a net underneath *and* seen the Fiordland landscape, to appreciate fully the difficulties.

The rewards were so good that it was not unheard of for rival teams to clash over territories. In many cases, this was because no clear borders could be drawn between hunting blocks in this landscape. In some cases, however, the attacks were deliberate and deadly. As if the battle against the landscape wasn't enough.

Hunting for deer (both alive and dead) by helicopter in New Zealand has arguably never ended, but the real innovations and fortunes were made from the mid-1960s to the mid-1980s. There are some frightening statistics, such as 208 helicopter crashes killing or seriously injuring fifty-seven pilots and shooters between 1976 and 1982 alone. Fortunes were made and New Zealand developed an industry that now has around half the world's farmed deer population (approximately 2.5 million) and the satisfaction of knowing that it not only makes money but helped save the country's valuable forests from being eaten to death.

However, the problem with trying to eliminate introduced species in the wild is that it is virtually impossible. Even for larger animals like deer, there is an awful lot of forest out there to provide food and cover.

Besides, it is in the interest of lots of Kiwis for wild deer to remain. Those most interested are the hunters. Wild deer are a pest in New Zealand and are legitimate and favourite targets for any hunter (with a suitable licence, of course). Venison is savoured; supposedly libido-enhancing deer antler velvet has a ready market in Asia; and deer antlers make magnificent trophies. Thus, a hunter wants to kill deer and therefore doesn't want all the deer to be killed.

From the top of Mount Luxmore it isn't possible to see the deer on the farmed plains past Te Anau or the takahe that are still rooting round the Murchison Mountains, the next range now visible to the north. Up here, my head throbs with the power of the natural forces around me. At 1,472 metres I am gazing out over mountain after mountain, each one a different shape and personality. The glaciers that strained at this rock must have made an ocean of ice. The rock that survived carries its age, strength and scars from the battle. Folds of vapour rush by me and I watch thick trails of it blow towards me, round me and on over the next peaks. I am inside the weather.

The cloud and I are swept forcefully by the wind. When a thinner vapour trail passes by, sunlight briefly reveals the shapes of the nearest mountainsides and peaks. In thicker cloud they are dormant outlines. When they suddenly appear I feel the need to sit down quickly. Everything is vast and powerful – the mountains, the vapour, the wind.

No one else stays on the peak for more than a few minutes and when I eventually descend back to the track I am alone. But I can't imagine ever feeling lonely out here. For one thing, there are too many preoccupations. First amongst these for the next few hours is avoiding falling off the side of the track.

The track is never less than a couple of feet wide and frequently more. I have seen photos taken by DOC staff when they were building this track. They drove mini-diggers – even on these ridges and even in the snow. Now that I'm up here, it doesn't matter that I have seen photographic evidence: I haven't the faintest idea how they did it. The ridge isn't level, either. The track slides down a hundred metres or so, then up again, then down, then up. It is extremely muddy in places, with respectable drops on one or both sides. For extra sport, the wind can reach up to eighty kilometres per hour across the most exposed sections. With every step my body makes a dozen adjustments for the wind, the gradient, the mud and the rocks. The conditions provide an acute awareness of life.

Every one of my senses is alert but I am unconcerned about the danger. This surprises me. In the most routine situations, my brain regularly invents amusing ways in which I might be about to die. While frying vegetables, I picture myself slipping on spilled oil, landing on my back and staring immobilised as a pan of boiling oil aims for my face. When walking along the side of a swimming pool, I glimpse the parallel universes in which I slip, hit my head and fall unconscious into the pool. Yet, when alone on a ridge on a mountainside, being battered by the wind and slipping on mud, I don't even pause to think of the colourful ramifications of a twisted ankle.

The sight far down to my right distracts my attention from the ridge. Gaps in the blowing cloud are releasing beams of sunlight onto the South

Fiord of Lake Te Anau. They look like celestial searchlights racing along the tousled surface of the lake.

There are two emergency shelters along the six-kilometre ridge from Mount Luxmore to the descent into the Iris Burn Valley. Unlike DOC huts, DOC emergency shelters are of a highly standardised design. They are essentially all roof – the roof being a steep-sloping inverted 'V' made airtight at either end by a wall. The doors to these triangular shelters are held on the firmest, tightest springs imaginable, because they have to withstand gale force winds without blowing open. This also makes them difficult for me to open. At the Forest Burn Emergency Shelter I tilt myself backwards at almost forty-five degrees to the floor, using the full weight of my body and pack on fully extended arms – only just prising the door ajar. Manoeuvring inside before the door springs shut is equally difficult. On my first attempt I become almost irretrievably wedged between the door and the wall. Of all the ways there are to die here, how ironic it would be to freeze to death whilst pinned by the door of an emergency shelter.

Inside, the tiny space smells just as it should, given that it is used by sweaty, steaming people and is designed to let in as little air as possible. An emergency would be exactly what it would take to make me sleep here.

The Hanging Valley Emergency Shelter lies about another four kilometres further on, near the end of the ridge walk. Outside it stands a cubicle for which the term 'long-drop toilet' is an understatement. Taut wire ropes either side of the door hold the cubicle onto the mountainside. Behind it are no ropes, just a drop of more than 600 metres. It is a brave person that makes use of this facility.

Yet these fancies of human construction are tiny blips along the day's hard tramp of more than fourteen kilometres. The big players are the mountains. With every twist, turn, rise and fall of the track, I see new peaks, new angles and new faces plummeting down to the valley floors. Hour after hour there is nothing but whipped air, mountains and physical effort. I don't think my body has ever before used its fuel so fully and so effectively. The world becomes a thoroughly different place in the space of one chocolate bar. An illicit snack in the office never had such an impact as this.

My mind is racing too, settling all sorts of unfinished thoughts and emotions from this new perspective. That man I was in love with and never told? Well, I'll tell him. It won't change anything, but how silly it was that he never knew. My old university tutor – he asked that we send him a postcard from time to time and in ten years I've sent none. Now I will.

The descent into Hanging Valley and round into the Iris Burn Valley is cripplingly painful. In several places the drops are so steep and the ridge so narrow that DOC has added ladders and steel guide-wires. Then come tight switchbacks so steep that with my feet flat on the track I am almost walking *en pointe*. There's a reason why ballerinas don't wear walking boots.

'Good evening everyone. My name's Pania and I'm your hut warden for tonight. This means that everyone *will* clean up properly after themselves and I want all the stoves wiped and the floor swept. And I'll be in while you have breakfast to make sure you do the same in the morning. The less time I have to spending clearing up after you, the more time I can spend in the valley.

'Now,' she suddenly smiles, 'how were the views today?'

Positive murmurs from all in response.

'And how are your legs?'

Groans from everyone. However toned the tramper, no calf or kneecap survives the 700-metre-plus controlled fall to Iris Burn Hut intact.

Pania's smile widens.

'Let me tell you about the Kepler Challenge. It's a race run every year on the track. It starts and finishes at the Control Gates, like many of you are doing. The difference is that these guys *run* the whole length of the track.'

She has everyone's undivided attention.

'Would anyone like to guess how long it takes them?'

'Ten hours?'

'Seven?'

'Nine?'

Pania smiles knowingly. 'Well, yes, there are some that do run it in those times. But the record stands at four hours thirty-seven minutes.'

Jaws drop. Limbs ache just that little bit more. A sense of inadequacy sweeps the room.

'In 2002 the winner of the women's race set a course record of five hours forty minutes. When she went up to collect her medal she confessed that she'd never been to this part of the world before and that she'd carried a camera and stopped to take photos at the top. She also said that she intended to return the following year and run without the camera. And she did. In 2003, she not only won the women's race again, but came second overall and took fifteen minutes off her own record.'

These are just some of the amazing stories that are added each year on the first Saturday in December. Two races are run on that day: the Kepler Challenge around the full sixty kilometres; and the Luxmore Grunt from the Control Gates to Luxmore Hut and back again. The quickest man and woman to reach Luxmore Hut (from either race) are crowned King and Queen of the Mountain. It's not quite the coronation that, say, an American event might have. It's a firm handshake from the race organisers, a round of applause from the assembled crowd and the award of a practical prize such as a racing daysack or a small tent. Somehow, the achievement of running up Mount Luxmore in little more than an hour seems to be reward enough. Having taken almost five hours to get there myself, I appreciate that.

The tramper's excuse is that the runners aren't carrying large packs. However, they do carry equipment, including waterproofs and food. I can think of no better testament to the extreme changeability of the weather in Fiordland: these people are extremely fit, they are fast, they complete the alpine section of the track within a couple of hours, they compete under the watchful eyes and radios of a team of race organisers and yet even they are in danger from sudden changes in the weather.

The slower 'challengers' and 'grunters' tend to carry more gear because they are out for longer. Those who take up to twelve hours carry a couple of light meals, warm clothes and waterproofs. They still cover in a day the same distance that will take me four. Oh, and the average age of the runners is currently around thirty-nine.

The Kepler Challenge has been run every year since 1988 and stories within stories have developed over the years. My favourite is of the three men who have run the Challenge every year since it began. Their times are lengthening but each is determined not to give up first. When one of them must eventually stop, the other two will be just as disappointed. That's one of the things I love about this place.

Neither is the Kepler Challenge the only race in New Zealand for the admirably crazy and the clinically bionic. Of the Great Walks, the Routeburn and Abel Tasman tracks also now host annual races and part of the Tongariro Northern Circuit has been incorporated into the new Tussock Traverse half marathon. Yet these are just the tip of the blister. Each year, thousands of New Zealanders race over scores of tracks and mountains – and they're not even trying to claim the first bunk.

I wonder whether I might one day be able to run the Kepler Challenge. Stories from the race are inspirational. Just to complete the race would be enough, even if I finished last. But then, I still have to learn to walk before I can run.

Kepler Track hut wardens go to extraordinary lengths to entertain their trampers. Tonight's show opened with Tales from the Kepler Challenge and continues with Pania's impersonation of the sound of kiwis, for which we are told to listen out in the night. She tips her head back, opens her throat and lets rip a piercing cry. Kiwis several kilometres away lift their heads.

The finale is a trip to meet the local glow-worm population. The tourist industry in New Zealand reaps millions of dollars a year from visitors to its glow-worm caves, most famously at Waitomo in the North Island, but also at Te Anau and a small number of other sites around the country. In the large caves at Waitomo, the glow-worm population is a miniature night sky that never turns off. Yet, in damp forests, hanging from rocks or under foliage across New Zealand are smaller grottos of pinprick lights that are free to view for the careful observer in the dark.

The New Zealand glow-worm is a quirky creature. It's not a worm, but a fungus gnat fly. It likes dark and, above all, damp places. It has four phases in its roughly one-year life cycle, but can only eat during one of them. As an adult it has no capacity to eat. Its entire purpose is to copulate, which it has been known to do continuously for up to twenty-six hours, and possibly longer. For the female flies, that's almost the whole of their adult life.

The glow-worm's Latin name, *Arachnocampa luminosa*, sounds like a spell. The pinprick of light is impossible to define between blue, green and white. The glow attracts insect food on to fishing lines and attracts males to the females. Glow-worms don't like to be disturbed (well, who would with so few, but sex-filled, days to look forward to?). The glow dims or goes out in reaction to noise or touch. This is marvellous because it means that viewing glow-worms is best done whilst creeping silently through dark, damp places, using your senses rather than a torch to stop from banging into a branch or tripping over a root.

Day three: Enchanted forest

On the third day the designers of the Kepler Track seem finally to have taken pity on trampers after the flamboyance of yesterday's route. Perhaps even they anticipated the strained calves and bruised knees with which we creak from our sleeping bags this morning. Today's route is flat.

At least, that's what the guidebooks say. In a tramping context, I am learning that 'flat' is defined as follows:

> **flat** *adj.* Containing individual ascents and descents of anything up to 200 metres, yet with roughly constant average altitude over the full distance. Commonly used in ironic context.

I hobble up and down, patiently reintroducing leg muscles to gradients. Once again I am at the back of the pack. Most trampers stay just three days on this track and are today on deadlines to meet with transport at the intriguingly entitled Rainbow Reach, some twenty-two kilometres away and six kilometres further than the next hut. They are up and away at the crack of dawn, factoring in the impact of yesterday's strains, twists and snaps.

A few of us take the side trip to the Iris Burn Waterfall – one of so many ground-level Fiordland outpourings that look like they could single-handedly power a small town. At the waterfall two women approach me, one Italian, one Israeli, both trying hard to look nonchalant.

'Do you have any – er … women's things?'

'Yes, we are desperate. We didn't anticipate.'

I break it to them that I didn't anticipate either. Yesterday I deliberately didn't drink enough water in order to force my body to delay the onset. It is not a tactic I recommend. Standing in front of surging great waterfalls doesn't help.

Most books offering advice to trampers contain a discreet, euphemistic section on 'Women's Health'. In this section they fail to offer any inspired, practical advice to the women who find themselves improvising outdoors. Constant inhalation of oxygen-rich air and prolonged physical exercise provide perfect conditions for events that many of us don't anticipate. So, just as all those deer hunters improvised net-guns and patched up their own helicopters, the female tramper becomes similarly resourceful. She just can't tell anyone about it.

Over the sixteen kilometres between Iris Burn Hut and Moturau Hut several strange landscapes exist. The first is well marked and not just on maps of the area: it is so well marked on the landscape that I saw it from the ridge yesterday, even through the cloud. The Big Slip was a landslide so enormous that even unassuming Kiwis gave it capital letters and a minor adjective.

It is easy to see the broken-off nose of the mountain – or, rather, the bit where the 'nose' used to be. Twenty years after the break, none of Fiordland's contortionist vegetation has yet managed to recolonise the triangular wall of exposed rock. The forest on the valley floor is only just beginning to reappear. The track crosses the resting place for the thousands of tons of rock and vegetation that 'slipped'. Looking around, it is impossible to understand how the nose laid waste to such an immense area of land. The area that was flattened includes several acres running a couple of hundred metres up the wall of the valley on *this*, the opposite, side of the valley. It takes around twenty minutes to walk the length of the debris along the valley floor.

Fortunately, the 'slip' happened four years before the Kepler Track was built and apparently in the middle of the night, so no human lives were lost. I'd be willing to bet, though, that several metres beneath my feet are a few crushed somethings with surprised expressions on their faces. At the new ground level, we trampers enjoy the rarest of sights in Fiordland: a low-altitude track with a clear view of the sky.

The more familiar low-altitude view of forest reappears quickly. However, there is never a truly familiar view of forest on a new track and something about this place is to become quite unique in my memory. It isn't the rolling carpet of ferns. It isn't the coloured mushrooms or the great height of the trees. Less than an hour into this forest, I admit to myself what I really think about this forest: it is enchanted; the trees are magical.

Perhaps I am overtired. Perhaps I am light-headed. I rest and eat chocolate and feel exactly the same afterwards. This forest is full of magic, good magic. It makes me deeply peaceful and happy. It tells me that my deepest, darkest fears can't hurt me. Things happen for a reason. Ultimately, everything will be all right. And, most importantly, this place, this forest and this magic will survive everything.

It is suddenly quite overwhelmingly important to me that this place survives. We trampers are just visitors – as are the hunters, hut wardens, track builders and other human beings who come here. We may think that, as a species, we dominate and own huge portions of the Earth's lands and seas. But as I walk through this forest I know absolutely that we will never own this place. It tolerates us. If inclined, it helps us. That is all.

The feeling that this magic will ultimately survive is intensely comforting. Maybe if I look back on this from the lofty perspective of my office window in London, I will think that for a little while back there I went bush crazy. But here and now, I couldn't feel less crazy. I haven't eaten anything different from all my other tramps. I haven't smoked or drunk anything more stimulating than rain water. I'm no more or less tired than I have been on many other days. This forest simply is enchanted.

I become even more convinced when I pass into an area of the forest that feels as if it holds darker magic. There has been no sudden change in the weather, the light, the temperature, the contents of my stomach or anything around me except the individual trees, ferns and rugs of mosses and lichens. I try to analyse the smallest changes, but I can't work it out. Here the forest feels just as powerful, but far less lenient towards the likes of me. Instinctively, I speed up.

As I am fearfully admiring a giant with two thin trunk-legs, a pelvis joining them at about twice my height and long arms waving from a short body, I hear a rustle in the ferns around its feet (sorry – roots). I wait. Another rustle. I stay still and silent, waiting for the bird – that I'm convinced is a kiwi – to show itself. The creature rustles a few times only about a metre away from the track, but firmly hidden in the thick ferns. I can wait for hours but I can't step into the undergrowth. It is not for the tramper to crash around on the local plants or scare the local creatures. It would be the equivalent of barging into the host's kitchen at a dinner party and rooting around in his cupboards: there's a slim chance that you might see something surprising, but you're more likely to end up feeling guilty and foolish. The more convinced I become that this is a kiwi, the less I want to disturb the poor endangered thing.

So I walk on, until after about five hours in the enchanted forest I meet the lower reaches of the Iris Burn and emerge on the shores of Lake Manapouri.

Most trampers on the Kepler Track don't stay at Moturau Hut. Tonight there are just nine of us. I arrive last, with the dusk sandfly swarms (indistinguishable from the morning and afternoon sandfly swarms).

Going from fifty people down to nine suddenly makes hut life human again. When there were trampers everywhere, it was hard not to see them as an amorphous mass. It was hard to take an interest in them. It was impossible to hold a decent conversation with more than a few. With nine people I can chat to everyone. I can take an interest in all of them. We can and do form our own little community. It epitomises in microcosm what it's like to go from the UK to New Zealand.

There are probably many reasons why Kiwis are such friendly people. My top theory, however, is the numbers game. Fewer people are easier to be friendly with by an exponential factor that somebody someday might capture mathematically in a General Theory of Relatives. If I walk down the main street of one of the small towns in the South Island of New Zealand, I can smile and say hello to everyone I meet and still reach my destination on time. If I were to try the same in London, I would be immobilised and probably arrested for suspicious behaviour. In a small town, I can remember everyone's names and personal details and become interested in them as people. In London my human brain could only manage this for 0.001 per cent of the population before it imploded or began dangerously to misremember things.

Of course, London is not the whole of the UK. A fairer comparison would be with small English towns and villages. Yet, there remains a difference in scale. The largest towns in the South Island of New Zealand are Christchurch and Dunedin, with about 330,000 and 110,000 people, respectively. These are roughly equivalent to Cardiff and Oxford. On an island whose area is roughly twice that of Scotland. In fact, the combined population of Glasgow and Edinburgh exceeds the total population of the South Island of New Zealand. The towns through which I have been travelling – Kaikoura, Te Anau, Wanaka – have fewer than 5,000 people

It's not just that it's easier to get to know and care about other people if there aren't that many of you around. In small towns, it is so much more obvious that we need each other to survive. In big towns and cities this critical dependence is hidden behind supermarket shelves stocked by anonymous someones with food produced by other anonymous someones, where the combined cost of all the items essential to physical survival is a ridiculously small proportion of the money most people earn. And if I am violently attacked on the way home, then I dial 999 and more anonymous someones come to help.

In some faraway part of my London brain I know that I depend on others for almost everything. But I don't know their names. Without realising I am doing it, I smugly assume that enough of the billions of other people in the world will forever continue doing whatever it is they do for me to have access to a never-ending supply of life's essentials at knock-down costs. Why should I care if Deepak Patel trips over a trolley whilst attempting to stock aisle 39 and impales himself on the toiletries display? My only link with his life is that we occasionally pick up the same potatoes. In his absence, surely someone else will put them out for me instead.

It is not so easy to think this way in New Zealand. Here, there is a far stronger appreciation of the people who produce our food and a far greater awareness of the links in the chain. Oh, there are supermarkets. There are even people who stack shelves in these supermarkets. But there are also noticeboards on which staff handwrite 'Happy Birthday Steve!' or 'Happy Birthday Clare!' before they open. The same noticeboards carry displays of 'Te Anau (or wherever) In The News!'. Newspaper clippings celebrate the recent reopening of the town's launderette, the departure of a local teenager to university or the building of a new wing for the community centre.

New Zealanders also have a long cultural tradition of welcoming others and putting the needs and comforts of visitors above their own. Maori tradition places great emphasis on welcoming visitors and although Maori officially comprise only about fifteen per cent of the population, Maori culture has an influence on life in New Zealand that belies this statistic. As long as a new arrival observes certain protocols (and this is where several early European explorers went spectacularly wrong) they will be welcomed into a Maori community and treated as a member of the family – that is, the kind of member who doesn't visit very often and who everyone likes.

So it may not just be a numbers game. Even if the population of New Zealand continues to rise and even if all the small townships disappear, there's a chance that this country might still have the friendliest supermarket staff and customers in the world.

Day four: Going all the way

My final day begins when the collective bangs and shuffles of cooking and packing seep through my ear plugs. I am no longer woken early by the light because the light no longer wakes early. We are nearly at the end of the official walking season.

The most wonderful thing about today is that I don't have to meet any transport deadlines because I am walking every step of the way back to my hostel in Te Anau. The least wonderful thing about today is that thick white cloud begins just above tree-level and blots out a view of anything other than the ground, the lake and the trees. The cloud doesn't even look like cloud. It has no contours, no colour variations and no movement. A blank expanse of ceiling has been lowered to within reach of the treetops.

An old children's story tells of an enthusiastic but ultimately misguided chick called Chicken Licken, who thinks that the sky has fallen down when an acorn falls on his head. He runs around shouting 'The sky has fallen! The sky has fallen!' like a – well, like a headless chick. This is how I feel as I stand on the beach outside Moturau Hut and look out over Lake Manapouri.

I shouldn't feel frustrated by this. I should enjoy the eerie feel and the greater sense of isolation. I should be positively ecstatic that the ceiling is white, not grey and leaking. I should, in short, give thanks for another wonderful day in the wild. I do not. I am annoyed and frustrated. Somewhere out there are small, densely wooded islands floating like dumplings in the lake and by all accounts looking quite charming. Beyond are even steeper, more jagged mountains. Some of these mountains even have interesting names, often courtesy again of Mr McKerrow – Cathedral Peaks, Precipice Peak and the little Camel Backs and Beehive. I have tramped through rain and wind and cloud, but this is the first time I have wanted to shake my fist at the sky.

One thing makes up for only being able to see the ground today – and that is what is on the ground. The track passes through a sphagnum moss bog, traversed by boardwalk (to protect the bog, not the tramper), with a small lake in the middle. Whilst everything above the treetops is a dull and dirty white, the ground is a disco of colour. Reds, oranges and neon greens predominate. Even if I hadn't become worryingly enchanted with moss on the Milford Track, I would still be impressed by this display.

I recently made the surprising discovery there are people on this planet who openly describe themselves as appreciators of moss. A few weeks ago, whilst sitting on one of the fleet of InterCity buses that are the backbone of the public transport network across much of rural New Zealand, I overheard an American tourist asking the bus driver to point out some of 'your special New Zealand sphagnum moss'. Now, InterCity bus drivers know a lot about their land. In fact, part of their job is to provide a commentary for their passengers – an activity they seem genuinely to enjoy and that would probably bring their counterparts in the UK out on strike. Admittedly, many coach passengers in New Zealand are tourists, but plenty of locals use the services too and I often wonder what they make of their coach-wielding historians.

The driver in question knew all about a nearby sphagnum moss farm and described how the moss is harvested, dried and sent round the world to help indoor plants to grow or to appear as the extra bits in bouquets of flowers that, until now, I had severely under-appreciated. The American Moss Appreciator was brought almost to tears at having received such a full and instant response from what must have seemed an extremely unlikely source and without a snigger from anyone on board. Some of their enthusiasm even rubbed off on me. And now that I'm standing in amongst the stuff, I can *so* see what the fuss is all about. Even the name is cool. Sphagnum. The name is Sphagnum. Sphagnum Moss.

A number of geese and scaup are paddling around on the unnamed lake while flying visibility is so limited. The scaup are merrily diving for food and every time they duck down it seems they have drowned, until they suddenly pop up again, like a floating toy held under water in the bath and then suddenly released. Supposedly, scaup can sustain a dive for up to thirty seconds. I count these boys down and up. Whole minutes elapse. In this small corner of Fiordland, six scaup are quietly rewriting the record books.

Of the fifty people who began the track three days ago and the nine people who stayed at Moturau Hut last night, just three of us are walking all the way back to Te Anau. The others are tall, fit Australians who have long since overtaken me. Most trampers meet transport at Rainbow Reach, which is linked to the track by a long swing bridge across the Waiau River. I'm not stopping here, but I cross the bridge to discover that the place with such a great name is nothing more than a small gravel car park.

The riverbanks look bare and unhealthy – a hangover from early experimentation to see what volume of water could be released in one go from Lake Te Anau to Lake Manapouri. Judging from the erosion it looks as if you could have surfed the wave of the first attempt.

The Waiau River has another recent claim to fame. In 1986 it was cited as the boundary in one of the claims lodged by Ngai Tahu with the Waitangi Tribunal (Ngai Tahu being the lead tribal name for most South Island Maori). The claim filed was enormous, having approximately 200 grievances split into nine main areas. One of these concerned the Crown's purchase of land in Southland in 1853. Ngai Tahu argued that the land west of Waiau River was wrongfully included in the purchase deed and never sold. If this claim were upheld, perhaps the Kepler Track should never have been built.

The Waitangi Tribunal is an ingenious and practical Kiwi invention. Many countries have had (and still have) issues between indigenous peoples and 'later arrivals', but none that I know of has taken quite the same approach as New Zealand to resolving these. Europeans (and particularly the British) settled into New Zealand, as elsewhere, in the nineteenth century and began to deal in earnest with 'the natives' – trading, befriending, sparring, killing, marrying and so on. A treaty was signed in 1840 between British and Maori leaders, setting out the principles by which New Zealand would be governed and protected and by which the rights and authority of Maori tribes would be preserved. Unfortunately, the British and Maori versions of this treaty – the Treaty of Waitangi – differed. Some would argue that the fundamental differences in opinion, interpretation and cultural frameworks have never been resolved. However, the British, and other nationalities, kept arriving. Within just a couple of generations, the non-Maori population had grown from around 2,000 to more than 600,000 and land and resources had been variously bought, claimed or otherwise acquired by them and by that other new arrival, 'the Crown'. Not all transactions undertaken after 1840 were entirely clear, honest, free from differing cultural interpretation *and* self-evidently compatible with the principles of the Treaty of Waitangi (which was itself not entirely clear or free from different interpretations). Politely put, grievances arose.

By the late twentieth century the world had a new view of the rights of indigenous peoples and Maori grievances had not disappeared. However, by then New Zealand's population had grown to more than 3.5 million and daily life had changed dramatically. Could anything be done to resolve old grievances once and for all? How do you right a wrong when so much has changed? How do you work out right from wrong in the first place, with two such different cultures?

New Zealand's answer was – and is – the Waitangi Tribunal. The Tribunal comprises a group of up to sixteen experts. 'Expert' is defined according to the particular matters before them, which is fortunate because there are a lot of cases and the same sixteen people would be dead before they finished if they had to hear them all. The Tribunal began its work in 1975 and currently estimates that all claims should have been heard by around 2015.

The scale and scope of the claims that have come before the Waitangi Tribunal is breathtaking. The Ngai Tahu claim alone related to more than half the landmass of New Zealand and the inquiry lasted five years. If anyone were to recklessly and grossly simplify the findings into one sentence it would be this: Ngai Tahu were badly done by and the Crown should make amends, through financial compensation, reimbursement of expenses and restitution of rights. However, with regard to the particular claim about lands west of the Waiau River, the Tribunal found that the land was indeed sold to the Crown. It perhaps wouldn't have been, if Ngai Tahu had been properly advised about what they were signing, but this southern end of Fiordland was included in the sale.

I still have fourteen kilometres of ground to cover before I reach the hostel spa pool and the terrain is genuinely flat. The sun finally appears and sends down spotlights on to the vibrant green mosses that once again cover every sliver of spare space in the forest. Even my naked, untrained eye is impressed with the huge number of different types of moss that exist.

Two elderly ladies approach, just as I'm beginning to wonder if I'll ever see the Control Gates again.

'Oh, well done, dear!' exclaims the first, noticing my pack.

'You've not far to go now. You're almost there,' smiles the second.

They seem to know that I'm walking out from the Kepler Track ('walking out' being tramping lingo for finishing a track). It is lovely to be told 'well done'. Could someone please arrange for these ladies to arrive near the end of every tramp?

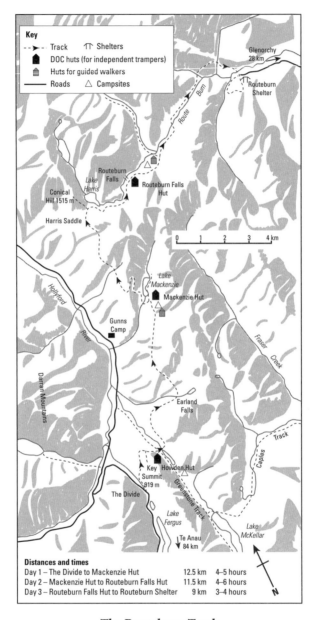

The Routeburn Track

6
Into the long white cloud: The Routeburn Track

Further additions to kit

- A small camera tripod

Otherwise, none. Have I finally cracked it?

'You're on your own then,' my driver observes companionably.

'Yep. Best way to tramp, I reckon, although I thought there might be others on the bus.'

He smiles.

'I run another shuttle to the Divide in a few hours, so there may be more passengers later. But this is the end of the season.'

The Divide marks one end of the Routeburn Track. At a mere 532 metres it is described as 'the lowest east–west crossing of the Southern Alps'. I'm sceptical.

The Southern Alps are the spine of the South Island, albeit a spine that has grown down the left-hand side of the back rather than in the conventional central position. Along the 850-kilometre length of the South Island just four road passes link the squeezed west coast to the roomier east – the Lewis Pass, Arthur's Pass, the Lindis Pass and Haast Pass. The Divide is unlike any of these road passes. From here the Milford Road runs west and south, but not east. Three tramping tracks – the Caples, the Greenstone and the Routeburn – lead east, but only to the next mountain range. It's hardly an east–west crossing of the Southern Alps. Even for New Zealand, 'the Divide' seems an odd name.

I look for clarification to the omniscient Kiwi bus driver.

'Why is it called *the Divide*?'

'Well, it marks a dividing point between … Well, between one valley and the next.'

That's clear, then.

I hitch myself forward on the seat. It is after 8.00 am, I have been up since 6.30 am, it is pitch dark outside and yet I feel wide awake and chatty. How can this be? Is New Zealand weaving its magic on me?

'I'm Gillian, but I guess you already knew that.'

'Hi Gillian. I'm Dave. Or Ferg.'

'OK.'

He laughs. 'The name's Dave Fergie, but people tend to call me Ferg. Or Dave.'

Clarity is obviously not up yet.

'So, Ferg – what will you do when the season's over and you're no longer ferrying tourists up and down the Milford Road?'

Today is Tuesday and tomorrow is the last day of the official tramping season.

'I keep busy. Thursday I start helping out with the cattle steering.'

'What will that involve?'

'Oh, rounding up cattle and getting them to the saleyards. A lot of cattle.'

'I thought the main stock was deer, not cattle.'

'Yeah, that's about right. It started in the 1970s. Some made their fortunes catching wild deer and bringing them down from the mountains. They got up to $3,000 per animal. As long as the animals survived, that is. Lots didn't.'

'Was it shock that killed them?'

I imagine I'd be shocked if I were minding my own business nibbling the peaceful Fiordland forest and a deafening large bird appeared, from which first a net and then a man jumped on top of me. I'd be even more shocked when, within the space of a few minutes, I found myself swinging from the bottom of the strange bird, with the forest rushing by at a hitherto unknown speed and angle.

'Shock was part of it. They kept them in the dark for the first few days to combat the stress. It wasn't just shock that killed them, though. Lots died trying to run through fences they weren't used to.'

May I be forgiven by animal rights activists everywhere, but I smile discreetly at this image.

'You'll be hearing a lot from the stags about now. We're coming into the height of the Roar.'

The way he pronounces 'Roar' is indistinguishable from 'Raw' and I spend a few moments imaging all sorts of meanings for the latter before I realise that he means the former. The Roar is the season when stags stand around literally roaring – as loud as they can to attract the ladies.

I picture the hinds grazing and chatting.

'Oh, there they go again. Honestly, what a racket.'

'I can't believe they still think we fall for that stuff.'

'Best to let them get on with it. It keeps them out of mischief.'

'I know. Oh well, we'd better line up, I suppose.'

I begin to wonder what human society would be like if women were always attracted to the man who bellowed the loudest. Then I spend quite a lot of time worrying that this might actually be the case.

As Ferg and I chat about the mating habits of deer, the Eglinton Valley quietly enacts a spectacular dawn. Mist hovers above the valley floor, white and still. Skimming over it, two paradise shelducks fly determinedly by our side. There are no clouds. The sky trembles from pale yellow into pale orange and finally, blue. Colours slide down the mountains as the sun rises.

By the time we reach The Divide the world is perfect. Our goodbyes are warm and friendly and I'm sorry I won't see Ferg on my return. Not only will he be doing manly things with cattle by then, but I'm not coming back this way. The Routeburn is not a circuit, but a line. Near its other end is the tiny town of Glenorchy and, forty-eight kilometres further on, the bustling metropolis of Queenstown.

This isn't sarcasm. Queenstown is *the* party town of the South Island and the high-adrenalin capital of the New Zealand tourist circuit. It could have an outdoor population clock in its main square, showing the number of inhabitants ticking inexorably upwards as the locals find ever more ways of building on ever-dividing sections. The diminishing plots of land are squeezed between the shores of Lake Wakatipu and the craggy peaks of yet more amazing mountains. These include the best-named range in New

Zealand: the Remarkables. They rise so steeply up from the lake shore that no other name would do.

However, I'm worried about my ability to cope with Queenstown. Doesn't it have bars and clubs and a non-tramping dress code? Won't I have to wash my hair and dress in the kind of clothes that I don't carry over mountains?

Yesterday I spoke to a man named Wattie, who confirmed my fears.

'Hi, Wattie? This is Gillian. I called the other day about transport out from the Routeburn Track?'

'Oh – yes. Hello, dear.' Wattie sounded kind and nice, with the wobbly vocal chords of an octogenarian.

'I've decided to start the track tomorrow, which means I'll be at your end on Thursday. Will you still be able to pick me up on Thursday?'

'Yes, yes. That's fine. Thursday.' I got the impression he was writing it down. Carefully.

'Also, I wanted to ask your advice about where to stay on Thursday night. In Glenorchy or Queenstown?'

'Oh, you'll love Glenorchy. This is a wonderful place. Queenstown is all right, in its way, but you mustn't miss Glenorchy. Much smaller. Friendlier. You'll want to stay here.'

'Great. Thank you. So, what time should I be at the Routeburn shelter on Thursday?'

'Thursday? Oh yes, Thursday. How about a quarter to two?'

'Great. Do you want to take my name and credit card details?'

'I've got your name,' he replied, before adding doubtfully, 'It's Gillian, isn't it?'

'Yes.'

I'm still not used to the fact that everyone on the South Island works with first names only. It is almost impossible to interest anyone here in your surname, never mind credit card details.

'So, I'll make sure I'm at the Routeburn shelter by 1.45 pm on Thursday.'

'Yes. Have a great walk. It's a wonderful track.'

'Thank you. Um … are you picking anyone else up from the track on Thursday?'

'Oh no, dear. It's the end of the season.'

I hung up and stared at the phone. Is he really as old as he sounds? Did he write everything down? What if he loses the piece of paper?

I shouldn't worry. Wattie's number was near the top of the list of track transport outfits recommended by DOC. He does this all the time. Plus, he's a Kiwi. Kiwis are reliable.

Day one: To the edge

From whichever end you approach it with your fully loaded pack, the first few hours of the Routeburn are up. This morning I don't mind. The track is enclosed by forest, but above is deepening blue sky. Waterfalls splash towards the track but run harmlessly under or alongside it. Foliage dangles between me and mountainous views. Sunshine glints from snow-capped peaks like a smile in a toothpaste advert.

Forty-five minutes later I am less bouncy. At ground level the track is clearly marked, but the air space has been colonised overnight: scores of spiders' lines snap with every step. I wave a dead branch in front of my face like a Catholic priest genuflecting on speed, trying to stop any more of the floss sticking across my nose, eyes and mouth. I am snared by the collective drag of Lilliputian lines. As I tire, I begin to begrudge the extra weight I must be carrying from the hundreds of surprised spiders I'm dragging up the hillside behind me.

I know that I am slipping into my tramping head when I begin to wonder strange things. Water runs along the side of the track, but which came first: the water or the people? I now consider myself an expert on Fiordland 'rain'. It takes the path of least resistance down the mountainsides and uses the tracks as highways, where the largest volumes of traffic travel at the fastest speeds. Did those who first cut this track use the path of the water, or does the water use the path we made? And why – oh why – does this single topic consume my thoughts for almost half an hour?

These thoughts evaporate when I climb beyond the treeline on the sharply zigzagging switchbacks to the top of Key Summit. Exposed to the full blast of the sun at barely 9.00 am on a late autumn day, I appreciate for the first time the strength of the sunlight here. Under sunhat, sunglasses and sunscreen I feel myself ageing like a special effects sequence.

The hole in the ozone layer that we are notoriously bad at tracking, still less caring about, is at this end of our globe. The hole itself still seems to be well to the south of New Zealand, yet the ozone here has been thinning. It doesn't help that the Earth is closer to the sun during the southern hemisphere summer. Despite New Zealanders' best efforts to use the world's oldest cars, there simply aren't enough of them to create the clouds of pollution that in other parts of the world protect their creators from ultraviolet radiation whilst doling out other illnesses. As a result, New Zealand has one of the highest rates of skin cancers and some of the most technologically advanced sunscreens in the world.

Slip, slop, slap and wrap, runs the much-repeated advice. Slip into a shirt and into some shade. Slop on the sunscreen. Slap on a hat. Wrap on the sunglasses. Or, in my case, slip into layers of clothing even when doing strenuous exercise in the midday sun (I burn here even through trousers, so I wear my fortunately breathable waterproof overtrousers as protection from the sun as much as from rain). Slop on the sunscreen every hour on the few patches of skin allowed out. Slap on a hat. And wrap on sunglasses whose boundary encompasses eyebrows and hairline, giving me a look that combines practicality with much-needed anonymity.

Key Summit in the sunshine is worth the squint. Jagged peaks and ridges surround it, many with permanent snow-hoods. What makes this particular summit 'key' is that it is the point from which river systems flow to the east, west and south coasts of the South Island. Only one of the three rivers can be seen from the 'summit', slinking down the Hollyford Valley, almost 2,000 metres below the gaze of white-topped mountain men lined up on both sides.

Key Summit is an odd place. It isn't a summit, but the flat-topped end of a ridge. It is also the lowest ridge in sight – a mere 919 metres. Standing on Key Summit is like being a child near the stage at a rock concert: the view is great, but all the important things seem to be happening somewhere above you.

Odder still, at the top I find a wooden box containing five A4-sized plastic nature walk guides with the kind instruction to 'please take one to be your guide and return when finished for the next person'. The walk winds round the flat 'summit', where numbered poles stick up at intervals to show where to read each section of your laminated friend. I can't believe that no one has stolen or vandalised these guides. They simply sit in their wooden box, being obediently used and returned by the thousands of people who come here each year. This would not happen in England.

I learn from the handy guide that gentians are one of many alpine plants that can change sex. Fortunately, I cannot see any gentians today, otherwise I would spend the next several hours trying to discover whether this is a trick you can watch with the naked eye. Sphagnum moss, meanwhile, can hold up to twenty-five times its own weight in water. Not just a pretty name, then, although here it looks like it shares a line of evolutionary descent with abandoned foam mattresses. In order to pass the long, winter days, it seems that alpine plants have developed eccentric habits, a love of sex and a complete disregard for image. I think I'm becoming a fan.

Inevitably, there are also 'facts' about who climbed which mountain first. Amazingly, these mountains were first climbed by Europeans, despite the fact that the track was used by Maori to access Fiordland pounamu long before the Europeans arrived. My favourite is Mount Christina – a wopping 2,332 metres of jagged ice and brittle rock that was 'first climbed in 1925 by Grave, Moir, Sinclair, Roberts and Slater'. It sounds more like a law-firm outing than a mountaineering expedition.

Key Summit is only about an hour's walk from the Divide and is therefore a popular trip on a clear day even with non-trampers. Other people begin to arrive soon after I have completed my second circuit of the nature walk and long before I've finished staring at the mountains all around. They dutifully pick up the laminated guides. I replace mine, smile and slip away.

It is increasingly important to me that I tramp alone. It's not because I dislike the people I meet. The mix of faces, cultures and nationalities is striking and greetings are always friendly. I suspect that everyone here – Kiwi, Japanese, American, British, German, Dutch and more – could tell me something fascinating about their land, their families, their beliefs or their traditions. The problem is, they won't. We are trapped in a layer of protocol, held there by lack of time, language barriers, and the unacceptability of probing into strangers' emotions. We ask the questions to which I least want to know the answers: where are you from; how long are you in New Zealand; isn't it a beautiful day? I don't ask the questions I want to: does our presence ruin this place; do you see gods in the mountains; what are you feeling?

I may be suffering from too many years spent with so many people all around me, all the time, and yet knowing so few of them properly – millions of them at work, on the tube, out on the town. It is hard to value the presence of others when there are so many of them and the connections are so slight. How odd it is, I realise now, that we seem to place no limits on human population when we have such strong ideas about the populations of other species. Too many possums and deer, so we hunt them. Too few kiwis and takahe, so we protect them. Too many human beings? And if not already, then when?

Having crept away to hear my own thoughts, I give myself nothing to listen to for several hours. I pass Howden Hut, which marks the meeting point for the Routeburn, Greenstone and Caples Tracks, boasts a wonderful view along Lake Howden and is a little shabby and faintly smelly. I climb up on to the side of the Hollyford Valley and make my way in to and out of the creases and folds of the Humboldt Mountains, just below the wavering line at which all but the shortest, toughest vegetation gives up. I climb up over boulders to reach the base of Earland Falls, where the spray bounds up to meet the slightest glimmer of sunshine with a grin and a rainbow. In today's bright, uninterrupted sunshine, the rainbow plays with me – disappearing when I get too close and simultaneously reappearing just beyond reach.

The pool at the base of the falls is turquoise-blue, clear and deep. The water falls eighty metres down an almost flat cliff face, directly above the track. When I crane my head back with my neck crumpled up in worthwhile pain, my bottom jaw drops down and my mouth hangs open like that of a dumbstruck child. This is the only feasible look to have when gazing up at Fiordland waterfalls.

The sun dazzles, the air is thick with cleanliness, my body is in full tramping flight and my mind is empty when a deep, male voice suddenly says 'Hello!'

I jump so violently that I almost fall off the mountainside.

The stranger laughs.

'I've been walking towards you for several seconds, but something told me you hadn't seen me.'

I'm laughing now. Not out of embarrassment at my squeal, but simply because it's funny.

'No – I didn't see you. I was in a world of my own.'

He laughs again. He has a large pack, well-worn boots, a youthful air and a lovely smile.

'It must be something about this track. You're the third person I've done that to today.'

We smile together, but neither of us stops. There is hardly anyone to be found on this long section of track today and yet neither of us feels a lack of human contact. It's not a day for chat. It's a day for laughing with strangers and passing by.

For around ten kilometres after Key Summit the Routeburn Track winds along the side of the Hollyford Valley. Some 1,000 metres below, the Hollyford River glints towards the sea.

Two days before the start of the off-season in Fiordland, the main company on the Routeburn Track is provided by birds. New Zealand boasts an enormous variety of unusual, outsized birds, but even its more common, small ones are fascinating company. I swear they are following me. When I walk through a pocket of whistles in the forest, I try to mimic the calls and often find a few curious chaps whizzing along the path beside me. They're cheerfully patient, stopping on overhanging branches while I catch up.

A common companion is the rifleman, or titipounamu (both names referring to its striking green colour). An average rifleman is just eight centimetres long. Now, some New Zealand birds lay eggs that are a phenomenal proportion of their body weight. Kiwi eggs, for example, can reach up to twenty-five per cent of the female's weight – compared with something around five to six per cent for human babies. Kiwi houses throughout New Zealand have diagrams showing the size of an egg within those enormous kiwi bottoms. The proportions are enough to make any grown woman cross her legs. The female rifleman, however, typically lays a batch of three eggs that together comprise eighty-four per cent of her bodyweight. Eighty-four per cent! This is not laying eggs; this is shedding an outer skin.

The good news for the female rifleman (and kiwi), however, is that once they've delivered their eggs, the father takes over as chief incubator. I'm never likely to witness first-hand the post-natal trauma of any of New Zealand's birds (and neither would I wish to disturb those exhausted females), but I already have a sense of the scene: father sits proudly warming and turning the eggs, while mother lies on the floor like an abandoned glove puppet.

The riflemen that accompany me to a place called the Orchard are bouncy, whistling, happy birds. The scene is faintly surreal: 1,000 metres up the side of pointy mountains the track passes through a large, meadow-like area dotted with ribbonwood trees. Birds chirp, the sun shines and the terrain is temporarily un-mountainous. Perhaps I have sunstroke. Perhaps even the surprising stranger wasn't real.

Here, suddenly, are deciduous trees. Unlike the vast majority of trees in New Zealand, ribbonwood trees shed their leaves for winter. Relatively few native tree species do so, which is great news for someone who will be doing the rest of her tramping in winter. I won't be buried under several tons of rotting foliage and the winter views will be as green as the summer ones. Just a lot colder.

At Mackenzie Hut I find Evan, the hut warden, standing on a stainless steel work surface in the kitchen, fiddling with the solar-powered light fitting.

'Hi there.'

'Hey, how're you doing?'

'Great, thanks. This is a *fabulous* hut!'

I mean it. The kitchen–dining area looks like it has been designed for a magazine feature. The stove takes central place in the large room. Forming a 'V' behind it are two reflective walls with wooden rungs, for hanging clothes to be dried by the heat from the chimney. Not for this hut the bits of string, nails or frames on pulleys hanging from the ceiling, which are the normal means for making cold, wet garments into warm, steaming, smelly garments. The floor, walls, tables and benches are of scrubbed wood. The kitchen is a triangle of gleaming work surfaces. Everything has been scrubbed and tidied to within a scratch of its varnish.

Only one thing has survived: a cutting from a local newspaper pinned neatly to the wall. It tells of an Israeli woman who recently walked the Routeburn Track. On a cold morning, with snow forecast, she prepared to cross the Harris Saddle (tomorrow's test for me). The DOC warden at the Routeburn Falls Hut advised her and her companions not to attempt the Saddle because they did not have the right clothes or equipment. The Israeli woman retorted that they were confident that they would have no problems. A few hours later she was being helicoptered off the saddle suffering from hypothermia.

The article presents all of this in a very factual manner. Its presence on the hut wall does the rest.

I unpack my billy.

'Oh yes,' says Evan, jumping down, 'I need to put some of the gas rings back. I thought it was the last day of the season today and no one was here last night, so I've done the clean-up. When I radioed in this morning, I discovered that the last day is tomorrow. So I'm making a few adjustments.'

Evan is fiftyish, with the energy and knees of a schoolboy. The others gathered here tonight are three Europeans (who are remarkably shy and soon revert to talking quietly to each other in a language I can't identify), two young Englishwomen (who are self-confidently lovers) and one half of a pair of rugby-sized Australians. The Australian talks proudly and confidently of his country, but his tone changes when we turn to tramping.

'Y'know,' he says quietly, after we've talked for a while, 'last time I was here – last year – I walked the Kepler Track. It's a great track – lots of great views from the tops all right. But it was the lower section that got to me. There's a section of forest after the Iris Burn Hut that felt very old. And magical. Don't reckon I've ever been in forest like that. Before or since.'

With that, he turns his attention swiftly to brewing up.

Well, quite.

I take my tea and go to sit on the lake shore.

Evan joins me, showing me in passing the spacious hut warden quarters.

'This is the best hut in Fiordland,' he grins proudly.

He doesn't just mean the interiors. The positioning is excellent. A few seconds' walk from the hut is Lake Mackenzie, held in a stadium where the stands are made from hard rock and anyone sitting in the highest row would need binoculars to identify their team.

'That's Emily Peak up there,' he says, pointing to the one furthest right. 'And that one in the middle we call F Knob.'

I lose my fascinated visitor expression. 'Er – "F Knob"? "F" as in …?'

'F as in F. As in A, B, C, D, E, F. I figured whoever was naming them got bored.'

I daren't ask where A, B, C, D or E are located. Still less dare I wonder aloud if they stopped at F.

Evan continues, 'That one on the left is Ocean Peak.'

'Oh yes, that makes sense. It looks like a cresting wave about to break.'

'Well, no – I think it's called Ocean Peak because if you climb to the top of it you can see the ocean.'

Kiwi Practicality 1:English Romanticism 0.

A figure arrives, scrambling round the rocks at the edge of the lake with a fishing rod in hand. The Aussie joins us and calls out to his mate, 'Did you catch it?'

'No. Nothing biting.'

They go back inside and Evan laughs.

'I told them about the Big Fish. Clive started the story, not me.' (Clive, I have learned, is the other warden at The Best Hut in Fiordland.)

'He told a tramper there was an enormous trout living in the lake. The guy came back with his fishing gear and spent ages trying to catch it. He didn't, of course. Where was an enormous fish going to come from up here?'

Clive and Evan clearly have a few laughs at the hut. Evan tells me of his favourite day this season. 'We weren't sure we'd be able to open on time at the start of this season. There were heavy snowfalls at the end of the winter.'

'So the snow was too deep on the track?'

'It was quite thick, but that wasn't the problem. The problem was the risk of avalanches. They were going to keep the track closed for another week or so, until the really bad stuff had fallen or melted. So, me and Clive went up with some dynamite and made our own avalanches. Cleared all the worst bits and opened the track on schedule.'

Clive seems to be a permanent fixture in the Mackenzie basin – he may even pre-date the hut. Evan arrived two years ago, after thirty years in the police force.

The paths to becoming a DOC hut warden are many and varied. There are those for whom it is their first job and those who come to it after a typically Kiwi career, encompassing everything from sheep shearing to bus driving to local politics (and that excludes all the voluntary work like firefighting, search and rescue and raising families). There are wardens in their early twenties, late sixties and everything in between. Neither gender dominates. They can be chatty or shy, straight or funny, bossy or gentle.

Despite the variety, I can't help thinking of them as a breed apart. It's not just the uniforms. These are all people who walk to work – often over mountains and carrying food to last up to eight days. They live half their lives in the wild and half their lives in towns (and lots of them seem to have great relationships and healthy sex lives, which leads me to wonder whether this isn't an underused model for marital harmony). These are people who share the joint privileges of having some of the world's most stunning landscapes as a workplace and having to empty out toilets for the tourists. They like their own company and yet always have a friendly word for those whose mess they may find themselves having to clean up (particularly on the Great Walks, where trampers don't always leave huts as they find them).

Perhaps above all else, however, DOC hut wardens are people who seem to have no idea how fit they are. When Evan tells me about some of his excursions, I make some mental calculations about the distances he covers – *steep* distances. He moves roughly three times faster than me.

'So, what will I find tomorrow night?' I ask. 'Is the Routeburn Falls Hut as nice as this?'

'I don't know,' Evan replies. 'You're in Fiordland here, but tomorrow you cross into Mount Aspiring National Park. They run things differently over there.'

As the sun slips from the tops of the mountains behind us, Evan returns to his packing and I sit on a rock and drink hot fruit tea. I taste the tea. I stare at the mirror water. I stare at the snow splayed in the crevasses of the shadowed valley walls of rock in front of me. Not a thought enters my head. I stay like this until the sun has gone from the valley and I can barely lift my bones from the rock.

Day two: Crossing over

The dawn view from my sleeping bag is incredible. Through the windows at the top of the hut I can see a row of peaks silhouetted against the sky. The sun doesn't reach Mackenzie Hut until late in the morning. This is not dawn so much as the start of light.

I am still surprised by how big the horizon is when there are no buildings in the way. I abandon my synthetic cocoon and quickly freeze, but it's worth it to stand on the porch watching colour emerge.

I arrange to meet Evan on Friday night in Te Anau for a beer to celebrate my return from the track, the end of the tramping season and the start of the duck-hunting season. For the whole weekend the small towns of the South Island will be in party mode, with everyone gathered together to roast, barbecue or otherwise sizzle the captured game.

It will take me more than twenty-four hours to get 'home' to Te Anau from the end of the track. The Routeburn, Greenstone and Caples Tracks are the only way to cross these particular mountains. The roads linking Glenorchy, Queenstown and Te Anau steer around the mountains and lakes. Wattie will pick me up from the end of the track tomorrow lunchtime, but the length of the journey and the timing of the daily buses mean I won't get back to Te Anau until Friday afternoon at the earliest. I love it. It feels like it's quicker to walk than to drive.

The DOC guides for independent trampers on the three Great Walks in Fiordland all show cross sections of the tracks. They look like settings on a high-tech treadmill. The Milford Track setting is for those who like their workouts easy: a barnacle-shaped hill in the middle, but with lots of flatness either side to warm up and warm down. The Kepler Track setting is for those who like to burn hard and early. Indeed, if this were really a setting on a treadmill, you would either tumble off the back or into the control panel at the front, or both, when the poor machine tried to adjust for the almost vertical climbs and descents. Condensed from a four-day walk into a thirty-minute workout, the first ten minutes of the Kepler Track would be little more than a bucking bronco ride.

The Routeburn setting, on the other hand, is just what a workout should be: a long, slow burn. As I begin yet another climb, I travel so slowly that I notice something strange about the terrain under my feet. I thought that I was walking up a valley wall. I'm not. This is a giant rockery, where the smallest rocks are the size of those four-wheel drive vehicles that tiny women drive in London. The layers of moss, plants and tree roots obscure the truth, but underneath there are gaps through everything – between boulders, rocks, roots and leaves. The track consists of smaller rocks squeezed together in between the bigger rocks. This whole mountainside could be just great boulders piled up like a harbour wall.

Beyond the treeline, the track passes beside overhanging boulders with horizontal lines that show how they were formed and vertical lines that show where they will break. The horizontal lines, or striations, were caused by glaciers moving down these valleys like thousands of nails down a blackboard. The vertical lines are pressure cracks – and in these wounds are traces of green. Rock rust, otherwise known as lichen.

One of the comments on those laminated guides at Key Summit was that 'life begins with rock'. So is this rock rust the first step on the evolutionary trail? I quite like the idea that I am related to rock. My school textbooks told me that my earliest landed relation was a fishy creature that heaved itself out of the ocean to lie around a lot, looking exceedingly unattractive. I would far rather be related to a mountain. Who knows, Maori beliefs that mountains and rivers are our ancestors could be scientifically true. At the very least, they make me feel part of something bigger and more powerful than simply being the latest in a long line of ugly fish.

As I clamber up the rock I do feel that I am part of it. We are both moving and changing, but I do so with greater speed and less time. The climb brings me back on to the side of the Hollyford Valley. At which point my legs give way. Not because of the strain, but because I have just become the luckiest person alive. This is Fiordland and it's not raining. In front of me, behind me and to all sides are mountains. The valley crumples down some 1,000 metres below my feet and I can almost look the mountains opposite in the eye.

From left to right is the full line of the Darran mountain range. Several peaks rise beyond 2,500 metres, all the way up from the Hollyford River between us. Thick greenery reaches up to their bellies. Tussock tints the next layer yellow. Towards the top blades of bare rock slice through struggling tussock, but in turn are defeated by thick snow – even in sunshine, even in summer. Several small glaciers have the final say on the highest peaks. I don't know who Darran was, but his luck was in to be a friend of whichever European surveyor was drawing this map.

To the right, at the end of the range and around thirty kilometres away, lies Lake McKerrow, which covers almost all the remaining twenty kilometres to a glinting sliver of the Tasman Sea.

Everything is perfect. I sit on a rock without guilt because I don't have to leave the track to reach it and it's not covered in crushable lichen. Its shape fits mine perfectly. From my personal armchair I eat a second breakfast and address the mountains.

'You're so beautiful. Do you know how beautiful you are?'

It is well documented that human beings generally feel humbled when they come face to face with things that are much bigger than they are. Feeling suddenly small supposedly makes us humble.

Well, I feel small most of the time. Next to the average man in the UK, I feel small. Next to the average man from America or Holland I feel even smaller. But I never feel humbled in their presence. Maybe this is because they aren't big enough. However, buildings don't do it for me either. For the last nine years I have lived in a city full of big and imposing structures. I am impressed by many of these. I frequently wonder how (and occasionally wonder why) man has made them. But I have never felt truly humbled by them.

Mountains are different. Perhaps because they are *so* much bigger. You can stand at the bottom of a skyscraper and look up and measure yourself against it and think, 'Wow, that's big'. Whereas, when you stand at the bottom of a mountain, it's invariably so big that you can't see it any more.

It's not just size that matters. To date, mountains have lasted longer than anything made by a human being. Along with oceans they are the closest things we know to being permanent – and oceans are hard to think of as anything other than, well, fluid. Planets, moons and suns have a greater theoretical claim to permanency, but for practical reasons they are nowhere near as good as mountains: they move around a lot and are, frankly, too huge for us to remember most of the time.

Maybe this is the secret of mountains: they are the biggest, seemingly permanent objects we can see with our eyes and fit into our brains.

Nevertheless, when you've spent time in their close company it is obvious that mountains change frequently. They are continuously losing their battles with the weather – shrugging off great chunks of themselves as forfeit, or splintering from their slow-motion scraps with glaciers. Neither do they look the same from one hour to the next: a slight change in light can make a previously magnificent chunk of rock look pouting and puny.

So, if it's not simply a matter of size and permanence, what is it? I have a few ideas. First, there is the question of strength. Losing out to the weather may be inevitable, but mountains make the weather really battle for its victories. Key Summit is far from being the highest mountain in this community, but it defeated the efforts of three glaciers. This rock is *hard*. I admire toughness. It is the quality shared by all hut wardens that impresses me most. Particularly when they don't even know they've got it.

Second, there is the small matter of Newtonian physics. The greater the mass of a physical object, the greater its gravitational pull. The Earth keeps me glued to its surface because it is *so* much bigger than me and (without wishing to boast) much denser as well. Maybe the reason that I feel so drawn to these mountains is because I am actually, physically being drawn to them. And I am more drawn to the Darran Mountains than to the Humboldt Range on which I am standing because the Humboldts are composed of schist and sandstone, whereas the Darrans have the gravitational trump card of granite.

Something that bears no scrutiny, however, is why people (or, at least the vast majority) think that mountains are beautiful. Not just powerful presences, but visually beautiful. Much money has been spent around the world on investigating what makes us think another person is beautiful and we have discovered that the answer has a lot to do with symmetry. The same cannot be said for mountains. It is the opposite – the odd angles, gravity-defying outcrops, jagged edges and unsymmetrical everythings are the most beautiful.

Here's something else I don't understand about the power of mountains: they make humility feel marvellous. I mean, we, as good human beings, are supposed to enjoy feeling powerful. We love feeling like we're the best, the strongest, the cleverest. Yet, people who walk amongst mountains leave feeling happier and more at peace with themselves. They look these beautiful giants in the eye and they come away thinking 'I am truly tiny, and, heck, that feels good'.

So, why does the sight of this land in this sunshine make me want to cry with happiness? I have no idea. I sit for more than an hour at the edge of crying. I could never have anticipated the emotion these mountains create in me. That such a world exists. And I get to carry the sense of it inside me for the rest of my life.

The only sign that this is later than about 1900 is a group of well-maintained, matchbox-shaped buildings, arranged in military fashion around a grid of paths near the river. This is Murray Gunn's Camp, described on the map as

'Museum, Store and fuel'. There is a road down there – the Lower Hollyford Road – but it ends about seven kilometres past the camp and long before it reaches the sea, which was its originally intended destination. The Lower Hollyford Road is a weaker, younger sibling of the Milford Road, dating back to the era when Kiwis were directing their entrepreneurial outlook, outdoor skills and physical strength to laying miles of gravel through unfeasible terrain.

Murray Gunn's Camp was where the road builders lived and its museum records stories from those Herculean days. From 800 metres up, the Camp looks the perfect place for misbehaving boy scouts. I'm told that it's still possible to stay at the Camp, even if you're a tourist. It doesn't advertise, though. You drop in if you happen to be travelling down the Lower Hollyford Road (rarely). Or you book ahead, if you have access to a local telephone directory and already know that the Camp exists and does take bookings.

From above Gunn's Camp until the descent into the next valley is the section of track that earns the Routeburn the title of 'serious alpine crossing'. The track has been cut, carved and blasted into the sides of mountains, far above the treeline. Thirty-two different avalanche paths cross the track between Earland Falls and the Routeburn Flats. A signpost at the Divide told me so and I love its precision.

The words used to describe the Routeburn Track in summer are: magnificent, breathtaking and impressive. The words used to describe the track in winter are: hazardous, wild and impassable. Well, today I have one of the last great summer days on the Routeburn Track all to myself. This is no small miracle.

The Routeburn is the second most popular track in New Zealand. Both Independent Trampers and Guided Walkers flock here. Its popularity soared with both tramping species when booking a slot on the Milford Track became more difficult than retying a bootlace whilst standing in a river. Even the creation of the Kepler Knee-Crunch didn't diminish bookings on the Routeburn, which is still, for many, the 'next best thing' to walking the Milford Track.

In the Mackenzie basin a Guided Walks Hut is carefully concealed from the DOC hut by a short distance and some strategic vegetation. However, the key division between trampers on the Routeburn is not money, but whether or not they have already walked the Milford Track. For those who haven't, it can be an obsession. Greeting a fellow tramper they rush the standard greeting etiquette to arrive at the main agenda, 'Have you done the Milford Track? And is it better than this?'

This is an impossible question to answer. It's like asking who is sexier: Brad Pitt or Clint Eastwood? The answer depends on personal preference and timing. And, unwittingly, I have timed this tramp to perfection. A pocket of high pressure has brought me a Fiordland tramp without rain (thus far). No group of Guided Walkers started the track on the same day as me. Tourist numbers have dwindled as winter arrives. And, above all else, the local trampers are waiting for the end-of-season free-for-all.

For two or three weeks immediately following the end of the official tramping season in Fiordland, the Great Walks become more popular with the locals than the nightly edition of *The Simpsons* is with backpackers in hostels throughout the land. Regular trampers flock to take advantage of cheaper huts before the tracks become impassable. During the tramping season, a night spent in one of these huts costs $40, which is roughly double the cost of a night in a hostel, with their proper beds and hot water. Out of season the price not only falls to around $10 a night, but is free to those in possession of the serious tramper's identity card: the Annual Hut Pass.

The Annual Hut Pass is a piece of thick plastic in the shape of a hut. The 'hut' has a window in the middle, to allow the tramper to secure the Pass to the outside of their pack. Possession of this plastic hut permits you to stay in almost all of New Zealand's real huts, subject to certain restrictions to prevent severe enthusiasts setting up home in them. The small list of huts excluded from this arrangement consists mostly of every single hut on a Great Walk in season. Popularity has its price.

Thus, the local trampers have a short window in which to exercise their plastic huts on the Great Walks of Fiordland. In these two to three weeks before the heavy snows arrive, standard tramping rules apply. To claim a mattress for the night, you must be amongst the first fifty to reach the hut. The slower ones claim the benches, tables and floor. Camping is allowed only in a couple of small, designated spots, so there is suddenly a very practical reason to try to walk faster than your fellow trampers.

I didn't want to wait for the cheaper tickets, when the gas would be gone, the water supply restricted and I would be thrust into a speed competition with the real experts. However, I did not imagine that coming here in the closing days of the season would give me this wonderful place to enjoy gloriously alone. I have the whole of the Hollyford Valley to myself. Fifty kilometres of it, clear from the Tasman Sea back to Key Summit.

Until I reach the Harris Saddle. Here, 1,255 metres up and with mountains on all sides, sounds of electric power tools drift on the rising wind towards me. I battle uphill through the wind tunnel that is the Harris Saddle to find a small generator and several large cables straddling the Harris Saddle Emergency Shelter. Inside are three abandoned backpacks, stacks of wood and a young man watching a DVD of a mindless Hollywood movie on a laptop. Somebody pinch me.

Next to the temporary cinema, a second structure is rising. It looks exactly like the existing shelter, but bigger and shinier. Over the noise of the wind, the power tools and the DVD, conversation is impossible, so I leave my pack in the cinema and make my assault on Conical Hill.

Conical Hill is a side trip from the saddle, the purpose of which is to get an even higher view of Fiordland mountains and the sea beyond. It is a scramble in many places, where, if you move as slowly as me, you can see the remnants of the cylindrical holes bored for dynamite sticks to blast a track through the rock.

My limbs are aching, but I'm trying to beat the clouds that are now gathering around the peak. The owners of the abandoned packs come sliding down the hill in front of me.

'Hi there,' I smile at the excuse to stand still. 'Is it worth it?'

'It's misty at the top. But if you wait a few minutes it clears to give you a view,' comes the reply.

'Yeah – great views! Well worth it. Although you've got at least another twenty minutes to climb.'

When I finally haul myself to the top I am more than ready for the view. Unfortunately, it isn't ready for me. Cloud roars past me. In occasional glimpses of the next mountain I can see that there's plenty more cloud yet to pour over the horizon. The cloud isn't high: it is sidling over the next ridge and then falling into the Lake Harris valley and fluffing past my lower peak. It looks as if someone has lost control of a dry ice machine on the other side of the ridge.

Today, it is widely accepted that the Maori name for New Zealand is Aotearoa and that this means 'land of the long white cloud'. From my observations to date, this is a fair summary. When the sky here is not just a blanket of wet and it is possible to discern individual clouds, they are invariably of the white and long variety. Often you cannot see their beginning and end because horizons get in the way. Aotearoa is a name based on sound observation, if not easy enunciation.

Maori is a language that takes its vowels seriously. They are generally pronounced individually rather than blurred together to form new sounds. Aotearoa is thus pronounced 'Ay-oh-tay-a-row-a'. Pronouncing the word 'Maori' itself is tricky. Most visitors say it as 'mow' (to rhyme with cow) '-ree'. Locals enunciate the vowels separately but so quickly that you can barely catch them at it. The 'a' is pronounced as in 'man', the 'o' as in bold. Furthermore, your teeth should not touch your bottom lip for the 'r'. Instead, try simultaneously flicking and curling your tongue at the bottom of your mouth. Start slowly and then work your way up to saying 'Maori' twenty times in ten seconds. Alcohol won't help, but may provide some comfort. (Oh, and by the way, the written form of Maori was devised by the English. You would never guess.)

By the time you've learned how to spell and pronounce Aotearoa, you could be forgiven for feeling a little bit proud for having learned the 'native' name for New Zealand. Unfortunately, this is not strictly true. Before Europeans arrived in New Zealand, Maori tribes had different names for their land. Aotearoa was, at most, the name used by a small number of northern tribes to describe what is now the North Island.

Over time, however, first Europeans and then Maori began to consider Aotearoa the Maori name for New Zealand. And so it came to pass. The Land of the Long White Cloud. And here I am, standing in it.

I wait for nearly eighty minutes before abandoning hope of the view reappearing. It is too cold to wait longer and I still have another two hours of walking before I reach the next hut. The time has come to cross over.

The Routeburn Valley is virtually perpendicular to the Hollyford Valley and the Harris Saddle marks the end of the ascent out of the Hollyford Valley and the beginning of the descent into the Routeburn. Today, this also means the end of sun-soaked views and the start of chill mist. I am crossing over. I am leaving Fiordland National Park and entering Mount Aspiring National Park. I am leaving Southland and entering Otago. I am also crossing into the second half of this Great Walk and am well on my way to meeting Wattie tomorrow.

Being halfway through my fifth tramp means I'm now halfway through the nine Great Walks. This is not strictly true, because I've now tramped little more than 200 kilometres and I have nearly 350 kilometres left to cover, and some interesting wintertime challenges to face in addition. Right now, however, such technicalities don't matter. A threshold has been crossed. Or, to be more precise: a threshold has been exhaustedly stumbled over.

Lake Harris is the first landmark on the Other Side. Trapped between the mist above and the mountains around it looks vast and eerily grey. Could its name honour an unrequited love or a stillborn child? Of course not. Harris was yet another European explorer whose name is now attached to a piece of the Earth like the scrawl of the world's worst graffiti artists. Perhaps Otago isn't so different after all.

When my trembling knees finally straighten on the deck of the Routeburn Falls Hut I have set a new record in competitive tramping: today I have made a five-hour tramp last nine hours. Now *that's* what I call good tramping.

Tonight's warden is not the real warden, who broke his arm two weeks ago. I don't ask how because I can imagine a large number of ways in which wardens break more than just their arms. Instead, I tuck into the enormous plate of pikelets (small, sweet pancakes) that his replacement has made for the trampers. The gift is a celebratory gesture to mark the end of the season. It is also the best way to dispose of the remaining eggs, flour, milk, sugar, butter and jam in the wardens' hut. Unfortunately, with a ration of around twenty pikelets per tramper, we are all defeated. Not even the stuttering fire can swallow the remains.

After a long, emotional day under searing sunlight, I am excessively ready for bed. No matter that the sleeping quarters don't look promising. Thin, dark spaces separate the three-high stacks of bunks in the tall, dark room. It's like sleeping in a cash-and-carry warehouse.

Except that I don't sleep. I lie huddled in all available clothing, sleeping sheet and sleeping bag – and I shiver. Soon it won't be possible to pretend that it's still autumn. Occasionally I try to warm myself up by means of frantic movement. This is made difficult by my desire not to arouse attention or misunderstanding amongst tonight's hut-mates.

Day three: The easy way out

Eight hours later I stop shivering and get up. I don't recall sleeping at any point during the night. Slow thawing and weighty tiredness add yet more time to my morning routine, so that I'm the only tramper left when a helicopter lands seemingly on the roof.

When the noise stops I venture outside and find two men drinking tea with the 'warden'.

'Morning.'

'Morning.'

'Are you giving him a lift out?' I ask, indicating pikelet man.

'No. We've been up tracking tahr. They've got radio transmitters attached to them. We've been out for two hours and thought we'd stop in for a cup of tea before the next circuit.'

'I have to walk out,' adds the warden. 'We all do. Choppers pick up the rubbish, but we don't get a ride.'

'Are you going up the saddle today?' asks one of the hunters.

'No. I've come the other way.' With a smile, I use the now familiar tramping lingo. 'I'm walking out today.'

I am dying to stay in the company of these men, who spend their days working in some of the world's greatest remaining wilderness. All three of them look tough and hardy, but none of them has the cowboy swagger that says they know it. I can tell, however, that although they have been polite, our conversation has just ended. Here, at least, are three people who have no intention of asking me where I'm from or how long I'm in New Zealand for.

I leave them to their tea and tall tales.

By the time I'm back on the track it is just past 10.00 am and I am slightly concerned that I may not finish in time to meet Wattie at 1.45 pm. No dawdling, stopping or side trips for me today.

Fortunately the route is a gradual downhill under a shady canopy. The sun dazzles in yet another clear sky above and makes me want to turn around and try another assault on Conical Hill. Too late, too tired.

I find a piece of local vandalism at Israeli Creek. Here, one of DOC's handy wooden footbridges crosses the tumbling waterfall–stream. The creek is named after an Israeli couple who apparently decided to deviate from the Routeburn Track. Their aim, I believe, was to cross from Lake Mackenzie over Emily Peak into the Routeburn valley – probably to try something different from the masses, to get their own views of the mountains and to cut a few kilometres off the route. Now, I'm not in favour of people crashing off-track in this otherwise undisturbed wilderness. Hut wardens and hunters earn the right to do so, but are few in number and DOC wisely discourages anyone else from doing so. I have been quite pleased to learn, therefore, that this particular couple became hopelessly lost.

They eventually found a waterfall and surmised that the water may have found a route down into the valley that they could follow. This worked up to a point – and they ended up huddled together on that point, as darkness and water fell around them. I can afford to be grossly unsympathetic because they were rescued by DOC. As I pass the creek, I notice that someone has tried to scratch out the name Israeli Creek from the signpost. Perhaps I'm not alone in thinking that selfishness and stupidity should not be commemorated.

This is rapidly becoming another day in which people are absent, for which I am extremely grateful. One of my less noble reasons for this obsession with solitude is that I still dislike being overtaken. Something inside that I haven't yet fully squished interprets being overtaken as meaning that I am too slow and therefore inferior. This competitive curse is well known to me.

At school and university the rules of the competition were clear: get the highest marks, have lots of friends, be as physically attractive as possible and, at every opportunity, display how 'cool' you are. I didn't exactly come top in each of these categories, but I always knew what they were and I always knew what was required. After university the rules were still clear: get the highest salary, have a wonderful network (some of whom you can still call friends if you wish), be as physically attractive as possible and, at every opportunity, display how successful you are. Again, I didn't win many gold medals, but I knew what was required and I knew that gold medals were out there to be won.

There were, in fact, dozens of events I could enter: the Career Ladder

Sprint; the Marvellous Girlfriend hurdles; the Glorious Lover Gymnastics; the Potential Daughter-in-Law High Jump; and even the Faithful Friend Marathon. No athletes are to take drugs, knobble other competitors or unduly influence the judges, except in the Career Ladder Sprint, where anything goes.

I regularly entered these events and obeyed the rules. Until recently, that is. As I walk down this valley between so many calm and quiet trees, I wonder what the goal is now. I've left the games with a few bronze and silver medals but I have no desire to compete again. I'm not even sure I entered the right events. Even if being competitive is a good thing, towards what am I competing? To earn the most money? To mate and have the most children (which would perpetuate my genes but probably wear me out)? To be happier than everyone else? Perhaps, but what do I mean by happiness?

Hugging a tree stops these scurrying thoughts and makes me feel peaceful again. It's enough for now that I've posed the questions. The answers will come.

A helicopter breaks the forest quiet, following the river now on my right down the centre of the valley. Trailing below it is a bulging net. Is this the rubbish from the hut toilets? Or the wardens' knick-knacks? On its second fly-past I see a hut and some cars on the opposite bank and watch the pilot swing the cargo into the back of a truck before returning into the mountains. Disorientated, I check the map. No clearings or huts are marked. Unless… no. This can't be the end. Today's route was supposed to require three to four hours and I have been walking for barely more than two.

I return to the undergrowth on my side of the river, only to emerge soon afterwards at a footbridge, followed by a sign welcoming trampers to the Routeburn Track.

So, this is the end of my fifth tramp. I have sneaked over the finish line as the season closes, despite a carefree approach to planning in the face of the Fiordland Great Walks booking system. As I stagger, DOC staff across Fiordland are now cutting off gas and water supplies to the huts and removing the wooden footbridges, to be stored safely away from avalanches over the winter.

At the Routeburn Shelter elderly couples drive up, sit in the sunshine, smile at the mountains and avoid the crashing air as the helicopter continues its work. With more than an hour to kill before Wattie arrives, I chat to all of them, dawdle around the short loop-walk for the non-tramper and then go to talk to the white-haired man in charge of the truck. The helicopter has disappeared again.

'Hi there.'

'Hello.' His round, reddened face smiles back. He looks to be in his sixties, but fit.

'Do you do much walking here?' I ask.

'I've spent the last fifty years walking all over these mountains,' he replies.

I feel very small.

'I don't do as much these days because I run the Guided Walks outfit. I've got around seventy-five staff and run both tracks and also three ski fields around Queenstown. You just come off the Routeburn, have you?'

'Yes, but not as one of yours, I'm afraid.'

'No, you would have started on Tuesday. Our trips this week started on Monday and Wednesday.'

I'm feeling rather overawed by this man.

'What happens to all your staff in the winter? What do they do when the tracks are closed?'

'A lot of them are young and go travelling, often to Europe for your summer. Some of them work on our ski fields. The rest get other winter jobs.'

'And is the helicopter bringing out the week's rubbish?' I figure that Guided Walks lodges generate a lot more rubbish than DOC huts. Soiled satin sheets, the remains of three-course dinners ...

'No. My men have just finished building our Emergency Shelter at Harris Saddle. They're bringing down their tools and materials. Later, I'll go up to inspect their work.

'Our Walkers will now have their own shelter. It will be better this way. It doesn't work when Guided Walkers and Independent Trampers have to share.'

He tells me about his daughter who has now lived for several years in London and loves it there. God, London. I can barely remember my life there.

'Have you been to England?' I ask, hoping I may sound more competent on this topic.

'No. Maybe, one day.'

I'm not fooled. He's being polite. He has no interest in leaving his life here. And why should he?

By 2.30 pm the elderly couples have disappeared, my white-haired friend has flown into the mountains, I have been killing time for almost two hours and Wattie is extremely late. It is twenty-eight kilometres from the Routeburn Shelter to Glenorchy, the nearest settlement.

I start to walk. I haven't got far before I flag down a minibus with 'Backpackers' emblazoned on the side and an elderly couple in the back seat. Yes, of course the driver will give me a lift. He looks me up and down, then insists I sit up front.

Ten minutes later he puts his hand on my knee and says, 'I'm very attracted to you. Sexually.'

I glance behind at the old couple in the rear of the minibus, who can neither hear nor see what is happening.

'Well, that's very kind of you,' I respond in a tone I hope to be amiable and utterly non-sexual.

My strange saviour, I correctly guess, is harmless. Lonely and harmless. But even if he weren't harmless, there is not much that can be achieved in pursuit of *amour* with a minibus, a trailer and an elderly couple in tow. He can't even afford to keep his hand on my knee as we swing round Kiwi road bends.

My only struggle is not to laugh. He is young, lean and good-looking, albeit behaviourally a little odd. I, however, have greasy hair escaping from under a smelly, red bandana. I'm wearing baggy tramping clothes. Moreover, I'm wearing baggy waterproof trousers over baggy cotton trousers in bright sunshine. Oh, and I smell. Is my sweat irresistible? Perhaps I could make my fortune by selling it to French *parfumiers*.

I half-listen as my saviour describes his major sexual experiences in chronological order. I offer brief but friendly comments as my side of the conversation, trying desperately not to laugh, or to become depressed by the disaster that seems to have been his life to date. He is harmless. When he drops me off in Glenorchy, I shake his hand in a firm and friendly goodbye and he gets the message. The couple in the back are still staring out of the windows.

My thoughts are elsewhere. Winter is arriving and tramping is going to get tougher. More worryingly, if I'm going to attempt the Whanganui River Journey, I'm going to need to find a canoe partner. Someone who is willing to canoe for five days in a remote spot in the middle of winter with someone they've never met before. And who isn't a nutter. Now, that is going to require a whole new set of survival skills.

Fortunately, my next tramp is in the sunniest, smallest, flattest, most touristy National Park in New Zealand. I should be safe there.

7

Unexpected guests:
The Abel Tasman Coastal Path

Further additions to kit

- ❧ New 'waterproof' jacket
- ❧ Second sleeping bag (never again will I be as cold during the night as at Routeburn Falls Hut)
- ❧ Two spare torch bulbs (my torch bulb blew in a hostel one night. How easily might it have gone on a track, when I would have had no idea that a spare bulb is concealed in the torch base, as the nice man in one of Nelson's gazillion outdoorsy shops gently pointed out)
- ❧ Three small candles
- ❧ Swimming costume

Abel Tasman National Park is New Zealand's most popular National Park. Every year, more than 180,000 people tramp, kayak, pothole or simply loll within its boundaries.

There are many good reasons to do so. The Park's outer edge comprises low, leafy headlands separating scores of bays and small golden beaches, of the kind that make holiday brochure photographers weep with joy. The walking is easy, with the crests of the Coastal Path all peaking below 200 metres and the highest peak in the park barely scratching 1,200 metres. The kayaking is good, with safe currents, sandy beaches and New Zealand fur seals all largely guaranteed. The bedrock is entertaining, with air and water having beaten up the wimpy limestone. The location is excellent – at the top of the South Island and easily accessible from Wellington. And local tour

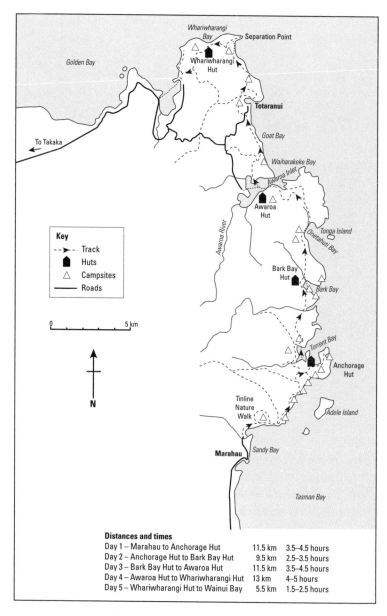

Golden Bay

Whariwharangi Bay

Separation Point

Whariwharangi Hut

To Takaka

Totaranui

Goat Bay

Waiharakeke Bay

Awaroa Inlet

Awaroa Hut

Awaroa River

Tonga Island

Onetahuti Bay

Bark Bay Hut

Bark Bay

Key

---▶-- Track

🏠 Huts

△ Campsites

—— Roads

0   5 km

N

Torrent Bay

Anchorage Hut

Adele Island

Tinline Nature Walk

Marahau

Sandy Bay

Tasman Bay

Distances and times

Day 1 – Marahau to Anchorage Hut	11.5 km	3.5–4.5 hours
Day 2 – Anchorage Hut to Bark Bay Hut	9.5 km	2.5–3.5 hours
Day 3 – Bark Bay Hut to Awaroa Hut	11.5 km	3.5–4.5 hours
Day 4 – Awaroa Hut to Whariwharangi Hut	13 km	4–5 hours
Day 5 – Whariwharangi Hut to Wainui Bay	5.5 km	1.5–2.5 hours

The Abel Tasman Coastal Path

operators offer a range of trips by foot, kayak and/or water taxi, for as little or as much time as the visitor wants.

However, the single, most important factor behind the popularity of Abel Tasman National Park is this: it hardly ever rains here. Well, this is New Zealand and leafy headlands don't exist without rain. But here, at least, rain is measured in millimetres – around 1,800 of them per annum. Moreover, these 1,800 millimetres usually arrive in winter and over a small number of days.

Day one: Learning to dance

Twenty minutes into the start of this Great Walk, I am wrapped in full waterproofs and getting wet. Rain doesn't come here often, but when it does it makes an effort.

I was warned. The weather forecasts issued by the DOC office in Nelson consistently promised 'unremitting, torrential rain on Friday'. However, the biggest challenge here is not surviving the weather. It is surviving the sea.

The Abel Tasman Coastal Path has four tidal crossings, two of which have no high-tide alternatives. Attempting the full track in winter has had me locked in a series of calculations with tide tables, maps, weather forecasts and daylight hours. I must time my tidal crossings such that I don't have to swim, and can reach the next hut before dark. Worse still, I want to walk from south to north, which is best done when low tides occur in the morning – and low tides are rapidly slipping towards the afternoons. I have little choice but to brave the weather.

Besides, Fiordland-style rain provides the perfect test for my newest item of kit. My second greatest ambition (second only to completing the Great Walks) is now to tramp through torrential rain with a dry bottom. I have purchased a waterproof jacket made by a Kiwi company for Kiwi trampers. It is my new line of defence against the waterfall that appears at the base of my backpack in heavy rain.

Of course, 'waterproof' is a relative term. 'Proof' seems so reassuring. It sounds definitive, but it isn't. Outdoor clothing declares itself to be waterproof, but dangling from even the most expensive waterproof jackets in the world is small print saying something like, 'waterproof to a minimum of: 2.8 bar; 40 p.s.i; 28 metres of water column'. This is more technical than meteorology.

The problem is that under enough pressure, water can get through virtually any fabric in which it is comfortable to walk. The more water a fabric can withstand under the greater pressure, the more 'waterproof' it is (and, generally, the more expensive it is too). Fiordland-quantity rainfall applied under the pressure of a loaded backpack will defeat most 'waterproof' fabrics. But all I want is a dry bottom. My new jacket reaches to thigh level, so the rain will have to percolate the 'waterproof' jacket *and* the 'waterproof' trousers before it can reach me now. Its odds are probably still quite good.

At the start of the track I delay stepping into the downpour. I huddle under the Marahau Information Shelter adjusting my now strangely shaped backpack. It holds barely two-thirds of my vastly expanded tramping equipment. The excess is tied, strapped or otherwise clinging on, underneath the flappy, king-size 'waterproof' pack cover. The effect is unbalanced, lumpy and wobbly.

Of course, tramping out of season and in torrential rain is perhaps the only way to get New Zealand's busiest National Park to myself. But even I am not that desperate to be alone. Not yet, anyway.

The Abel Tasman Coastal Path is well manicured. At its southern end, it begins with around 500 metres of good quality boardwalk across Sandy Bay, which is usually a vast sun-drenched tidal flat, but today is a blurry smudge of space. Once over the park's threshold on the far side of the bay, the track cut into the headland is wide and smooth, with none of those slashed edges of rock or tricky tree roots I've found before. Better still, its colour is true gold.

Now, almost every sunny, yellowish beach in the world will, at some point, be called 'golden'. This has as much to do with the impact of sunlight and the dreamy tendencies of the human spirit as with the colour of the sand. Today, pelting rain has smothered both the sunlight and any dreamy tendency in me. Yet, the colour of the sand on Abel Tasman beaches and of the track that joins them comes from the local granite and is unmistakably golden, even under dim light and pouring rain. The track is a yellow brick road for the super-rich.

Less than three kilometres in, the Tinline Nature Walk is a thirty-minute looping side trip and I refuse to be deterred by the deluge. Neatly printed labels crouch at the base of trees otherwise difficult to identify because leaves, blossoms, fruits and other distinguishing features hang far beyond sight. I adopt the now familiar head-back-drop-jaw position. Shafts of rain batter my eyes shut.

The Nature Walk exists because this is one of the few pockets of untouched native vegetation in this area. Modern populations are not alone in being attracted by the beaches, climate and low-lying headlands of Abel Tasman National Park. Maori tribes lived here and Europeans were swift to join in from the 1850s – logging, burning and engaging in all the usual landscape-shredding activities. The campaign that led to the designation of this National Park in 1942 was mounted to preserve the remaining modesty of this land and to give it a chance to grow some new clothes. In small pockets – like the Tinline Nature Walk – it is still possible to trip over old roots and sink into rich mud. Elsewhere the soil and vegetation is not so feisty.

Of all the Great Walks, the Abel Tasman Coastal Path is the one most closely associated with the arrival of Europeans off the shores of New Zealand. Or, to be more precise, the arrival of Europeans off the shores of two large islands that they presumed to be one and for which the 'natives' had no common name.

The first recorded European arrival was that of the eponymous Abel Tasman – a Dutchman who is erroneously reported in at least one well-known guidebook as having given New Zealand its name. He didn't. Apparently, New Zealand takes its name from the scribbling of a seventeenth-century cartographer in the Dutch East India Company.

Abel Tasman did navigate the west coast of what we now call 'New Zealand' (both main islands), but he mapped it as one long squiggly line and thought it was Staten Land, an island off South America, previously seen only from the other side. Many months later, somebody realised that Abel Tasman's squiggly line was not Staten Land after all. An anonymous cartographer renamed it Nieuw Zeeland after the Dutch maritime province, Zeeland. Thus, Abel Tasman not only failed to name New Zealand after his king, himself or his boss. He failed to name New Zealand at all.

Who knows how different things might have been? Perhaps some earlier explorer reached New Zealand, named it something wonderfully creative but sank on the way home. Or perhaps the first arrivals didn't believe in naming and claiming. Perhaps they simply settled down here to live, giving practical names to identify the features of the land in the local areas where they lived. Which, it seems, is precisely what the Polynesians did, hundreds of years before Abel Tasman showed up.

The names currently scattered on maps of the Abel Tasman National Park are a mixture of Maori and English. However, many of the apparently English names were bestowed by French explorer Dumont D'Urville, when he arrived some 127 years after Abel Tasman, in 1769.

The southern end of the Abel Tasman Coastal Path is more closely linked with D'Urville than with its namesake. Unlike Tasman, D'Urville seems to have spent a great deal of time on land here, admiring trees and chasing birds. He also did something of which I had thought early European explorers incapable: he named a place after his wife. Adele Island is a large chunk of the view from the beaches at this southern end of the track.

I drop down onto a beach, hoping to find shelter to eat lunch. I try standing in the lee of the large boulders and trees high up on the beach, but the vegetation above does a collective dog-like shake in the breeze and douses me in water. Having taken off my pack, its hitherto dry belly is now sponging up the rain water. Delving inside for honey-smeared bread I feel water trickling from my sleeves. I pull food out and feel the rain pour in.

Why was I so determined to start tramping today? It's not just the new kit I wanted to test. I haven't forgotten a chance conversation a few weeks ago with a DOC track-worker halfway up a mountain at Arthur's Pass, near the top of the Southern Alps. He was coming up as I was going down. Strapped to his back were a canvas tool bag and planks of wood, about two metres long and at least an inch thick. He looked to be in his forties, with a round face, thick moustache and a healthy glow in the midday sun. He had leaned against the weight of his load as I enthused about the Southern Alps.

'Yeah. Reckon I've got the best job in the world,' he grinned.

'Absolutely. Although there must be some bad points?' I asked, wondering if he'd even noticed that he was climbing 1,000 metres with planks of wood strapped to his back.

'Aw no, not really. Maybe sometimes when it's cold. When you're out for a few days with heavy frosts or snow it can get cold. It can get wet sometimes too.

'I remember once I was working on a track down in Fiordland. There were a few of us, but all in different places. Every evening we had a radio call for the weather forecast, although there was a lot of banter too. It was on the edge of the season and we had a lot of rain. One night I remember was particularly bad. It had been raining for about twenty-four hours. Real hard rain.

'The guy up at the furthest hut had been there for years. Hard as. Nothing bothered him. But this one night, when we asked him how the weather was with him, he said, "Even the ducks are running for cover".'

He laughed. '"Even the ducks are running for cover." I liked that.'

'Well,' I replied, 'as the saying goes, "There's no such thing as bad weather; only the wrong clothing".'

I laughed, confident that this guy would never have the wrong clothing. He laughed with me. Then he said:

'Don't hide from the storm. Learn to dance in the rain.'

Ten days on, his words are still fresh in my mind. Inspired, I hitch my wobbly, dripping pack onto my back, march out on to Stilwell Bay and attempt to dance on the sand in the rain. From under the bottom of a large, bulging tarpaulin, two short legs with big heavy boots jig, kick and boogie. At the sides two short arms waggle and wave. Using the weight of my pack I jump big footprints in the soggy sand and fling myself round in circles. The extra weight gives me wild momentum and grinds me into the sand, so that I have to stagger out of each twirl.

When I'm all laughed out, I turn back towards the track. Only then do I spot the campsite shelter along the beach.

This landscape copes less well with rain than Fiordland. Here there are few diverting waterfalls carrying water efficiently downhill. The track is one long golden puddle.

Two girls approach, each with soaking trainers, dripping daysacks and grim expressions.

'How far is it to Marahau?' they demand.

I've already forgotten. 'Maybe a couple of hours?'

They splash on before I can suggest a dance.

After four hours, new items of equipment are proving to be less than entirely waterproof and items that were previously waterproof are faltering. My right foot feels distinctly damp. When I finally descend down the soggy sand to Anchorage Hut, even my dancing spirit is glad to strip off the wet layers. Carefully and with dread, I disassemble the backpack. My sleeping bag – no, both my sleeping bags are dry! My spare clothes are dry! A momentous achievement.

Tonight's hut-mates are a young Frenchman and two Kiwis, Peter and Corran. We gather round the heater in the main room, reading the notice lodged on top of it: the heater is broken. It will not be fixed for another week. Faced with the prospect of an intimate group hug to keep ourselves warm until dinner time, we retire to our sleeping bags.

The hut is cold, dark and damp as we prepare our evening meals. Peter is a lawyer (quite a senior one) and Corran a journalist and former lawyer. Even though they're both experienced trampers, they giggle like excited children staying out in a tent in their garden for the first time. Kiwis really do love their tramping. Only one topic of conversation brings sobriety and reveals the age gap between them.

'How's the Queen?' Peter asks, quite seriously. 'We were all very sad when the Queen Mother died. A wonderful woman. A real loss.'

'No we weren't,' Corran interrupts. 'We don't need a royal family – and especially not one that lives on the other side of the world. New Zealand should be a republic.'

Corran's views on independence are clear and passionate. Peter's are equally and charmingly strong, but in the other direction. Peter initiates discussions about everything English – places he's visited, people he admires, English country gardens, cups of tea, the romance of the royal family and even some of the specific romances of the current royal family, although he is understandably disappointed with the course of many of these. He wants news from England and is eager to talk of his time spent there and plans for future trips.

Corran cannot allow a single positive comment about Britain to go uncorrected. When Peter praises Britain's democratic tradition, Corran expounds examples of British governmental incompetence. When Peter admires the extent of British influence on world history, Corran is ready with facts about concentration camps and other seedy contributions from the British Empire. When Peter talks of the pride of New Zealanders fighting for 'the mother country' during two World Wars, Corran stops just short of rubbishing this sentiment. And when Peter waxes lyrical about the English countryside, Corran eloquently conveys his view of New Zealand's vast superiority in this regard. Yet, they get on famously with each other.

As Peter and Corran cook they discover that the Frenchman has no food. In broken English he relates that he wanted to travel light and has just four energy bars to last him until he is picked up by water taxi tomorrow. All three of them are staying out on the track for only one night, but Peter and Corran are carrying almost as much food as me. They improvise a third plate and feed the Frenchman.

I reflect once more on the sociability of trampers in general and Kiwi trampers in particular. Later that night, huddled for warmth in my sleeping bag and with rain still drumming hard on the roof, I begin to write down my observations on this most generous of species.

> One of the most distinguishing features of the Kiwi Tramper is that this unique creature can – and frequently does – transport up to a quarter of its own body-weight in food across vast distances. Frequently observed amongst its victuals are pasta, noodles, potatoes, meats, porridge, scroggin and Milo. The mix of nuts, seeds and dried fruit known as scroggin is usually prepared to personal recipes, although Kiwi Trampers are sometimes sighted buying pre-packaged scroggin from shops. Milo, meanwhile, is almost always bought and transported in powder form. Every night, in huts across the land, this chocolaty powder is mixed with hot water. In overcrowded huts, where distinguishing between different species of Tramper can be difficult, the Kiwi Trampers are the ones drinking Milo.
>
> Kiwi Trampers are rarely sighted alone, but both pairs and larger groups are common. Their highly social behaviour is further shown in their use of communal nesting sites. Each night Kiwi Trampers converge on the same sites to eat and sleep in close contact. They rarely stay more than one night in the same place, but these communal sites mean that minimum effort is expended in re-nesting every night.
>
> Inside these huts Kiwi Trampers can also usually be identified by their 'polypros'. Polypropylene is a manufactured material that pretends to be wool, but is thinner and repels

water. Standard hut-wear for the Kiwi Tramper comprises polypro long-sleeved top and polypro long-johns, mixed and not necessarily matched from the standard colours available in New Zealand's outdoor shops. These are relatively conservative blues, greens and clarets, but also the local favourites – thin bright stripes of yellow-red-purple-green or blue-green-purple-red or, for the really wacky, a combination of both.

Kiwi Trampers' favoured habitat is wilderness. They are accustomed to travelling long distances across unpopulated, untamed terrain. Yet, they almost always use the same tracks across these landscapes. Where one pair or group of Kiwi Trampers leads, others will follow. Once a route has been established, Kiwi Trampers rarely, if ever, deviate from their track.

Many Kiwis Trampers wear polypros for tramping as well as nesting. Polypro clothes are designed to be a snug fit. A softer, warmer lycra, leaving no room for vanity. Not only are underwear lines visible, but sometimes so is the underwear, should there be any. To allow for this, cotton shorts are worn over the top by Kiwi Trampers striding up and down mountains.

These are modest supermen and superwomen out to rid the world of evil. Or, at least, a good proportion of its Milo supplies.

Day two: Something strange approaches

In the morning we run from the hut to the beach, where we leave our boots to steam in the returned sun and take photos of each other grinning in our polypros.

It is immensely pleasing to wander around in the same clothes in which I've just been sleeping. Tramping is highly liberating in this regard. Day after day with no advertising or marketing messages within sight or hearing. A dress code with only one requirement: practicality. Corran augments his outfit with plastic bags on his feet, tied at the ankles (a technique for preventing blisters when wearing wet socks and boots – the plastic apparently preventing wet fibres from rubbing against the skin).

The roar of engines breaks the peace. The noise is coming from the other side of Pitt Head, the promontory that shelters The Anchorage from the sea.

'The British are coming!' giggles Peter.

If they are, they sound like tourists on a flotilla of jet skis. We can't see the boats, but the intrusion should not be surprising. Of all the Great Walks, the Abel Tasman Coastal Path is the least isolated. Even in winter it has a holiday-camp atmosphere. Tourists come from all over rest of the world and from all over New Zealand too.

There are also many blocks of private land here, privileged to be surrounded by National Park and sea. A speed boat is anchored nearby, probably sharing an owner with the house that overlooks The Anchorage from the far end of the beach. In the summer the owners must have hundreds of neighbours: at the border of their private block lie twenty-six-bunk Anchorage Hut, a sizeable campsite and hoards of wooden supports for storing kayaks.

I have a military schedule in this holiday camp. The first of the tidal crossings is Torrent Bay, which is just beyond a squiggly promontory from the Anchorage. It may safely be crossed within two to three hours of low tide, which today is happily at 10.47 am. The tide is my excuse for today's late start.

I have taken barely ten steps off the headland before my feet sink in the gloopy, greying sand-mud.

A voice hollers, 'Where have you come from?'

The accent is American. Squinting ahead I see three men approaching with baseball caps, baggy shorts and no packs.

'Just Anchorage Hut,' I reply, feeling slothful.

'Are there any more tidal parts back there?' they shout.

'No. No – nothing tidal to cross.'

'Well, I hope you've got some shorts. Good luck!'

This last is hollered in an exceedingly patronising tone, as they saunter past, still some ten metres away from me. Hmm. Patronising and rude. They didn't even say hello. This is not any species of Tramper that I recognise.

At Torrent Bay, the strict route of the Coastal Path crosses almost a kilometre of sand, which is not even the widest point of the bay. Trampers follow the lollipop – a big red circle on a stick where the track joins the shore on the other side.

The terrain is not really sand at all, but billions and billions of small shells lying waiting to be crushed. The closer I get to the midpoint of the Bay, the greater the density and depth of the thick, crunchy carpet. The shells are all roughly the same size and shape – the shape now poached by the oil conglomerate. Clearly, the popularity of Abel Tasman National Park is not confined to those of us with spines.

I reach the middle of the Bay at the exact point of low tide but the water still covers my knees. At least the freshwater channel isn't too swollen with sea water. And at least I now know what brownish water means.

Past the lollipop comes an even stranger sight for a Great Walk: a village of private baches (small holiday homes), all deserted. The broad, sandy track doubles as the high street in this nameless village. Most of the houses are simple, single-storey wooden constructions, varying in shape, size and colour. The only signposts are no-nonsense, emphatic, humourless instructions for trampers to stick precisely to the path.

I'm good with rules, so I wander only to the jetty, where two wooden benches look over Torrent Bay and back towards the Anchorage. A small island of rock crowned with trees sits in the path of the waves, magnificently picturesque in the sunshine. Click, click, click. I take the latest additions to the millions of images of this scene that must surely already exist.

There are side trips from Torrent Bay to intriguingly named places like Cleopatra's Pool and Falls River. However, I no longer feel the need to take every side trip. I lie flat-out on a bench and let the sun dry my feet and bottom. The new jacket is good, but, alas, not that good.

The buzz of tiny craft wakes me from my steaming daze. A line of small boats appears around Pitt Head and buzzes back towards the Anchorage. These are no jet skis. They are nine black, motorised dinghies. In each sit three figures. Only their heads and torsos are visible and they are completely black. I can't even see the whites of their eyes. It's like a scene from a James Bond movie. Perhaps Ursula Andress will shortly rise up out of the sea wearing her white bikini and sexy smile. She'll be disappointed to see me.

Ruling out aliens, sunstroke and dreaming, this is either part of filming for the latest movie to use New Zealand as a studio, or the country is being invaded. By twenty-seven blackened men. Of course, New Zealand *is* being invaded, but they call it immigration rather than invasion and the people who move here from all over the world don't arrive blacked out in small dinghies. At least, I presume they don't. Perhaps this particular group have heard about the All Blacks and become confused?

No, it must be filming. I just can't see the camera unit. Or hear the director. Suddenly it hits me. A notice in the DOC office in Nelson was the clue. In amongst those chronicling the history of hut heater breakdowns and assuring trampers that all were now functioning, there had been another notice. It read:

Important notice to visitors

Between 28 May and 1 June the New Zealand Army will be on a ground patrol exercise in Abel Tasman National Park. Up to 60 troops will be exercising in the area between Anchorage, Harwoods Hole and Wainui Bay. Some troops will be dropped off along the coast by navy inflatable boats while others will be moving cross country from Harwoods Hole. Troops will be fully equipped including weapons.

This is real life James Bond.

Kiwis are extremely proud of their military history, albeit understandably prouder of some parts than others. Almost every township, town and city in New Zealand has a war memorial in prominent position. New Zealand's history of conflict and war is, unsurprisingly, as long as its history of human habitation. Maori legends recognise this link in the form of Tumatauenga, who is both god of people and god of war.

Few records remain of the inter-tribal battles that took place when only Maori tribes lived on these islands. However, the scale of conflict really got a boost when European settlers provided muskets to make conflict more deadly, more people to make it more likely, different customs and values to fuel its causes and pens and paper to write about it.

First came the musket wars in which Maori fought Maori over land, honour or to settle other grievances. These peaked in the 1820s and 1830s. Then came the New Zealand Wars in the 1840s and again in the 1860s, in which Maori and Pakeha broadly fought each other, but sometimes also among themselves, over issues such as those that the Waitangi Tribunal is even now still trying to resolve. Next, New Zealanders fought in a succession of wars in other countries, on behalf of first Britain and later America: the South African War, the First World War, the Second World War and conflicts in Malaysia, Korea and Vietnam.

New Zealanders' contributions in the First World War became a defining moment in the emergence of New Zealand's national identity. At Gallipoli, a blend of strategic blunders, tactical errors and unfortunate accidents left troops from the Australia and New Zealand Army Corp (Anzac) having to dig in on cliffs, with superior numbers of Turkish troops attacking them from above and nothing but the sea behind. They held their position in conditions that few of us will ever appreciate. Flies swarmed around casualties who could not be moved. Food and water were limited. Dysentery, fevers, frostbite, diarrhoea and bullets were relentless. When finally the survivors were evacuated, Anzac troops had held their position in the deadlock for just under eight months. Nearly ninety percent of the New Zealand soldiers were either wounded or killed.

Kiwis commemorate their casualties of war each year on the anniversary of the day when Anzac troops were dropped by boat at Gallipoli – 25 April. Having experienced numerous Remembrance Sundays in England, Anzac Day in New Zealand came as a surprise to me. In Britain – a nation that has lost many more people in many, many more wars – Remembrance Sunday falls on the Sunday nearest 11 November and involves a respectful two minutes' silence observed at 11.00 am. There are local and national services of remembrance, but most people don't attend one of these and many don't observe the silence either. Moreover, none of this involves shops closing. The silence is announced over supermarket tannoys for shoppers to pause momentarily from their purchases (when it is announced at all).

In New Zealand, Anzac Day is always 25 April, whenever it falls, and is a national holiday. My first Anzac Day happened to fall on a Sunday – moreover, the Sunday immediately following Easter Sunday. On both of these Sundays, I was in Te Anau, trying to buy food from the local supermarket for the Kepler and Routeburn Tracks, respectively. On Easter Sunday, I expected all the shops to be closed, but every one was open. Pleased, I then expected the shops to be open on Anzac Day. They were all closed.

A nation was too busy remembering its dead to shop. And more than 17,000 kilometres away, hundreds, perhaps thousands, of Kiwis were standing at Gallipoli in Turkey to honour their dead. Now, that is respectful.

I watch the activities of the blackened troops with interest and from a frustrating kilometre away. Having seen how regular New Zealanders operate in the bush, I imagine these guys take toughness to extremes.

One boat zooms towards the rocky shoreline – did a dark figure just jump out? – and then zooms to the other side of the bay. One by one, the other boats follow. Next they test who can buzz between two rocks the fastest. More bouncy zooming. Then they speed off around Pitt Head and out of view. Nine boats, three men in each, all in a line. I wonder what threat to New Zealand is being rehearsed. Are the French coming back for more nuclear testing? Or is this an anti-tourist operation, preparing to cut off the army of summer kayakers from the fur seals?

Another hour passes before my socks and pants are dry and I concede that the entertainment is over. Beyond the unnamed village, the track winds over headlands away from the shore. Its route across gullies and rises is squiggly to say the least.

Postcards of the Abel Tasman National Park show vistas of low-lying green, crinkled headlands, smooth, sheltered beaches and calm, blue sea. From the Coastal Path, however, these views lie somewhere beyond the tunnel of green above and gold below. Marked on the park map are two short side-trips to allegedly panoramic viewpoints, but these are elusive. I turn onto one possible side path but abandon my pack after ten minutes because the tunnel between branches and prickles is too small for both of us. I end up, heavily scratched, standing on a large, slippy boulder with prickly bushes and trees blocking views of the coast on all three sides. The only view is over the forested hills of the hinterland.

I hear a chuckle nearby. It's a rude, deep laugh and I assume it's directed at me. Further along the main track I hear the same voice. The Abel Tasman Coastal Path seems bereft of the small, friendly birds I've found elsewhere and, until now, the only birdsong I've heard is from further back in the forest. Looking up, I see a bird shaped like a slimline raven or crow. This is a tui.

Its colours are dark except for the blobs of rounded white feathers that protrude from its neck, as if it's playing that game of trying to pass a table tennis ball from one person to the next without use of hands or arms. It isn't the smallest of New Zealand's bush talkers, but is often seen attacking larger birds, such as the morepork, harrier and even the New Zealand falcon. However, the most interesting thing about the tui is its voice. It sings in the descant range, shrill and long and apparently sometimes hitting notes undetectable by the human ear (although I've no idea, therefore, how we know this). Then suddenly it makes deep croaking, chuckling, barking and wheezing noises like a short-band radio being flicked between channels. Its odd croaks and sudden switches across octaves mean the tui sounds more like a pubescent boy than a pirate in the forest.

At Bark Bay Hut it begins to rain again and a notice on the gas heater relates that it is not working. For the first time whilst tramping, I set about boiling my drinking water.

DOC diligently warns trampers to guard against giardia on every track and in every National Park, but this is the first time I've felt the need to act. At least 30,000 people stay overnight on the Abel Tasman Coastal Path each year and many of these camp, either in the official sites or surreptitiously on the beaches. Toilet facilities are provided at the official sites, but I have a strong suspicion that my fellow human beings may not be entirely fastidious in their use. I also suspect that they aren't all familiar with the rules for personal waste disposal.

The main rule is simple: dig. The problem is that there are lots of clauses and subclauses to this rule. The depth to which one must dig one's hole varies according to the composition of the soil, rock or other ground matter beneath one's firmly planted feet. Six to eight inches is a general guide, but based on many assumptions that may not hold true in any particular terrain. Fairly complex scientific calculations are required to deduce the real answer. Worse still, being near a water source makes the calculation so much more complicated that even the wildly scientific counsel avoidance. Yet, on the crinkly Abel Tasman coastline, it's difficult not to be near a water source. Campers even make a special effort to stake their pitch right next to a source of fresh water. After all, who wants to go on a long walk to fetch water for drinking and cooking? When the local kayaking outfits hire out their kayaks to the holidaymakers, I don't imagine the standard equipment includes a trowel for digging.

Giardia is like a lottery: the more people there are playing, the more people there are losing. And it's not just humans who can carry giardia; animals can too, with the result that an indiscrete toilet trip may pass the baton to a passing possum, who may hop upstream and do his bit for the cycle.

No one seems to know exactly how many cysts must be consumed before interior redecoration becomes unavoidable. It may take lots and lots. Or it may take only one – and giardia cysts are so tiny that the odds of imbibing one could be even higher than winning the lottery. Apparently, around a million of these DIYers could fit under a fingernail.

The general rule is that the greater the number of campers, the greater the risk of giardia. Even with more than 30,000 people tramping or camping here each year, the risk may be small, but it's not as small as it would be if fewer of us came. My billy whistles away, making it even smaller.

Unlike a lottery, giardia is not entirely a game of chance. The recommended precautions against giardia are filtering (bulky equipment), chemical treatment (ick – drinking chemicals) or boiling. Boiling must be for at least three minutes, which causes anguish over the state of my gas supplies. I carry only one canister. Boiling water and my new-found habit of cooking porridge for breakfast mean I could run out of gas before the end of this walk. Cold porridge is hardly a matter of life or death. Still, sighing deeply, I wonder if I will ever be a fully prepared tramper.

I chat to Carly, an American girl brewing up next to me. She is also tramping alone and has done several other tracks.

'Where are you going tomorrow?' she asks.

'To Arawo – Awawo – A-w-a-roa Hut,' I reply. 'For some reason I can't seem to pronounce it. Where are you heading?'

'I'm going to the end of the track. I'll leave real early because I have to cross Awaroa Inlet before eleven o'clock to catch my water taxi from Totaranui.'

'Totaranui? But you're walking the Coastal Path?'

'Yes. Why?'

'Well, Totaranui isn't the end of the track. It carries on up and over the headland with Separation Point and round into Wainui Inlet.'

She looks at my map, horribly disappointed.

'I thought it ended at Totaranui,' she says glumly. 'Maybe I could come with you instead.'

I panic slightly until she adds: 'But no, I can't. I've booked the taxi and there's no way of cancelling it now.'

Many people think that the Coastal Path ends at Totaranui. I don't know why: the parkmap and track guides all clearly show that it continues north of Totaranui. However, Totaranui is the furthest stop for the regular water taxis and for the many trips and tours offered by local entrepreneurs. As a result, the northernmost section is quiet by local standards.

Carly enthuses about tramping. She whispers how much she enjoys the simple pleasures like going to the toilet al fresco. Oh dear. The poor girl now hears my monologue on sanitation, giardia and digging. Being a responsible tramper is harder than it looks.

'Sorry,' I conclude, sympathising with her despair in my British way. (Britons seem to be the only English-speaking people in the world who use sorry to mean that they are sorry that something has happened, without meaning that they consider themselves to blame. Confusingly, we also use it to apologise for personal guilt, like the rest of the English-speaking world.)

Over candlelight and cards Carly discovers that one of the German contingent will shortly visit her home town, San Francisco.

'I'll give you my address,' she offers.

'Thank you. That is very kind,' the German girl replies.

'You should come and stay with us when you're over. I'm sure my boyfriend won't mind.'

What Carly means is that she is free to offer accommodation even though she shares her flat with a boyfriend who is not present to be consulted. However, the German girl interprets Carly's offer somewhat differently.

'No, no, no,' she replies urgently. 'I shall stay somewhere else. This will not be a problem.'

Carly realises the mistaken interpretation, but now can't bring herself to explain the misunderstanding because she is too embarrassed. Somebody changes the subject. No one swaps addresses.

Day three: An unusual set of circumstances

As I lift my food bag down from its lofty hook away from scurrying creatures, I notice a pile of strange fluff on the bench underneath. My food was hung up, wrapped in layers of bags and packed inside my sleeping bag stuff-sack, with the cord drawn tight. Yet something has climbed up (or possibly down) the wall, sat on the top of my stuff-sack and patiently nibbled through layer upon layer of plastic before tucking into the sunflower seeds, pumpkin seeds and ginger biscuits that were on top. Mice.

'Oh yes,' says one of the boys from the German group, 'I thought I heard something in the night.'

Grrr. None of their food has been attacked. However, one of them had propped their pack on the bench to help the mice gain access to my food bag.

I am still sorting edible from suspicious food when everyone else begins to haul their large packs onto their backs, ready to rejoin the track. The table is littered with hard balls of candle wax that they absent-mindedly picked to pieces last night. The floor is covered in dried mud from the boots they failed to take off. Energy bar packets litter the bunkroom floor. The stainless steel kitchen surfaces have bits of dinner dried to them. The mattresses are all lying flat.

'Right!' I say, cheerfully, grabbing a broom. 'I'll do the sweeping. Who's going to wipe the tables? And the kitchen area? Then we just need to stand the mattresses up. Oh, and are these your empty packets?'

I smile broadly and leave them no room for manoeuvre. Perhaps they think that their hut fee not only pays for the maintenance of the track, the hut and its water supplies, but also covers the cost of someone to come all the way out here every day and clean up after them. Assuming, that is, that they've paid the hut fees. I daren't ask. I'm angry enough as it is. These people have clearly never observed hut etiquette before. They're about to start.

Today's tidal crossing is right outside the hut door. The track across the centre of diminutive Bark Bay is reportedly passable within two to three hours of low tide. About two hours further north, the tidal flat at the northern end of Onetahuti beach must be crossed within three hours of low tide. At Onetahuti beach no high-tide route is available, so I have a deadline for my third day of slothful tramping.

Sheltering most of Bark Bay from the sea is a long, sandy spit and deserted campsite. Beyond, at the edge of the waves sit two large shags, like a pair of bookends. I watch them for more than half an hour, creeping ever closer. They sit still, a few metres apart. Occasionally one moves its head. Then the other does. Less often they strut a few steps before settling once more into stillness. I am not used to such stillness in creatures awake. Surely there is always something to be done – some nest to build, young to feed, or perhaps even some young to create? These birds seem to have nothing to do. Their stillness permits mine. The three of us shuffle in slow motion around our small patch of beach. The waves lap lazily away from us.

Near low tide I find I cannot cross Bark Bay after all. At least, not without getting my bottom wet again. I don't know how the guides can all be wrong, but even close to low tide the channel in the centre of the Bay remains deep and strong. Fortunately, there is a high-tide route and Bark Bay is so small that this is little longer than the low tide route. I am soon up on the headland, where the track weaves like a drunkard finally sobering up after yesterday's much unsteadier progress.

With time to kill I pull out the book I have brought deliberately for this purpose. It is high time I got to know New Zealand's trees a little better.

Manuka and kanuka are easy. Star-shaped clusters of thin green leaves riddle the branches and the thin trunks have flaky, black and silver bark. Less easy is identifying manuka from kanuka and vice versa. The easiest way to do so, I read, is by the flowers and seed capsules, neither of which are available in winter. The other trick is that manuka leaves are soft and kanuka leaves are spiky to touch. However, all the leaves are so tiny that nothing pricks me, despite my best efforts.

Sadly, my guide doesn't incorporate some of the best information about New Zealand's vegetation. Taupata (a hardy coastal shrub) was used by Maori to treat cuts and sores. A lotion made from rata bark contains astringent tannin, which can treat wounds, aches and pains. Nectar from rata flowers is a remedy for sore throats. Cabbage trees can be used to treat colic, dysentery and diarrhoea. Flax makes clothing. Ferns make houses and shelters. Totara, if only I could spot it, makes a mean war canoe (a totara being a giant tree with great practical and spiritual significance for all Maori tribes).

Young lancewoods are easy to identify with their spindly stalks and extremely long leaves, drooping at forty-five degree angles down to the ground. Then there are the beeches – hard, red, silver, black and mountain. All have tiny green leaves, indistinguishable to my untrained eye, even when I read that the edges may or may not curl under very slightly and they may have different teeth. Teeth? I'm finding this hard enough as it is.

I try a different approach. I choose a specimen from the jostling bush around the track and stand in front of it in deep contemplation. Then I raise my book and follow the step-by-step guide to tree identification. First, the characteristics of its leaves – narrow, long, small, broad, hand-shaped etc. But which do I pick if the leaves are both narrow *and* under five centimetres? I choose narrow. Next decision: are they white-ish underneath or not white-ish underneath? Not. More or less than four centimetres long? Less. Aha! That means it must be a kauri tree. But no. Kauri trees are only found in the northern half of the North Island.

I met some kauri trees a few days after I first arrived in New Zealand. The two largest remaining kauri trees to have escaped the widespread logging activities of European settlers are now one of Northland's most famous tourist attractions. Tane Mahuta, or God of the Forest, has a trunk girth of 13.8 metres and stands 51.5 metres high. That's tall enough to tickle Nelson's nose on his Column. Nearby, the Father of the Forest, or Te Matua Ngahere, is a mere 29.9 metres tall, but with a trunk girth of 16.41 metres, making it not much thinner than the Leaning Tower of Pisa and without the slump. If there were staircases up these trees, they would run to about seventeen flights, and running would be the last thing on your mind by the time you reached the top.

Reading the DOC notices around these trees I made the surprising discovery that hugging trees might not be an environmentally friendly thing to do. Although these trees are immense and more than 1,500 years old, their roots are shallow. The hug itself may not hurt them (if, indeed, you can use the word 'hug' for the act of flattening yourself against a barely tapering surface), but footsteps will. Imagine balancing on one leg for half an hour and then having someone tread on the arch of your balancing foot. It would hurt. The sinews and muscles on the top of your foot would scream with pain. Well, apparently, trees with shallow roots have a similar reaction to well-intentioned huggers.

After more than an hour of further tramping and unsuccessful tree identification, I reach the disused Tonga Quarry, still practising the name of New Zealand honeysuckle – rewarewa. This is now the second Maori word that I shall never successfully articulate.

If it weren't for the base of a winch and some suspiciously uniform blocks of stone near the track here, the quarry would now be obscured under the returning forest. Stone from this quarry features in tourists' photographs of nearby cities. Probably its most regular photo shoot is in Nelson, around fifty kilometres from here by sea, on the opposite side of Tasman Bay. There, Tonga granite is better known as the Cawthron Steps, which are the perfect foreground frame for the art deco Cathedral with its strangely hollow spire.

From the winch base, Tonga Island is visible across Tonga Roadstead, which is the strip of sea between the shore and the island. In a roadstead, the sea is theoretically calm enough for a ship to rest safely at anchor. Today the sea waters in Tasman Bay look calm enough for a ship to rest anywhere, but there are no vessels to be seen.

These waters are part of Tonga Island Marine Reserve, which runs from Bark Bay in the south to the unpronounceable Awaroa Bay in the north. The Reserve stretches out in places more than three kilometres from the shoreline. It is one of twenty-eight marine reserves (and counting) in New Zealand waters. New Zealand has been quick to realise the importance of conservation compared with most other countries. However, it has been slower in realising that conservation could extend beyond its shoreline. It was 1993 before the waters around Tonga Island were designated a marine reserve – the same year that Milford Sound became a marine reserve and some forty years after the completion of the Milford Road and Homer Tunnel opened up Milford Sound to mass tourism.

Today, around thirty per cent of New Zealand's landscape, but little more than three per cent of its marine environment, is protected in parks and reserves. Still, this is good compared with other countries. Around nine per cent of the UK's land area and less than two per cent of its marine environment is in protected areas. Moreover, the number of marine reserves in New Zealand is growing faster than the country's film credits.

I drop down to Onetahuti beach, the long strip of sand opposite Tonga Island. Confident that no one else is around, I strip naked, pull on my swimming costume and run into the sea before the sun can burn my china-white thighs. Despite dazzling sunshine, the water is a whack of cold. I swim furiously up and down the beach with an enormous grin on my face, wondering how many people ever have one of the largest beaches in Abel Tasman National Park entirely to themselves. It would be rude not to make the most of it, even if this means ignoring instant numbness in my fingers and toes.

I daren't swim out towards Tonga Island because that way lie fur seals. I'm a little afraid of New Zealand fur seals, or, rather, the impact we might have on each other. A week ago a theoretically harmless afternoon's walk on a public footpath brought me into direct confrontation with several hundred unimpressed fur seals.

I was on the coastal path at Kaikoura, that great haven of marine life on the north-east coast of the South Island that is also not a marine reserve. I had set out correctly with the low tide, only to find myself with sheer cliffs to my right, an advancing sea to my left and a large number of fur seals lying all over the track in front of me. If a seal feels threatened on land it warns its ostensible attacker by barking and then, if necessary, by biting.

The track behind me was being covered by the tide and signs warned not to go within five metres of a seal, for fear of alarming it. I calculated a route forward across the promontory that would work well, so long as none of the seals moved and the one asleep at the far end didn't wake up. There followed a nerve-wracking twenty minutes as I tried to cover the one hundred metres to the next promontory. The largest seal sat up and barked at me. I tried singing, because I once read in a book written by a woman who lived with a seal (I'm not kidding) that music always had a soothing effect on it. My singing induced more frantic barking, so I gave a calm-voiced commentary to let each seal know where I was and that I posed no threat. This worked well until I rounded the headland to discover yet more seals camped around the track. Now there were dozy seals in front and alert seals behind.

This hour was one of the most frightening of my life. When a seal barked it was all I could do to move gently around it and maintain my calm-voiced commentary. When I returned to the local DOC office some three hours later to recommend that they advise walkers against using the track at all, I was still giving a calm-voiced, hysteria-belying running commentary on my movements.

I was furious that it was somehow deemed appropriate to pass a walking track through a colony of fur seals. Of course, it could have been a freak occurrence. The waters had been stormy for several days and few others had been out walking that day. Even so, I was far more angry than relieved.

Seals quickly feel threatened when approached on land because they feel cumbersome and slow out of water. Even on land they can probably move more quickly than me, but I suppose they don't know this. In any case, much of the history of interaction between humans and fur seals in New Zealand has involved humans wielding clubs and seals yielding skins. They have good reason not to trust us.

The first European settlements in New Zealand were sealing stations. Men (and occasionally women) were dropped off by boats that promised to return within a few months to collect them, along with the thousands of sealskins they should by then have assembled. The number of seals killed by these sealing parties around the turn of the nineteenth century reaches into six figures. Yet, the sealers arguably had as bad a time as the seals. Not only did they have to fend for themselves wherever they were dropped, but sometimes the ship that was due to collect them would sink on its way back, or forget to come back at all.

These days the fur seals that live off the coast of the Abel Tasman National Park are used to the presence of human beings for different reasons. Boats and kayakers deliberately head for Tonga Island to splash amongst the seals. Fur seal pups have even been known to play with paddlers or sit on the prows of kayaks looking cute. Day after day nobody bops them on the head. The seals are quick and graceful in the water and largely tolerate the intrusion. Even so, I don't intend to approach them in their natural habitat. They may feel less threatened in the sea, but I don't.

After half an hour it occurs to me that I should perhaps get out, because the water really is rather chilly and I must by now be cleansed of tramping odour. As cold-thickened fingers struggle to pull off my swimming costume, I notice that it is full of greenery. (I will be finding seaweed and marine life on my person for the next two days.) I towel myself dry and pull on my clothes, but I can't feel them. My body is numb with cold. I've gone from invigorated to numb without noticing.

Fortunately, I have another two hours' walking to warm me up. The northern end of Onetahuti is an intensely picturesque meeting of forest, stream, sand and sea, offset by a skeletal carcass of a dead goat lying in the middle of the beach. The sun is blinding as I walk over the low-lying Tonga Saddle and down towards Awaroa Bay. The track here is even wider than before and the trees on either side even shorter, offering little shade.

Awaroa Bay is another of those spots that others might call oases of civilisation in Abel Tasman National Park. A side track to the right leads to a lodge, a café and a small airstrip. Back at sea level again is a row of private baches with gardens that end just above the high tide mark. Even today smoke curls from a chimney and a man stands in his garden watching the sunset and returning my wave.

Each step of the final kilometre sinks into soft sand. Awaroa Hut lies about a third of the way back on the south side of this inlet. From its narrow neck, Awaroa Inlet creeps inland for around three kilometres, nosing so far into the surrounding hills that it is more than a kilometre wide in several places. The current at its much narrower neck is strong and deep. The safe crossing for tomorrow is further back.

At Awaroa Hut the light is fading fast and I should start the evening duties as soon as possible. I don't. I drop my pack on the veranda and go to stand on the sand. A full moon is rising from behind the hut, the sun is setting behind the headland on the opposite side of the inlet and the clear sky is a battle of colours.

Awaroa Inlet is so vast, wide and smooth that the leading edge of the incoming tide is as thin as a sheet being pulled along by a line of thousands of tiny crabs. As the water silently covers the sand, bubbles rise the short distance to the surface and pop like small rounds of applause. These are probably just pockets of air being released, but it's as if a colony of creatures lives just below the surface of the sand, each one exhaling as it feels the long, slow inhalation of the incoming tide. Phew. The water is returning.

A man stands about one hundred metres away from me, also absorbed in the stillness. Suddenly I cannot bear the prospect of hut protocol. On such an evening I don't want to talk about where we're both from and how gorgeous New Zealand is. I can't bear it. I won't. So I plan a daring speech for when I enter the hut. 'Hi there. I'm really pleased to meet you but I have to ask you a favour. Let's not introduce ourselves. Let's not tell each other our names, or where we come from, or how much tramping we've done. If you want to ask me a question, ask me what my biggest fear is, or whether I believe in God, or how many times I've been in love. Let's talk about big things – about things we rarely tell even our friends. What do you think?'

I enter the hut. There is no one inside. I check the bunkrooms and find no backpacks. I am alone.

I make dinner and delight myself by laying a good fire in the hut stove. Who needs broken gas heaters instead of matches, kindling and a few hefty logs?

On two sides of the hut lies the forest. On the other two sides long windows look out over the estuary, whose waters have now crept up to the edge of the grass outside the front of the hut. The cloudless sky has a white pallor against the black landscape. The full moon lights the outlines of the water, forest and hills. I can see almost as well as in daylight.

With few chores remaining, I sit in front of the stove and reprimand my wandering thoughts. Now is *not* the time to ask myself whether or not I believe in God. Or gods. Thinking about the existence of gods is a slippery slope that leads to thinking about devils and demons and ghosts and all kinds of spooky things that could well go bump in this particular night. No. If I'm going to assess my spiritual beliefs, I must do it in daylight, when I can think rationally. Imagination is a dangerous ingredient in this situation. I forbid my imagination from taking control. I am going to wash up. I am going to tend the fire. I am going to go to bed early. And I am *not* going to spook myself.

To fetch water, wash or go to the toilet I must abandon my fire and the safe walls of the hut to walk the short distance to the toilet block on the edge of the forest. I saunter to and fro, swinging my billy and my fake bravado.

New Zealand forest is not a quiet place at night. The kiwi really does scream keee-weee in a high-pitched shriek (even though it wasn't named for this noise, but from the Polynesian name for another bird, the kivi). I've heard several different noises that I've been told by hut wardens and local trampers are uttered by kiwis. The most chilling one sounds like a small girl screaming, but I'm told that it's a kiwi call and I'm clinging to that knowledge tonight. In fact, with screaming kiwis, munching possums and hooting moreporks, New Zealand bush is noisier at night than it is during the day.

Dusk is possibly noisier still. I imagine the shift-change. 'OK boys. Last few cries before the shift is over. Let's make them good ones.'

'Right, make way – we're up now.'

'It's all yours. Oh, and there's a woman in that hut entirely on her own. You should have some fun tonight.'

'All right, lads, you heard the man. Give it all you've got.'

Fortunately, I am inside the hut when I see a large, dark shape run across the grass next to the hut and spring up onto the incongruous picnic bench. It looks and moves like a giant and obese squirrel. It is a possum, grown large and fat.

If I were a true Kiwi tramper I would now seize the broom or a large log, run outside and club it to death. I am as yet a wimp, scared of being scratched, bitten or visited by a delegation of its seventy million friends. Still, at least I recognise the enemy. If this were my first night in a DOC hut, I'd be in trouble.

Yet, even armed with a real fire, the walls of the hut and a fair knowledge of the creatures around me, I feel uncertain. It's not fear, but an acute awareness of everything that's going on around me, both inside and outside the hut. If just one other person were here, I wouldn't feel like this. I would be distracted by them and by the interactions between us, however trivial. Who knew that other human beings were so distracting? On my own, the boundaries of my thoughts extend far beyond the hut.

'Don't you get bored?' people have asked when they find out that I tramp alone. Bored? No. Bored is certainly not the word.

When it's time to sleep, I can't decide whether to wear my ear plugs. Usually a defence against snoring, maybe I now need them to block out sounds that might keep me awake through misplaced fear. On the other hand, shouldn't I have all my senses available in the event of something approaching? After lying for an hour inside an overactive imagination I exasperatedly stuff in the ear plugs.

Thus, my sleep is not disturbed by pouncing possums, scurrying mice or visiting demons. My sleep is disturbed by my lovely fire, whose ashes I dutifully scraped before retiring to bed and whose cooling metal chimney emits a crazily loud, wailing clank every time I'm about to drop off.

Day four: The top of the park

Awaroa Inlet is the biggest tidal crossing on the Abel Tasman Coastal Path and has no high-tide alternative. The safe margins are reportedly two hours either side of low tide, but some wading is required even then. Today, low tide falls at 12.39 pm, which means that I have hours to kill this morning before I can cross safely. Then I'll have up to five hours of walking to complete before the sun sets just before 6.00 pm.

I choose to spend the morning neither lying slothfully in the sun nor walking the two kilometres or so further into the Inlet to see the remains of Awaroa's school and a steam engine site. I spend the morning cleaning my new-found home. I clear the ashes, sweep the fireplaces, wipe the work surfaces, stand up the mattresses and sweep the floor. It could be a scene from Snow White and the Seven Dwarfs, except that if it were, I would be auditioning not for the role of Snow White, but for that of an eighth dwarf – Frumpy. Still, the birds sing and the sun shines as if they haven't noticed. There is no need to collect firewood because the long chest is still brimming with logs and kindling. The hut gleams as I close the door behind me. I will never meet those who come after me, but it feels important to bequeath them a clean and happy hut.

Modern conventions of hut maintenance have much in common with traditional Maori values. Maori tribes living several hundred years ago in this and other parts of New Zealand observed the principles of utu (reciprocity, or balanced exchange), and mana (meaning authority, but as a wide definition, encompassing physical, spiritual, practical and moral authority). Utu meant that if one tribe or sub-tribe received gifts from another, then they would repay this in some way and at some unspecified time in the future. The mana of a tribe and its chief was expanded by the extent and value of its gifts to others.

These are strange concepts for those of us taught that accumulation of personal wealth is the key to greater power and influence. It is also easy to oversimplify. The ability to give food and hospitality to others comes from success in producing these gifts in the first place, so it's not entirely removed from the idea of accumulating wealth.

My hut-cleaning motivation has echoes of both utu and mana. I hope to find that the next hut has been left clean for me by some other sub-tribe of trampers. Furthermore, whoever next arrives here will see from the intentions book the name of the person who left this hut in such good condition. They will know that I had the energy, knowledge and consideration to create this simple gift. Yet, I give my labour freely and happily for the benefit of someone else and regardless of whether the next hut is clean or not, or whether anyone notices my name. There must be something to this mana business, because it feels marvellous.

Just as the water rolled silently and swiftly into Awaroa Inlet yesterday evening, today its edge seeps quietly outwards. The plug has been pulled and shortly before low tide I set off barefoot across the sand. I look like a one-man band: my backpack protrudes roundly from my back like a big, bass drum, while other instruments are strapped to every available joint and things clink as I walk.

Halfway across the inlet my feet sink into the sand and water rises up to my thighs. I'm not even at the deepest point. Piercingly cold currents buffet my legs, numbing them and pushing them into giving way. A flock of oystercatchers trots suspiciously away from me. They don't like humans, but they don't like to be seen to panic. Instead of running or flying away, they walk at a determined trot that is just short of a jog, with one eye fixed on my progress. Oystercatchers have been known to mount aerial and knee-level assaults on human beings who get in their way. These ones seem content with merely trying to stare me out.

Why are none of these tidal crossings quite as the guidebooks suggest? And why are the oystercatchers not drowning if the water is at my thigh level?

Of course. Guidebooks are written for the ninety-nine per cent of people who walk the track during the summer. The problem is not the tide. The problem is the recent and heavy rain that is still streaming off the land. Meanwhile, Awaroa Inlet is so wide that there are channels within channels. Standing now considerably less than one-and-a-half metres above sea level I can't pick out the best route, so I let the oystercatchers do it instead. I follow their lead across the sand banks, apologising profusely as they have to strut away from their best feeding grounds to let me pass. Even so, it takes me about forty minutes to reach the enormous red lollipop on the northern side of the inlet, a mere kilometre away from where I started.

Much of the next five kilometres involves popping down on to more lovely beaches. Waiharakeke Bay, Goat Bay and Totaranui Beach all have views of rocky, green-topped headlands up and down the coast. Three kayakers, far away from the shore and tiny to behold, plough their way towards Totaranui.

When D'Urville explored sections of this coastline in 1827 he was struck by the lack of butterflies, insects, lizards, mammals and even birds. He was used to finding forests, but he was also used to finding them packed with life. Being in New Zealand was like arriving between the fourth and fifth days of creation, when plants had been ticked off the list but animals hadn't yet been created. If D'Urville were to return today, he would find these forests more densely populated with animals, but only the human kind.

Totaranui has rocky headlands, a golden beach more than a kilometre long and a wetland area where tall grasses glisten and rustle. It also has houses, cars, a Visitor Centre, an Education Centre, an enormous campsite and even a few roads. The Visitor Centre is closed, but its toilets are always open. These are toilets like those in shopping malls and airport lounges. I feel extremely silly with bits of seaweed still clinging to me. There are even bins in which I can lose the deadweight of mice-nibbled food. I don't particularly want to. I can't get used to this constant popping in and out of populated areas. This no longer feels like tramping and I begin to understand why some people are fooled into thinking that Totaranui is the end of the track. I hurry on to the other side of the wetland, only to find a man in a digger cutting tracks and a couple out jogging as if this were Central Park in summer.

Once over the next headland this flurry of civilisation is gone. All is silence, ferns and forest. The two remaining beaches on this coast of the park are deserted. Limestone rocks have here been licked into odd shapes by the sea. Two sets of human tracks have been laid since high tide but both lead the other way, back to Totaranui. Another night alone becomes a possibility. I'm pleased.

I realise too late that the sun is setting on the other side of the headland. Instead of looping up to Separation Point to see the fur seal colony before the sun sets, I must now tramp furiously uphill as the forest darkens around me. Ow – I'm not used to this any more and I'm so stupid to have run out of light.

I catch up with the sun and skitter down to Whariwharangi Bay just in time to watch it smudge into a thin band of cloud on the very edge of the horizon. I won't be alone tonight, after all: a young couple wave hello before carefully placing themselves at the far end of the beach from me.

In theory, Farewell Spit is visible from here. This sand spit arcs nearly thirty kilometres northwards at the north-west tip of the South Island. It is a protected wetland and bird sanctuary, free from buildings other than a lighthouse at its tip, and traversed only by a small number of highly regulated tour buses. This is the tip of Aoraki's canoe. Being a sand spit, it is extremely flat. Thus, the 'view' of Farewell Spit from Whariwharangi Beach is like trying to pick out the edge of a piece of paper above the straight edge of the horizon.

There are four of us in Whariwharangi Hut tonight and it is not a typical DOC hut. It is a former farmhouse and stockman's hut, where most of the rooms feel haunted in the darkness. Maybe I'm just not used to company any more.

The small ablutions block is inside the edge of the forest at the end of a thin track from the house. Even under cover, the moonlight is strong enough to clean my teeth by. But as I straighten up over the sink, a large, black shape detaches itself suddenly from a nearby tree and springs out. What I thought was a large section of bush is now leaping towards me. It thuds onto the wooden floor. I scream – piercingly high, long and loud. The black shape stops, turns and disappears into the forest. My insides thud and bang together in alarm. My outsides are immobilised. I expect to hear the hut door open as someone responds to my scream. It doesn't. They don't. I felt falsely secure in the presence of others. We look after ourselves.

I'm deeply ashamed that all I did in the face of danger was scream. It was a good scream. I haven't achieved that velocity and pitch since the age of nine. But standing still and shrieking in terror surely isn't a sensible reaction to an oncoming threat.

What is the purpose of the instinctive shriek? Perhaps, like the appendix, it is a defunct evolutionary hand-me-down. It seems futile in all respects. If it were to call for help, then its effectiveness is obviously poor. If it were to sound the alarm for others, then that's very noble, but it doesn't help the screamer. No, the only practical use for my scream was to shock my attacker so that its superior defence mechanism made *it* run away from *me*. My defence mechanism is based on the hope that every other living creature has a better defence mechanism than me. On current evidence, this may be true.

Day five: Old habits die painfully

Whariwharangi Hut is just a few hundred metres inland from Whariwharangi Bay, the beach from where we watched yesterday's sunset and a likely candidate for the place where the first recorded fight between Europeans and Maori took place more than 360 years earlier. It was a one-sided fight, because the Europeans weren't aware that they had agreed to it. Considering this, the final score of Maori 4 : Europeans 1 wasn't too disgraceful.

Two Dutch ships, commanded by Abel Janzsoon Tasman, dropped anchor in the Bay on their 1642 tour up the west coast of what they failed to call New Zealand. The local Maori issued a challenge to fight, by means of blowing many times on trumpet-like instruments. We now know that this was a customary challenge to newcomers, denoting that the locals were ready, willing and able to fight if required. Not rising to this challenge meant that the arrivals respected the might of the home team and were not seeking to displace them – an ideal result for the home team and not a bad one for the visitors. Unfortunately, Tasman's men issued a return call, thinking that they were politely exchanging greetings.

The next day, Maori war canoes approached Tasman's ships. A cockboat was being rowed from one to the other. The war canoes rammed it and Maori began clubbing the sailors on board. Tasman had specific orders not to engage in warfare with local peoples, so he gave orders to set sail. The Dutch ships seem to have left just in time, as more Maori canoes were joining the attack. A potshot backwards at these canoes hit the single Maori casualty.

Funny, these cultural differences. The gap in understanding between Abel Tasman's party and local Maori lay in so many things: both sides were born and raised in different types of society on opposite sides of a much less travelled Earth than we have today. Yet, the gap in understanding between me now and me three years ago is about as big. If I were to meet London Me now, I would be baffled. We all assume that others think like us because we are our main or only frame of reference. What I haven't appreciated until now is that our own frame of reference changes.

All of which makes what happens next even more surprising.

Five days ago I booked a shuttle to pick me up today from the end of the Abel Tasman Coastal Path. It should arrive at Wainui Inlet at 11.00 am. According to the guidebook, I need between one-and-a-half and two-and-a-half hours to walk to Wainui Inlet from Whariwharangi Hut. I should leave by 9.00 am to be sure I'll make it. I don't. At 8.00 am I run in the opposite direction, carrying a water bottle and camera. I really want to see those fur seals. So much so, that I plan to get to Separation Point and back again in an hour. Separation Point is a good one-and-a-half hours' walk from the Hut. Somehow I think I can beat the distance.

Why do I do this to myself? I thought it was life in London that made me never want to be early for anything because being early means waiting, means wasting time. Perhaps it's life in me, not London. Or perhaps London is still in me and will take longer to shake out. Ten minutes short of the lighthouse and viewpoint I realise what I'm doing, laugh and turn round.

I have less than two hours left before my shuttle bus arrives. It is only coming out to fetch me and will leave without me if I don't meet it. I don't have enough food left to stay for another day. I must turn back now. Even if I do, I may not reach the end of the track in time.

I take the last and longest rise and fall of the Abel Tasman Coastal Path at commuter pace. There is no time to stop and stare. I feel a surge of stress adrenalin for the first time in months. What an idiot.

On the final descent, I sneak glances at the marine farms and sand spits inside wide Wainui Bay and at the next set of crinkly, forested headlands beyond, but mostly I jog and trot down the wide, windy, grassy track and hope that my lift will be waiting for me at the bottom.

'You are only just on time,' says the German lady as she climbs immediately into the driving seat.

It's strangely comforting to find that I'm not the only one here who hasn't entirely left their home culture behind. What I don't know yet is that I'm now in the multicultural, nay *uber-cultural* world of Golden Bay. I'm about to enter its capital, Takaka.

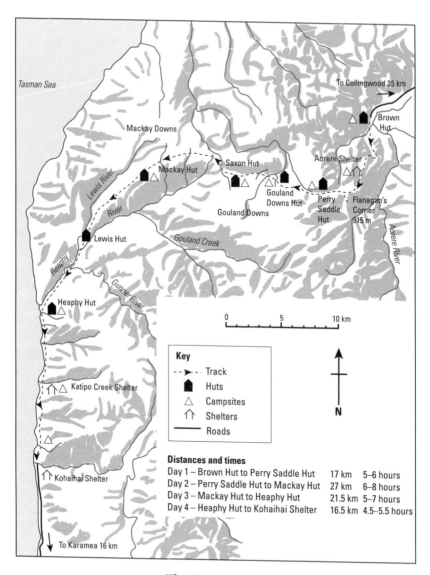

The Heaphy Track

8
There and back again:
The Heaphy Track

The only sizeable township reached easily from the north-west edge of Abel Tasman National Park is Takaka, with around 1,300 inhabitants. Takaka's population isn't swollen over the summer months as much as that of other towns in New Zealand, because it's not 'on the way' to anywhere.

Takaka lies on a fertile plain, shaped like a thin wedge of cheese, with tall, crinkly mountains on the long sides and sandy beaches at the crust. One road links it, fifty-seven kilometres eastwards, with the next biggest township, Motueka – a relative giant with around 6,700 inhabitants. The road is a challenge for any vehicle. Even the strongest engines need a drink and a rest when they reach the top of the mountain pass euphemistically named Takaka Hill. No road leads over the mountains to the west.

Takaka achieves the impossible dual identity of being both infamous and unknown. Those who know it know that it has its own rules. Those who don't know it are the majority.

When I arrive, I know only three important facts about Takaka: it is wedged between the Abel Tasman National Park and Kahurangi National Park, my next destination; it has a small supermarket; and it has hostels, one of which I can call home whilst replenishing food supplies and having a proper wash.

The first hostel I try is closed for winter. At the second a young man directs me round the back and invites me to sit down in one of the twenty or so different chairs in the yard.

'So, like, how *are* you?' he asks, lighting a joint.

A memory flickers; a comment in a guidebook about Takaka being a hippy hang-out. And here's me: matted hair barely concealed under a bandana; all my worldly goods in one bag; and wafting my unique perfume of sweat and seaweed.

I move to the last hostel (a non-smoking joint) and work on smelling once more of twenty-first-century toiletry products. Even so, it takes me less than twenty-four hours to fit in. Soon, I find myself spending my days eating organic food and admiring the work of the local artists and my evenings sitting on bean bags in the small cinema or drinking in the local bar and improvising jazz with the locals.

In December 2004 New Zealand became one of the first countries to ban smoking in pubs and restaurants, but this pub was non-smoking before the ban. Its patrons seem happy with the arrangement. My new friends take shifts with me at the bar, between trips outside to smoke various substances. They return smiling from their breath of fresh air and slip back into the jazz and latest topic of conversation.

I had thought that I would stay just long enough in Takaka to clean myself and my clothes and to purchase food for the Heaphy Track. Now I find it's hard to leave. Dire weather reports make me deliriously happy. Surely it would be foolish to leave Takaka and head into the mountains to the north-west only to be met by storms? I settle in a little more.

I feel intoxicatingly free here and not just because of the atmosphere. I am living from one small pack with the bare essentials. Things I normally consider 'necessities' aren't necessary at all when tramping – not least because they constitute Extra Weight. However, now I'm discovering that they're not necessary even in towns.

I have a second bag of belongings in New Zealand that contains such luxuries as a comb, books and respectable clothes. I left it in a hostel in Nelson before I started the Abel Tasman Coastal Path. They're relaxed about when I collect it; they know I've gone tramping for a while, but I expected to miss these belongings between tracks. I don't. One small bag of belongings is all I need in the world. It helps, of course, that Golden Bay culture doesn't place much emphasis on physical appearance.

On my umpteenth day in Takaka, I make what becomes a very important call.

'Hello. I understand you organise guided trips down the Whanganui River?'

(I don't have to phrase the question properly: I've been in New Zealand long enough now for my voice to rise naturally at the end of my sentences, which is one of the more pronounced Kiwi linguistic traits.)

'Yeah, that's right. Are you interested in doing one?'

'Yes. But I'd like to do it soon. Would one of your guides consider taking me out on the river in the next few weeks?'

'In winter.'

'Yes.'

'Are you on your own?'

'Yes. That's the problem. I don't think I'll find anyone to join me, but I can't go on my own, for safety.'

'Hell, no. You definitely can't go alone. Have you canoed before?'

'No.' I'm feeling desperate. This is the third outfit I've tried. 'But I do lots of tramping. I'm a strong swimmer. And I'll take full responsibility for myself.'

And I'll beg if necessary.

'Well, we may have someone. Yeah, I'm thinking Stewart might be game. But I'll have to check. Call again tomorrow and I'll let you know.'

Stewart is game. He has a two-week window in which to attempt the five-day journey, weather permitting. For $750 he'll bring the canoes, the tent, the food, the expertise and himself, full-time for five days. This is what scares me about the Whanganui River Journey in winter. I now feel equipped to deal with the dangers of drowning, hypothermia or being stranded by floods. I no longer feel equipped to handle the presence of another human being for five days. Particularly one I don't know.

Day one: Facing the weather again

Right now I need to drag myself away from Takaka to begin the Heaphy Track. It is the longest Great Walk that is properly a walk. After the seaside amble of the Abel Tasman Coastal Path, the Heaphy Track will be a marathon. Almost two marathons, in fact. With mountains.

Guidebooks relate that the Heaphy Track takes four to six days to complete and for the first time, I plan to complete a Great Walk in the minimum number of days suggested. I must atone for the Abel Tasman. Walking fifty-one kilometres over five days barely qualifies as tramping. Squealing at wildlife is even more shameful for a would-be tramper. It's time to take things seriously.

As further penance, I'm eschewing carrots. The first section of the Heaphy Track from its north-eastern end is a long, slow ascent that is forecast to take five hours. The apples may stay, but the carrots must go.

The north-eastern end of the Heaphy Track is the most difficult end of any of the Great Walks to reach. The road crosses three fords, any one of which could be impassable through flooding. The last of the three is often the worst. So, even if a vehicle navigates the first two successfully, it may have to re-navigate them sooner than intended. Much relaying of messages goes on between the drivers of sturdy, four-wheel drive vehicles and the helpful souls whose houses are dotted along this back-country road.

The sun has been shining for days in Takaka, but it has been raining in the mountains and as we approach them, the windscreen wipers whirr ever faster. A concrete floor lies under the first ford and our jeep driver grins as she urges the tyres through the current. The sudden shunt of water against the jeep is met with determined pedal work. We bound off on the other side.

'Are you on your own?' asks Shane, the tall, broad, red-haired Kiwi in the passenger seat.

'Yes,' I shout back, as friendlily as I can over the noise of engine, rain and river.

Four of us are starting the track today – and, for once, we are all solo trampers. Even more remarkable, two are Kiwis. Shane provides his explanation for this seemingly un-Kiwi-like behaviour. 'I'm tagging this on to a work trip. No one else from work came down, but I figured I'd be bound to meet people on the track.'

Shane is from Auckland, which for many makes him a JAFA (Just Another Something Aucklander). Books have been written (well, at least one) on the distinguishing features, habits and attitudes of the JAFA. The term has been coined because the population of Auckland is so very much bigger than the population of every other town and city in New Zealand. More than three times bigger than the capital city, Wellington, or the next biggest city, Christchurch. Moreover, Auckland lies at the north end of the North Island, and sometimes seems to be more connected with the rest of the world than with the rest of New Zealand.

'What is your work?'

'I'm an Ecology Technician. I work for Landcare Research. We do environmental research. I deal with plants, weeds and bugs.'

My bug-related small talk is limited. Fortunately, we meet Jane and Leon at the start point, Brown Hut, and Shane is full of questions for them. Soon, as we begin the ascent, I am already in need of almost all my breath for my muscles, so Jane takes up the baton.

'I've been living in Golden Bay for the last nine months,' Jane tells us. 'Before that, I lived in Australia.'

There's no mistaking her accent, though. Jane's roots are English, but she's been living down under for the last three years. The aura of serenity with which she greets us and the track are far more the product of nine months spent in Golden Bay than twenty years spent in Reading. As a tramper, Jane is everything I'm not – tall and willowy, with a long stride and all the right equipment strapped on in the right places.

The fourth tramper is Leon. Lean and dark-haired, he is a Kiwi. Like Shane he looks to be in his mid-twenties. Like Shane and Jane, he seems almost a foot taller than me. Leon is the most talkative of us all and yet reveals almost nothing about himself.

'I love tramping,' he enthuses, 'although I haven't done any for a while. I was worried about coming out on my own. I hoped I'd meet some people on the track.'

Yet, bonding on a tramp is not a simple matter. None of us is likely to need the others in order to survive. Each of us is carrying all we need and we wouldn't be here if we weren't comfortable with the prospect of spending several days in our own company (with the possible exception of Leon). Depending on the prevailing conversations and personalities, I may even need the *absence* of others to enjoy a tramp. Leon is the first person I've met who has come out into an unpopulated, near-wilderness area for the company.

'I'm really pleased you guys are here,' he continues. 'It's not much fun to tramp on your own.'

This is beginning to feel like a scene from *The Wizard of Oz*. If there were five of us, I would be Toto, given the size differential. As it is, I think I must be the Tin Man because I clearly don't have a heart. Instead of being pleased to have the company of these three people, I'm already wondering how soon I can drop behind to walk at my own pace and save my breath for puffing. If this is my response to Leon's enthusiasm for our company, then I am heartless. Also, I may need some oiling when my joints stiffen.

The Heaphy Track crosses the north-west section of Kahurangi National Park, which is itself almost the entire north-west corner of the South Island. Kahurangi is New Zealand's second largest National Park, but this is second after the vast space of Fiordland and thus not to be sniffed at. Or sneezed across. At around 450,000 hectares it is nearly two Luxembourgs or three Stewart Islands. At its centre lies the Tasman Wilderness Area, available for use by those whose survival skills are well honed and who *really* like to get away from it all.

Kahurangi National Park is full of mountains and frequently also full of wet. The rainfall isn't quite as all-consuming as in Fiordland: it might only, in any one year, fill a hole three or four times my height, so I am in slightly less danger here of drowning whilst standing up. Still, the pattern of Kahurangi's mountains on the map looks suspiciously like wrinkled skin.

Fortunately, the Heaphy Track is not about climbing mountains. Like many of the other Great Walks, it was devised as a route through mountains rather than over them. Once we reach an altitude of 915 metres later today, we will have passed the highest point. It won't be all downhill afterwards, but in theory the worst will be over.

This first section of track must surely be the long and winding road so lamented by that dirge. Round we go. Up we go. The only views are of banks of beech, rimu and miro trees stretching out of sight. Light rain falls. We space out and I fall to the back. Only Leon bounds as before. Like a happy dog he switches company between Jane, Shane and me, talking to each of us until we're red in the face, then moving backwards or forwards to the next in line.

The challenge here is mental. Break down the distance. Try to remember why you're doing this. Try not to think about wanting to be back in Takaka. Find a rhythm.

Left! Left! I had a good home that I left!

This was the marching song that Mum taught me and my sister to get us up hills when we were small. Small*er*, that is. At my current speed, however, it's more like:

Luh-e-e-eft ... Luh-e-e-eft ...

This is like dream running. I'm told that it's a common phenomenon in our dreams to discover that the world is somehow made of cotton wool or treacle when we want to run. However much we try, we can't move our legs through it quickly enough to escape whoever or whatever pursues us. As a child, my dreaming brain decided that if the air was too thick to run through, then it was thick enough to swim through. In dreams, I'd kick off from the ground and swim above the trees and houses, always escaping whatever was chasing me. There's no jumping off the ground here, though. The rain isn't quite heavy enough to swim through. Not yet, anyway.

As the hours slump by something strange starts to happen. I am now walking more quickly than the others. My legs seem to be made for this gentle yet unending upward slope.

Oh dear. It all fits rather too well: a certain comfort in carrying heavy loads; excellent stamina over long, gentle gradients; a dislike of steps; and all those carrots and apples ... I must have been a packhorse in a previous life.

Leon and I take the lead, desperate now to find the Aorere Shelter, under which we can eat lunch. Just as I am giving up and about to bring my lunch out in the rain, Leon spurts ahead and calls back to say that he has found it.

We also find a young Kiwi couple, Brent and Alicia, who are out on Alicia's first tramp. They now know that they won't have Perry Saddle Hut to themselves tonight, but they are still extremely friendly. We compare notes on the weather forecast.

'Mine said cloud with some sun.'

'I saw showers developing later.'

'Mine said snow, but only down to 800 metres.'

We munch sandwiches whilst staring at the wall of mist that is today's view along the Aorere Valley. That is, most of us munch sandwiches. Jane's lunch is decidedly different.

'What's that?' I ask.

'Oh!' she laughs. 'It's vegetables. I'm on an elimination diet. No dairy, no meat, no wheat, no gluten, no sugars and no fermented foods. Afterwards I'll introduce foods back into my diet one by one, to see the impact.'

'You tramp on an elimination diet?'

'Well, this is my first tramp, actually, but yes.'

'So, your backpack is full of vegetables?'

She laughs again. 'Yes. I'm finding it quite hard going. It's almost all vegetables – kumara, potatoes, carrots, rice and so on. I may have more than I need. I measured everything out for six days, but then I put more in on top.'

'Six days?!'

Jane explains her master plan to avoid the Heaphy Track transport issue. In this corner of New Zealand, the persuasive power of environmentalists, pragmatists and mountains have so far won out over the road builders. This means that from the western end of the track it takes the best part of two days, three buses and a fair few dollars to get back to the north coast. Instead, Jane is going to tramp to nearly the western end of the track, then turn round and tramp all the way back again. She won't stay in the same hut twice and will be back in Takaka within six days. By which time she will have eaten about ten kilograms of fresh veggies and tramped about 160 kilometres.

We leave Aorere Shelter and the rain turns to sleet as we ascend. At 915 metres Flanagan's Corner is the highest point on the track. A short, root-riddled side track leads off to a view of one of Kahurangi National Park's many jagged mountain ranges. After four-and-a-half hours of staring at ground and trees, the promise of a long-distance view is alluring.

The boys are coming back from the viewpoint as I approach.

'There's a lot of cloud,' enthuses Leon, 'but it clears every five minutes or so. Fabulous views!'

Dutifully, I stand at the viewpoint watching the wind punching the clouds. Snow starts to fall and still I wait. Perhaps Kiwis have a hereditary ability to see through clouds and don't realise that others are more visually challenged. Or perhaps enthusing about non-existent views is a tramping tradition that I should, by now, be able to decode.

A thin layer of snow on the peaks flanking Perry Saddle Hut makes it look as if lit by moonlight. The hut is cold and damp. A message on a whiteboard warns to guard against mice. We take turns stamping round to keep ourselves warm and to avoid trips to the toilet outside until the last possible moment.

Two hours after lighting a fire in the large stove, the only warmth to be gained is from sitting on it. Brent and Alicia retire to warm each other. Shane drags a mattress from the bunkrooms to sleep next to the fire. I zip myself into both my sleeping bags and am still warming them up when the storm really begins. Thunder and wind shake the hut. With eyes shut and head inside two sleeping bags, I still see the lightning. Shane desperately wants to stoke the fire but refuses to touch it for fear of electrocution.

Day two: Towards the Wet Coast

By morning our only casualty is Brent and Alicia's large bag of scroggin, which has been patiently nibbled by fearless mice. Otherwise, we are intact, if a little louder and wider-eyed.

Today we cross Gouland Downs, a plateau of tussock grasses, low shrubs, herbs and heathers, said to be golden in the sunshine. Gouland was a magistrate at Collingwood, the small settlement near Farewell Spit that is overshadowed by enormous Takaka. Fortunately his name was not Smith, so the Downs at least have a suitably spooky name.

Snow is still falling, but lightly now, with just a few inches on the ground. The wind must have blown the rest into the sea, some thirty kilometres and a couple of puffs away. Surely, of all mornings, this one would be a good one to force myself to walk with others.

I can't do it. I dawdle over breakfast and cheerily instruct the others to set off without me when they're ready first. Despite their polite delaying tactics, which include a snowball fight and making a diminutive snowman, they pull on their packs and hesitantly leave without me.

The track winds slowly downhill, across several small waterfalls and within a cocoon of stunted beech forest. It's impossible to see for any great distance until the track appears at the edge of Gouland Downs. The Downs are seemingly flat, but really are billowing up and down at around 700 metres above sea level. They are bordered by mountains that rise much higher but are mere shadows within this morning's weather.

When the weather forecast says 'snow down to 800 metres', it really means it. The mountains all around are of different heights, shapes, sizes and angles, but across them all the snow lies to a straight hemline. Where the track drops below 800 metres, rain replaces snow.

At this eastern end of the Downs stands a monument to human oddness: a tall pole decorated with shoes. These include several pairs of old walking boots now polished with lichen. There are assorted items of children's and ladies' footwear, some of which bear messages of names, dates and countries. The oddest entrants in this strange competition include a pair of grey, strappy, ladies' sandals, two non-matching children's shoes (one tiny trainer, one bootee) and a roller skate. How and why all these shoes were brought and abandoned here is not clear. Some were probably brought deliberately for this purpose. Others may have been abandoned once their owner realised they weren't good for tramping eighty-two kilometres. But who erected the pole for this purpose? And if you abandon your walking boots part-way through a tramp, then in what, if any, footwear do you finish the tramp?

We know little about the many Maori who traversed the Gouland Downs before the Europeans arrived. Like the Milford and Routeburn Tracks, the original Heaphy Track is thought to have its origins in the march towards greenstone on the west coast of the South Island. What is now the Heaphy Track may have been two tracks originally: one through the mountains inland to meet the Tasman Sea at the mouth of the Whakapoai River (now called the Heaphy River); and the other along the coast from the mouth of the Heaphy River, north round huge coastal bluffs and south to the Kohaihai River, which is the end of the modern Heaphy Track.

Major Charles Heaphy was one of the first Europeans to walk the coastal track, but never saw anything of the Downs or this inland section. That privilege fell to a Scotsman, James Mackay, amongst others. Mackay came to New Zealand aged thirteen and followed the new colonial career path of farmer, explorer, public servant and politician. Hearing rumours of hidden

Abel Tasman, Day 2. Perfect weather for drying socks and pants before the New Zealand army arrives.

Abel Tasman, Day 4. Sinking into the centre of Awaroa Inlet, until the oystercatchers show me the way.

Abel Tasman, Day 4. In the morning sunshine Awaroa Hut seems an undaunting place to spend a night alone.

Heaphy Track, Day 1. Perry Saddle Hut, seemingly sheltered as storm and snow clouds gather over the Gouland Range.

Heaphy Track, Day 4. Four solo trampers (though I clearly lower the average height), all still grinning with relief at having survived the storm two nights before.

Heaphy Track, Day 4. Waves so loud that trampers can sing without being heard.

Heaphy Track, Day 4. Point of no return for a mouse at the Katipo Creek Shelter. Point of return for the author.

Heaphy Track, Day 5. Winter dawn breaking across Gouland Downs.

Heaphy Track, Day 4. The world of the nikau palm is an exceedingly stripy place.

Heaphy Track, Day 3. A strong contender for Best Candelabra in the Gothic fantasy forest.

Whanganui River Journey, Day 2. A great walk: battling upstream on the Retaruke River to reach safety before the flood.

Whanganui River Journey, Day 4. The middle of Nowhere is surprisingly well engineered.

Whanganui River Journey, Day 5. The river is home to the people of Atihaunui-a-Paparangi, who continue to welcome visitors onto Tieke Marae.

Whanganui River Journey, Day 3. Tiny whirlpools open and close as still swollen waters carry us through the steep centre of the journey.

Lake Waikaremoana Track, Day 1. One last 'large hill', looking out over the 212,672 hectares of Te Urewera National Park. I was warned that in mid-winter there could be no one else here.

Lake Waikaremoana Track, Day 3. Korokoro Falls from the tree to which I cling for balance. The noise is overwhelming.

Lake Waikaremoana Track, Day 4. Calm water, a good place to reflect.

On the Great Walks most of the tracks are clearly marked, most of the time.

'meadows' amongst the mountains here, he came exploring, walked straight across the Downs and announced that he hadn't found them. Perhaps it was difficult to recognise a 'meadow' in this foreign land until his fellow countrymen introduced all those rabbits and hedgehogs.

The section of track across Gouland Downs is lengthy, particularly when staring at the ground is the only position in which rain doesn't sting the face or flood the hood. Even the snails are running for cover. Our hoods are drawn so tightly that they dig into the sides of our faces. It makes no difference. With so much rain-induced misery, I try not to be a misery-guts. I catch up with the others and walk with them.

Dry rest comes at Gouland Downs Hut. The track crosses the northern section of the Downs and the hut lies in the centre of this section. It does not have the alpine chalet feel of so many welcoming DOC huts. It is small and built from stone, with a large fireplace but no water inside. It is cold, damp, smelly and, fortunately, not our destination for today. We drip and snack under its gable until a rainbow sweeps over the Downs and makes me think of Takaka again.

Shane, Leon, Jane and I must pass by two huts today. Brent and Alicia are taking things more slowly. Even without the scroggin sacrificed to the mice they have enough food for a couple of weeks. They plan to stay on the track for six days, but unlike Jane, they're using their six days to walk the Heaphy Track once, in one direction.

'Are you guys going to Saxon Hut tonight?' I ask Brent.

'Yes!' he answers exuberantly. Then he pauses, looks confused and asks me to repeat my question.

'I just asked if you and Alicia are staying at Saxon Hut tonight, rather than coming through to Mackay with us.'

'Oh!' he laughs.

'Erm – what did you think I asked?'

Brent looks a little sheepish, then says, 'I thought you said, "Are you guys going to have sex in the hut tonight?"'

Around Gouland Downs Hut are limestone caves, worn out by the rain. Trampers are virtually encouraged to go wandering off-track to explore them. Instructions such as 'go in a group', 'watch out for potholes' and 'ensure to take torches' have an effect on the curious tramper like the words 'offer open only to the first hundred applicants' have on serial consumers. Brent and Alicia go off to explore together. We say our final goodbyes to them and continue along the track. We still have a long way to walk today.

Some caves are visible from the track itself, inside the small patch of beech forest that intrudes into this corner of the Downs. Here, for a short while, it's like being back on the Milford Track, with mosses and lichens draped over every twig, branch and trunk, be they alive, dead or leaning between the two. To be buried as a tree must be one of the noblest ways to rot – being veiled gently with lichens and moss, lying outdoors in dapples of sunshine whilst slowly collapsing into new life. Much better than a bonfire or a cold, dark hole.

Separated by the others again through our different paces, I find myself thinking about death. Not because of the rain-filled gloom, the cold air or the dark caves. Nor because I'm afraid – for, surely, last night's storm was the closest we'll come to danger. But because I'm surrounded by life that is built on decay. Decaying rock lets lichen in. Decaying trees feed insects. Decaying ferns feed the trees. It's impossible to think negatively about death when it's part of this.

I may be in danger of rotting myself if this rain continues. It lashes against us on the exposed Downs and the track disappears under two shallow but wide rivers, which are probably small streams in summer. The water is up to shin height and rising. Yet, this is a Great Walk and one of the most distinguishing features of a Great Walk is the effort to which its carers go in order to shield visitors from wet feet. They don't succeed, of course. But they try hard. Here, little trails of boardwalk lead over the tussock to two swing bridges. However, the next river is unavoidable. After the slightest hesitation I stride through. The cold water inflates my socks.

Spirits are dented as we sit at Saxon Hut, knowing that the Downs continue for another three hours for us today. They really are, apparently, most beautiful in the sunshine. Even in the rain each strand of tussock glows orange.

Trampers often cite weather conditions as a manifestation of luck. European trampers seem particularly obsessed with personal luck quotients and can be devious in showing them off. Often, for example, a fellow tramper will ask me if I've walked a particular track, whereupon I assume that they ask because they are thinking of walking the same track and want the inside knowledge on the terrain or facilities. A typical exchange goes something like this:

'Have you done the Routeburn?'

'Yes,' I answer, awaiting some relevant question.

'So have we. And we had the most *fabulous* weather. We were really lucky.'

They seem to believe that divine forces tailor our weather, sending rays of sunshine to light the favoured and clouds to sit on the rest. Perhaps someone could sell 'sunshine' badges to these people. They could have a little patch of sunshine to sew on to their packs for each gloriously sunny day's tramping they have been 'lucky' enough to experience, thereby advertising their enormous personal luck quotients quickly and effectively to everyone they meet.

I try not to associate weather with luck. In the first place, weather forecasts are often right – and tramping in sunshine should therefore be the result of good planning more than good luck. In the second place, I set my sights a little lower. I consider myself lucky when my guidebook and I agree on the definition of flat.

We reach Mackay Hut one by one. Jane first, with her long legs and strong back. Leon second, with his still undiminished energy. They are hard at work when I arrive. Jane is boiling water for all. We lower the clothes rack with numb fingers and pull and peel off our dripping clothes. We squeeze them out and hang them up.

'What can I do to help?' asks Leon.

'You could move a table and a couple of benches near the stove,' I suggest. The small room is packed with furniture at odd angles.

The coal bucket is half full with wet slag that won't light until Jane produces firelighters from her pack. Once the blaze catches, we lay out the scraps of coal around the stove to dry.

'Is this ok?' Leon asks.

Jane and I survey the now even odder angles of the benches.

'Um, well – I kind of meant near the fire,' I say.

Jane has the furniture optimised within a minute. Leon turns to hanging up the clothes that he's knocked down whilst moving benches.

We have changed, unpacked, snacked and lit candles when the door flies open and the rain sweeps Shane inside. He limps awkwardly across the room and sits down heavily next to the fire, dropping his pack into the second of two new puddles.

'God, are you ok?' Jane asks.

He does not look happy.

'Didn't think I was gonna make it,' Shane replies. 'I've torn something in my calf. I can barely put any weight on it. Shit, it's painful. And Jeez – the rain! I'm soaked. It's dark out there now. And I'm really cold.'

While Leon enthusiastically knocks down more clothes to make room for Shane's, Jane proffers a hot drink.

The problem is muscular, so there's nothing we can do other than keep it warm and think positively. I fetch Deep Heat from my medicine kit, but stop short of massaging it in. A man's sweaty tramping legs are his own affair.

Jane offers a distraction.

'I faced my worst fear about tramping today,' she announces.

Her worst fear? A woman who plans her first tramp as a six-day vegetable haul?

'I was afraid of getting my feet wet,' she continues. 'I'd been using all the bridges and skirting round all the bad bits. But that last stream – well…'

'There was no alternative,' we all agree.

About two kilometres before the hut, a deep stream crossed the track. It was too wide to jump and too deep for stepping stones. Even with all my practice at Straight Through Tramping, I had paused for a good look, then taken it at a run, sinking up to my knees and kicking up the water as I ran through, laughing like a small child in her first puddle. It will be days before my boots stop squelching.

'I saw you earlier,' Jane says to me. 'One minute I looked up and you were just before one of the deeper streams. The next minute you were fifty yards further on and I just knew that you had walked straight through. I thought, well, if you can do it…'

'And how did it feel?' we ask.

She laughs. 'When you've done it once, you can get quite into it, can't you?'

'Right,' I say decisively, once Shane is warm, dry and aromatic. 'I hereby volunteer to do the supply run.'

'The supply run?' asks Shane.

'Coal and water. We need more coal for the fire and water for cooking, washing-up and tomorrow's water bottles. The water supply outside may freeze overnight, so I suggest we bring enough inside for the morning too.'

They look at me as if I'm some kind of Bush Queen, rather than a slightly practised novice with a few mistakes behind her.

'Are you sure you want to go back out there?' asks Shane, in a voice that says he wouldn't.

'Yeah, I'll be fine,' I say, climbing into cold, sopping boots and waterproofs. 'But I'll need help. I'll bring stuff to the door. Could one of you relay from the door with the bucket and pans and let me know when we're full?'

Leon jumps up and quickly assembles a mound of pots, pans and billies. I head for the coal bunker.

The darkness outside is startling. I can see only what is in the path of the torch. The wind is cold and the rain nearly horizontal. The coal bunker is only ten metres away from the hut, but feels much, much further as I stand and scrape the slack away from its base. Were anything to take a leap at me now, I would neither see nor hear it coming.

I dig around, deliberately making lots of noise and expecting to dislodge fresh, dry supplies from inside. My arm has disappeared to the shoulder before I realise that there are no fresh, dry supplies. Scraping up enough wet scraps to fill the bucket takes longer than I'd hoped. At the door I am delirious to see Leon. We swap the bucket for the first of the pans.

One of the quirks of the Heaphy Track is that it seems to be the place where pots and pans go to retire. Each hut is home to a large population of them. Some of them are enormous – fit for the hefty stews of the Kiwi Tramper. Nevertheless, the water run will take several trips.

The main water tanks are out of action. A simple, open water butt sits at the back of the hut. As I scoop water out, I can't help but think that any old possum could perch on the side and pee into this.

Every time I return to the hut Leon hands me fresh pans and a comforting grin. Once all the pans are full I receive the empty coal bucket. Second time around, the bunker isn't quite so far away.

Plunging a numb, wet arm back into the bunker I reflect that if I were alone in the hut tonight I would lie in my sleeping bag for warmth and not bother with a fire. Yet I don't mind shivering in the rain and blinking furiously in the dark. We need the fire to be social and to keep Shane's leg warm while he eats.

An arc of water around the door inside the hut shows where Leon has enthusiastically hauled the pans of water. He knocks over a bench trying to make room for me to drip and strip. Then he makes more space on the clothes line and inadvertently brings a few more socks down.

'Sorry, sorry,' he laughs.

We all laugh as a final sock lands on the tables, just missing the candles. Over dinner Leon tries to manufacture new candles from old bits of wax, and we all take turns at spreading out wet slack to dry and stoking the fire.

Tonight I'm not quite the self-sufficient tramper I intended to be. I needed Jane for her firelighters and selfless efficiency at boiling water and ordering the hut. I needed Shane to remind me that my situation could be a whole hell of a lot worse. And most of all, I needed Leon to make me laugh.

Day three: The other side

In the morning things are not quite as they should be. Something is missing. A shout from outside gives it away. Sun! Sun, sun, sun! Blue sky! Sun! The rain and wind and snow have passed.

I have never before felt such intense delight. We thought we would never see the sun again. Our boots may even be dry before the day is out. We would dance around the hut if it wasn't still icy cold and if Shane wasn't limping badly.

'Do you need us to carry anything for you?' I ask Shane.

'No, I'll be right. I'll use a branch as a walking stick.'

The descending track would be ideal for a limping man if it weren't for the storm debris. The track is littered with branches, twigs, leaves and plants. They crunch and occasionally roll or slide underfoot, reminding us that we could all be limping if we don't pay attention.

Today's task is to descend around 700 metres to the edge of the Tasman Sea on the West Coast of the South Island (also known as the Wet Coast). To suit the packhorses and cattle for which the track was cut, the descent is long and steady. The track is remarkably wide, given that it was hewn out of the side of mountains and mostly by hand. The men who cut it developed a technique whereby they cut down trees parallel to the track and then used them as skids to clear the felled vegetation. Not much is known of those who worked this route, although I'd be willing to bet that nothing around here is named after them.

The development of the Heaphy Track since it was first cut has been the subject of much controversy. Or, rather, the *lack* of development has caused the controversy. There have been several attempts to approve the construction of a road near or along the track, linking Karamea on the West Coast with Collingwood and Takaka on the north coast. Local and national opinion has been divided. Claims and counterclaims have raged, sometimes quite feverishly and with decreasing sense.

Pro-roaders have cited the economic benefits of linking the north and west coasts of the South Island. Towns such as Collingwood and Karamea would no longer be end-of-the-road towns. Tourist buses could run the whole circuit of the South Island instead of lopping off its north-western ear. Jobs would be created. Money would come driving in. They have even suggested that trampers' enjoyment of the Heaphy Track would not be affected significantly by the presence of a road running next to the track. Besides, the track was constructed for economic reasons – to move livestock over the hills. It would be appropriate, they have argued, to maintain its economic focus, even if today's livestock are encased in aluminium and leave more toxic excretions behind them.

Anti-roaders have argued not just about the need to protect and conserve the natural environment and the habitat of important species such as kiwis, kakas (native parrots), parakeets, giant land snails, geckos and wetas (local insects, not unlike crickets but vastly bigger and possibly New Zealand's oldest unchanged species). They have articulated the enormous cost and practical difficulty of driving a road through the terrain in question, never mind maintaining it. Sections of the hills on the West Coast regularly tumble on to the tramping track or toss the track onto the beach. Surely the same would happen to any road. Besides, what would be the point of linking Karamea and Collingwood? Linking a township of around 700 people with another township of around 250 people isn't, perhaps, an obvious stimulant for a local economic boom.

Most arguments, both practical and loony, were silenced with the creation of Kahurangi National Park in 1996. A road cannot, surely, be laid through

New Zealand's second largest National Park. Fortunately, Karamea and Collingwood have benefited from those sought-after tourist and local dollars by the increasing popularity of the Heaphy Track.

We wouldn't want to hitch this morning, anyway. With boots and undergrowth gently steaming, we wind down the Heaphy River valley, still several hundred metres above the river itself. The Downs must be glowing bright orange in today's sun, but there's no time to go back to look.

Instead, we go downhill inside a gothic fantasy forest. Lacy veils of rimu drape the corridor of the track and roll back as we pass. Spindly stems support high, twisty street lamps of leaves. Individual stems rise up more than two metres high and are no more than an inch thick, yet on top of these fibrous rods perch exploded pompoms of leaves, cheekily indifferent to the laws of gravity.

Under the gothic street-lamps grow candelabras. These plants come from the same gene pool as their high-rise cousins, but have multiple stems bending gracefully up and out from the central stand. Each red-green ball of leaves looks like wax that has dripped from years of non-stop dinner parties. These are candelabras from fantasy castles, not for modern dinner parties: an urban dinner table with one of these on it would have no room for plates and food.

Above the lighting department are the upper floors of flora. The top floor is dominated by mature rimu trees, with their enormous dreadlocks of leaves, which begin and end far above my head. Trees have a very different approach to maturity than human beings. And these rimu trees do it most successfully. The mature trees rise straight up to around thirty-five metres high, with branches and foliage only beginning around halfway up. The baby versions, however, have stems and foliage all up their length. Contrast this with my own experience of growth from sapling size. Every single bit of me has grown bigger since I was born, albeit some bits haven't grown quite so much as others. But none of my bits has dropped off. I didn't rely on limbs as a child that I subsequently shed when I grew my adult limbs. Yet this, it seems, is what trees do.

At ground level, the cheeky youngsters jostle like market traders to be the first to offer you their wares. They wave young limbs up and out towards the track, offering necklaces and bracelets for sale. The young leaves are bright, tiny and delicate in their chains, but soon they'll be gone. Perhaps that's how the pubescent rimu lose their lower branches: they don't discard them, they sell them. Or perhaps I'm spending just a little bit more time alone in forests than my imagination should be permitted.

An over-active imagination gland is not the only condition I'm developing from prolonged exposure to fresh air, exercise and having nothing more pressing to do each day than to gaze at plants. I'm also developing a condition that is more physical and potentially a great deal more embarrassing: horniness.

Now, we all have our own natural background levels of horniness – our personal Geiger counters blipping away as we work, eat, sleep and take cold showers. We have our own cycles, when the blipping races or slows, whether or not we notice or care. And we have our momentary flurries of frenetic beeping – the ones induced by anything from a lover's eyebrow to the types of adverts that are placed wherever large numbers of bored people assemble on a regular basis (the London Underground being a particularly fine example of this). In this way, we blip...blip...blip our way through life, enjoying the blip...blip...BLI-IP moments wherever we can.

Out here I shouldn't feel horny because I certainly don't feel sexy. I am ignoring every last piece of mating etiquette taught me by the twentieth century, as well as the few I have noticed from the twenty-first. In place of figure-hugging and strategically skimpy outfits, I wear baggy trousers, a T-shirt and fleece. The same ones every day. They are not even colour-coordinated. In place of stockings, I wear socks so thick they would attract only an Eskimo. In place of make-up, dirt. In place of perfume, sweat. In place of clean, shiny hair, a matted mess flattened under a bandanna. In place of stilettos or kitten heels, I have my boots. These are not shoes that say, 'I am willing to undergo pain to make myself attractive to a man who will look after me – and I need a man because I am unable to walk long distances unaided'. No. My boots say, 'We are big and heavy and this woman needs us more than she needs you'. In short, I am as close to repulsive as it is possible to become without being shut up in a bell tower or hired as a nanny by a paranoid wife.

Faced with these new, repulsive attributes, two things astound me: first, that I don't care; and second, that I feel horny as hell. My background count seems to have moved from blip...blip...blip to blip-BLIP-blip-BLIP. And those are just the *background* readings. I am beginning to understand the call of the great outdoors for courting couples. This must be what those French *parfumiers* devote their lives to trying to recreate. Forget the bottles, *mes amis*. Head for the hills.

The gothic forest grows ever taller during the descent to Lewis Hut. I don't envy Jane the return journey. These pleasant three hours would be a gruelling three-to-four-hour test in the opposite direction.

DOC maps make few concessions to gradients. Timings are annotated on most track maps, but only one guide time is given per section. This means that the same guide time governs sections that are a descent going one way and an ascent going the other. It's as if these people don't operate within the law of gravity by which the rest of us are bound. For them, descending uses one set of muscles and ascending simply uses another set. For me, descending uses one set of muscles and ascending is a test of nerve and strength between me and the laws of physics.

At the foot of today's descent, Lewis River sweeps into the Heaphy River. At the junction, the walls and veranda of Lewis Hut itch with sandflies, even now in winter. Charles Lewis was another of those Brits who came to New Zealand in the mid-nineteenth century. Settlers like Lewis could choose from a variety of careers in their new country. They could survey the land. They could clear the land. Or they could farm the land. There were some alternatives, but most jobs involved heaving around bits of the landscape. Like many of the immigrants whose names are now closely associated with the Great Walks, Charles Lewis chose to be a surveyor. It sounds like the easy way out, wandering around the countryside deciding which sections someone else should clear and farm. It wasn't. Lewis spent numerous days and nights drenched and cold on what is now the Heaphy Track. On one occasion, he travelled the whole length of the track, from Karamea to Collingwood, expecting the trip to take three weeks. It took five – and the word euphemistically used to describe his condition on finishing was 'skinny'.

Perhaps the relatively low proportion of females to males in early immigrant settlements had something to do with the propensity of early European males to take long trips into the bush. Bush exploration may have been an early equivalent of the cold shower – involving, as it did, many a cold shower. Perhaps also it explains the tendency of explorers and surveyors to name things after themselves. After all, who's to say which is the more lasting legacy: some genes washing around in the next generation, or having your name on maps?

The remainder of today's journey to the sea is largely flat and is characterised by bouncy metal swing bridges and a strange sense of shrinking. Every species of tree, vine and flax is now taller and wider than it was before. The biggest change comes when we cross the second swing bridge, on to the southern side of the Heaphy River. Shane uses slow and deliberate movements to counteract the enormous bounce he triggers in the guide wires. It's like walking on the moon.

'Come and look at this,' he says on the other side.

I stare up into the thick arms of an enormous tree.

'That's a giant rata,' he says, with a touch of pride.

For once, I already know the name of this tree. This is no thanks to any improved skill in wielding my guide to native trees. Besides, detailed examination of leaves is not practical when standing ten metres below the nearest one. No, my fool-proof system for spotting giant rata is that they are the really big ones with hairy armpits.

As the name says, giant rata are extremely large. Southern rata grow up to fifteen metres high from the ground up, with trunks around one metre thick. Northern rata grow from the top down on other trees, reaching twenty-five metres in length and 2.5 metres thick, even here at the edge of their latitudinal limit. From the crooks of these giant ratas' branches, a parasitic plant grows its long, wavy leaves. Its living green leaves and dead brown ones hang down like thick strands of hair. Thus, when peering up in the impossible quest to see the top of a giant rata, the ground-dwelling tramper sees only a large number of very hairy armpits. It's an unmistakable sight.

By the time we reach the Heaphy Hut, the proportions of the local flora are faintly ridiculous. The flax on Gouland and Mackay Downs was barely half my height. Here, I am half its height.

Inside Heaphy Hut is another surprise: around twenty members of a local tramping club have made the hut their home for tonight. We are stunned by the presence of other people.

The Heaphy Hut is a popular destination for one-night-only tramping trips. It is only a five-hour walk from the Karamea road end and those hours are spent on virtually the only section of tramping track in New Zealand that runs along the West Coast of the South Island. In the last three days we have met no one but Brent and Alicia, who are now a day behind us and no doubt treating Trampers' Horn most effectively. We have completely forgotten that people might be joining the track from the other end.

'But it's our last night together,' bemoans Shane as we sit in the small space that the club members make for us.

Tomorrow, Shane, Leon and I will walk out to the Karamea road end, from where we will summon a taxi to transport us to spa pools and steak dinners. Jane will walk halfway with us, then turn round and walk all the way back to where we started.

'It's nearly eight o'clock!' announces one of the club members suddenly.

Several of them disappear outside with a mountain radio. It's time for the evening weather forecast, which is their main reward for carrying this bulky, heavy equipment. I turn to Jane. 'I really don't want to hear that you're going to have glorious sunshine for your trip back across the Downs.'

'You could always come with me,' she grins.

I laugh. It's impossible: I only brought food for four days; I need to reach a telephone within the next two days to communicate my continued state of not being dead, before my parents raise an international alarm; I have a rendezvous in the North Island in seven days' time with the only living Kiwi game enough to canoe down the Whanganui River with me in the middle of winter; and, darn it, I have a spa pool and a steak dinner in Karamea with my name on them.

I wish I could be the kind of person who makes spontaneous decisions to do crazy, exciting things.

And suddenly I realise that to become that kind of person, all I need to do is to make a spontaneous decision to do a crazy, exciting thing.

The club trampers return and announce that glorious sunshine is forecast for the next two days.

'Shane, do you have a ten cent coin?' I ask.

'Why?' he asks, passing one over.

'Heads I'm going with Jane. Tails I'm coming with you.'

We peer at the back of my hand.

Shane is tutored in how to contact my Dad without making him think that I have walked into a tree and killed myself, or been kidnapped and tortured by a strange, deep-voiced Kiwi calling to demand a ransom. Then we consider the food problem. Shane and Leon contribute most of their emergency food, safe in the knowledge that they will be in Steak Dinner Land tomorrow night, even with Shane's continued limp. Jane offers some of her little-diminished mound of vegetables and we lay everything out on a bench and take stock. After several conversations beginning with phrases like 'I could have the second half of the tomato soup for breakfast on the third morning…' we concede that I don't have enough food for the return journey.

Lack of food is a prominent theme in early written accounts of traversing this route. It took weeks rather than days to cross from coast to coast before the Heaphy Track was cut and even hardy Kiwi Trampers can't carry several weeks' of food. Instead, the explorers caught their food – deer, fish, eel, birds … whatever they could get.

Word spreads amongst the tramping club that I'm going to attempt the 'double Heaphy' if I can assemble enough food. Asking Kiwi Trampers if they have any spare food is like asking the European Union if it has any spare butter. One by one trampers approach me and press half-packets of dried foodstuffs into my hands. One elderly gentleman gives me his last three slices of raisin bread (slightly soggy) and apologises profusely for not being able to give more. Soon everyone wants to contribute to the mad scheme and I can neither refuse nor dispose of the gifts I don't want.

An hour later, I lie down amongst the snufflings and shufflings of trampers in their bunks and I think to myself: am I really going to do this?

I now possess a store of food heavier than any I have carried on to a track, even when indulging myself with carrots. Moreover, it is nutritionally unhinged. Pasta, bread, rice, bread and pasta.

'Don't worry,' Jane whispers in the darkness. 'I still have lots of vegetables.'

Day four: Am I really doing this?

I wake to the shoutings, stompings and bangings of a Kiwi tramping party being considerate of other hut users. I lie in my sleeping bag, mentally listing all the Kiwis I know and developing my working hypothesis that Kiwis are genetically unable to whisper. Then I remember that I'm not walking out today after all – and suddenly want to vomit.

I could change my decision. I eat breakfast, leave the hut and walk for twenty minutes still considering the coin toss. If I return to the Heaphy Hut now, I could collect my pack and still make it to the Karamea road end in time to hail a taxi.

I keep going. I *am* that crazy, spontaneous person. Really, I am.

The section of track from the Heaphy Hut at the mouth of the Heaphy River to the Karamea road end is accorded many fine adjectives by the guidebooks. A random sample includes: stunning, raw, beautiful and tropical. I would add: deafening.

The Tasman Sea is very excited at having found land again after its long journey from Australia. It beats against the South Island in one long line. Waves queue up to fling themselves onto the sand. At least seven tiers of froth stack up at any one time, making the sea seem strangely tall as well as shouty. I love noise like this. It lets you sing at the top of your voice without anyone hearing.

Even with blue skies and no wind, the spray that hangs in the air prevents anyone from seeing more than a few kilometres along this coast. The sea pummels the soft sand into troughs and crests, making it even more tiring to haul aching legs and wrinkled packs around.

I am heading south, with the Tasman Sea assaulting my right ear. To the left a row of forested foothills rises up sharply from beach level, albeit to a mere couple of hundred metres. The official track winds in and out of the forest at the foot of these hills, although most people plough along the beaches instead.

Inside the forest the world is a very stripy place. Thousands of nikau palm trees make it so. Their trunks have horizontal bands, alternatively light and dark browns. They look like so many thin legs in stripy tights – a convention of wicked witches of the west coast. From their tops, thin leaves splay out in long, green strips and sunlight slices between them in thick stripes. The sea spray that reaches even here is illuminated like a three-dimensional zebra crossing.

My decision is now irrevocable. I will be walking almost the whole length of the longest overland Great Walk twice over in one go. There's nothing to do now but relax and get on with it.

Unfortunately, one part of me relaxes too much. By the time I reach the Katipo Creek Shelter I am moving at a trot and overjoyed to greet its humid, midge-infested, un-lockable green outhouse and the wet toilet roll I find squatting under a layer of dead sandflies. If this is giardia, its sense of timing is impressive.

I wobble back to the shelter where Shane and Leon are valiantly fighting a mouse away from the chocolate bar in my coat pocket.

'You know,' says Shane, 'that by turning back now, you won't have walked all of the Heaphy.'

'That's true,' adds Leon. 'So you won't have completed all of the Great Walks.'

They're right. I am deliberately defeating my own objective.

I weighed this up carefully last night when trying to decide what to do. Walking all of the Great Walks was an idea that became a challenge that I wasn't sure I could meet. However, last night I realised that my odds had moved from unknown to slim to excellent. I had already tramped six tracks, which, a few months ago, I thought I would never complete. I was near the end of the longest, most gruelling overland Great Walk. I had found a guide to help me navigate the Whanganui River safely. Thereafter, the only remaining track would surely be no harder than the rest.

I had realised that the bigger challenges now for me lay in following Jane. That would be the biggest test of my physical stamina. I would allow myself to fail deliberately to complete the Heaphy Track.

'Look after him,' I say to Leon, nodding at Shane and his drooping leg. I think I might mean it the other way round.

We grin. We hug. Then I turn north and set off on another tramp, with a tight heart and loose bowels.

The Heaphy Track has had its fair share of deaths. In the last few years, the coastal section of the track has seen off the most trampers, mainly at Crayfish Point, which lies just beyond my turning point. The culprit is that excitable sea. Recent victims hadn't even been trying to swim in it. They were walking along the rocks when the waves grabbed them.

At the Heaphy River mouth lies further evidence of the sea's force. A Japanese trawler sank here, amongst others, and parts of its wreck can still, apparently, be seen against the rocks on the bank opposite the hut. I don't have time to look as I scamper to the toilet. For the last forty minutes I have been in bowel-clenching agony. Being a responsible tramper meant holding out. I was carrying nothing suitable for hole-digging; no trowel-like objects could be gleaned from the undergrowth; I couldn't easily work out where all the nearest water sources were; and if I had stopped moving, my bowels wouldn't have waited the time required to dig even the standard six to eight inches down.

I stagger from the toilet, wash my hands thoroughly, drink a large quantity of water, watch a helicopter landing large gas canisters next to the hut, and then set off upstream after Jane.

One reason this forest is so tall is that much of it grows out and up from limestone cliffs. What are tall trees anyway become even taller when their trunks start at the top of a cliff and their roots trail vertically ten metres or so down a rock wall before disappearing into the ground.

Limestone being the weak-willed rock that it is, these cliffs are full of caves. How many is unknown, but this doesn't mean they are undiscovered. When modern-day caving trips find a 'new' cave, they also tend to find bones inside it. Including human bones. Reason enough, I think, not to go disturbing all those nice roots.

Down at ground level I am befriended by a fantail. It takes me a while to notice because he seems shy. When I stop, he stops. When I walk, he flies with me, but never in full view. I have met friendly, fearless fantails on most of the other tracks. Legend tells that they got their distinguishing features from a run-in with Maui, a major figure in Maori legends with a predilection for mischievous experiments ending in great discoveries and lots of trouble.

Maui brought fire to man, but only by stealing it from his grandmother, the goddess Mahuika. In revenge, Mahuika tried to blow Maui up. She failed, but reclaimed the fire and hid it. The fantail knew where it was but refused to tell, until Maui squeezed it so hard that its tail popped out at an angle and spread out in a fan. The squeezed bird inadvertently avenged itself later, when the ever-ambitious Maui tried to kill Hine-nui-te-po, the goddess of death, by climbing inside her while she slept. The fantail laughed and woke Hine-nui-te-po, who promptly killed Maui.

Fantails may laugh at death, but they can't fly in a straight line. This fellow cavorts around at my knee level, executing flips and turns that would make an Olympian gymnast dizzy. Yet he giggles and stops when I turn to watch. When I stop, he lands, hops along the path in front of me, turns, looks at me and waits. When I walk on, he flies behind me. We repeat this sequence for about two kilometres.

Just as I am at my most delighted and enchanted with my new-found friend, whistling encouragement to him, walking backwards and forwards while he dances around me and about to hold out my hand for him to alight while we whistle Mary Poppins-like to each other, we meet Brent and Alicia.

'Hi there,' they smile. 'We met Jane a while back and she told us about your change of plan. She also said you're a bit short on fruit and veggies, so we've got something for you.'

They pull out an enormous bag of semi-dried fruit (the kind that is officially dried and yet still wet). They pile half of this into a second bag and hand it to me. The bags must weigh a kilo each. They've been tramping for four days and could still feed a passing rugby squad.

I look down at the contents of my new bag. Mostly prunes.

'I see you've found a friend,' Brent says, nodding at Boris. (I've named him.)

'Fantails are great, aren't they?' enthuses Alicia. 'The way they fly around you when you're walking, eating the grubs that your boots kick up. Particularly in this mud.'

Ah. Now I look again, Boris does seem rather well fed. He is clearly a master of the technique.

I carry on feeding Boris until we reach a swing bridge. I try to encourage him across by standing on the other side whistling our little cheep and squelching in the mud. He doesn't come. After ten minutes I give up and walk on, feeling lonely for the first time in two years.

At Lewis Hut Jane is boiling water for both of us, the resident sandflies are climbing over each other to get inside and an obviously frisky middle-aged Kiwi couple sits in the corner. They had clearly expected only the sandflies for company.

'I had a panic today,' Jane confesses quietly. 'I heard a helicopter flying above me, which went away but kept coming back again. I thought I must have inadvertently set off my Personal Locator Beacon. I didn't know what to do. Thankfully the helicopter flew off in the end.'

'What's a Personal Locator Beacon?' I ask.

She looks surprised. 'Don't you have one?'

'No.'

A Personal Locator Beacon, it turns out, is the 1980s in my hands. It is the size and shape of the first mobile phone and is neon yellow and orange. It would stand out anywhere other than a 1980s comeback disco or beside wet sphagnum moss. It also weighs about the same as a small possum, due in no small part to the gazillions of batteries it requires.

'So you've been carrying this as well as all your vegetables?'

'Yes.'

'Where did you get it?'

'The DOC office in Takaka told me to bring one with me. I hired it at the garage. I assumed they'd tell anyone tramping alone in winter to get one. I can't believe you don't have one.'

I don't know whether to be pleased or not. Do I now look like the kind of person who doesn't need a Personal Locator Beacon? Or did they like Jane better than me? Oh well, at least I haven't had to carry one of these neon bricks.

Day five: The long and winding road all over again

We wake tired, with a long day ahead. Breakfasting, packing and cleaning must be done quickly today.

I have been steeling myself for these few hours ever since the coin toss. The climb back up to the Downs will be the longest, most exhausting part of the return journey. The only small comfort will be in knowing the route this time round. Which means knowing just how long and exhausting it will be.

For once, I walk as quickly as possible. This is not a morning for staring wide-eyed at the world or for allowing imagination to burn calories. This is a morning for ascending as quickly as possible. For minimising the time between toilets. For single-minded focus on reaching Mackay Hut before lunch. And for having enough daylight left to reach Saxon Hut after that.

For three-and-a-half hours I do as good an impression of a racehorse as a packhorse can. I eat a precious chocolate bar when I feel I'm slowing. I stop only once, two hours in and only for a few minutes. A South Island robin kindly hops onto my pack for a pep talk. After another ninety minutes I know I'm nearly there from the changes in vegetation and the familiar twists in the track. I'm nearly there for almost half an hour. My bowel swoons at the prospect of a toilet that doesn't appear. All I want is rest, but every time I find a good rock perch it's too close to the sound of running water. The only thing I can do is to keep moving.

When, finally, I emerge at Mackay Hut, my concentration is so focused on one thought that I barely manage a 'Hi' to the man sitting outside before dropping my pack and, with trembling fingers, closing the lock on the toilet door.

Afterwards, we introduce ourselves properly. He is Julian, in his early fifties and a Brit on holiday.

'Look what I found,' he says excitedly, pulling a snail shell from his pack.

It belongs to one of the twenty or so species of giant snails that live in Kahurangi National Park. These are not garden snails. These are snails grown big in big forests.

Most people think of snails as small, slow, slimy and not much else. Crunchy, perhaps. Tasty, in France. Annoying for gardeners, but otherwise not inspiring much passion. No country would have a snail as its national emblem, even though this would provide some much-needed variety amongst all the lions and eagles. However, New Zealand's giant snails would be worthy challengers for the role of National Creature if only the country didn't have so many other unique, odd and endangered contenders.

Giant snails are not quite as large as their Latin name, *Powelliphanta*, suggests. However, their shells can grow as large as saucers. Better still, they are carnivorous, eating other snails and worms, which out here grow to pretty ridiculous sizes themselves. There's no evidence that they have a taste for human flesh and I could run faster than them in any case, even in my current condition. However, I can't help thinking of all those bones found in the caves around the Heaphy River – caves that we know giant snails like to use to renew their shells. We may not have any evidence of man-eating tendencies, but then who would be left to report it?

'You're not supposed to take things from the Park,' I say to Julian. '"Take only photographs, leave only footprints."'

Julian looks at me with disdain.

'It's not as if the snail is still in it,' he says. 'Besides, one shell isn't going to make any difference.'

He then tells me how he and his three companions were determined to get the full Kiwi tramping experience and how no one else with just four weeks to spend in New Zealand would bother to do that. He tells me how much easier it is than he expected, how he has been the first to reach the hut today, while his companions are dawdling across the Downs.

I don't partake in the conversation. All I keep thinking is: how do I persuade him not to take the snail shell? I must, but I can't. He has sized me up and determined that I have no authority over him. I am not a wizened old tramper. I am not a DOC employee or a local. I'm not an environmental scientist offering rational arguments on the practical impacts that will arise from his theft of the shell. I'm not even from a different country. I want to influence him, but I can't. He has dismissed me. He can't find a reason why he might learn something from me.

I have temporarily forgotten that DOC specifically forbids anyone from taking snail shells out of Kahurangi National Park and I don't yet know that a Kiwi scientist collected uninhabited shells for research and observed that the next generation of snails had deformed shells. It seems that some living snails eat the shells of their dead companions to grow their own shells.

Julian takes his shell. And if giant snails do ever schlurp human flesh, then I have a main course that I'd like to suggest.

An afternoon trip across Mackay and Gouland Downs in the sunshine is what I came back for – and here they are. This corner of Mackay Downs is full of low hills, round which the track winds like a Scottish reel. It is impossible to see more than a few hundred metres in any direction other than up. Thick crops of tussocks beam orange and gold in their sunny enclaves.

The transition from Mackay Downs to Gouland Downs is through forested, winding hillsides. Jane, Shane and Leon swapped stories of seeing hobbits' faces in the walls of moss at the side of the track here when we passed in the rain. For thirty minutes I stare hard at the moss to my left, examining every inch for traces of insanity, so that I am dizzy when I eventually find them. They are many faces of small stones pressed into the moss. Some passing sculptors have used the shape of the moss and rock wall so well that a pirate and a skull stare out a little too convincingly.

Through breaks in the trees I see cloud creeping up the valley. Oh no, not more rain? The light dims as I drag myself on to Gouland Downs. This really is a long, long Great Walk. Knowing the track a little doesn't help. Wasn't Saxon Hut just beyond this creek? No. Or this creek? No. The next one? No. No.

The exact length of the Heaphy Track is not known. After all, it's not as if someone can set their tripmeter and drive along it. Not yet, in any case. So we make calculations and estimate that it's about eighty-two kilometres long, give or take a bit. That is, the DOC Heaphy Track guide says eighty-two kilometres. The DOC Kahurangi Park map says seventy-seven kilometres. Guidebooks give figures between seventy-six kilometres and eighty-two kilometres. In 1971, the track was measured the hard way, using a bike wheel and mileage counter. It was announced to be 43.5 miles long, or just over seventy kilometres. This was '15 miles shorter than generally believed', which would put the generally believed distance at ninety-four kilometres. By tomorrow night, Jane thinks we will have walked about 160 kilometres. I think we will have walked until I can walk no further. There doesn't seem to be any reason to be more precise than that.

On the last stretch towards Saxon Hut I could be wearing a deep-sea diving suit for the effort required to take each step. Jane comes out to greet me.

'Well done!' she beams.

'Have you been here long?' I ask, then quickly add, 'No – don't answer that.'

I flop onto the veranda. I'll go inside when I've summoned enough energy to take my boots off. Jane fetches her drink and joins me.

'Aren't you tired?' I ask.

'Exhausted,' she sighs. 'But isn't it great?'

And it is. It really is.

Our hut-mates tonight are five middle-aged Kiwi men who joke about escaping from their wives and fill the hut with Tupperware containers full of pre-prepared food. They are friendly, but we fail to strike up much conversation. Jane and I are not at our sparkling best and I think the guys are trying very hard not to swear in our presence.

We sit on a thin wooden bench. On the table in front of me are my remaining food reserves: one sachet of boil-in-the-bag rice and the remaining third of a packet of tuna will be tomorrow's lunch; half a packet of pasta spirals and the remaining carrots and kumara are tonight's dinner. Each of the purple kumara tubers is smaller than my little finger. Tomorrow's breakfast must be a further donation from Jane – something called millet.

The men come to the table with their enormous pot of heaven-scented stew. I'm very good: I don't stare at it or make any comment. I'm so hungry and tired that just plain pasta tastes wonderful. They make no comment, but tuck into enormous bowls of steaming, fragrant salvation. When the last of my pasta spirals has gone, one of the men silently takes their enormous ladle and fills my plate with stew. My second dinner is to die for. After which, they insist on doing all the washing up. Who needs conversation?

Day six: Everything but the prunes

I don't know what wakes us. Jane and I are the first up – not the hulky Kiwi blokes who do this all the time, who instinctively rise with the dawn to walk all day and cook themselves hefty, tasty stews before the sun goes down. We rise *before* the dawn. It is dark and silent in the hut and we are tired. We wake early because we have to. We have about thirty kilometres to cover before 4.30pm when the sun sets and one of Jane's friends from Takaka is picking her up. I'll catch a lift with them back to Takaka, where I'll stand, smelly and bedraggled on the doorstep of one of the locals who said I'd always be welcome to stay, and see whether they meant it.

Outside the hut the temperature hangs just below freezing and thick frost covers every surface. The short strip of boardwalk leading to the toilets is slippy, but fortunately I'm no longer running for the outhouse. I leave the toilet door open because this wooden cupboard has one of the best dawn views on the track. The arrival of light is so clear and crisp that suddenly my thighs stop aching, my eyelids open properly and I can't wait to be back on the track.

From Saxon Hut, the track crosses a section of flat tussock land and winds up through a small beech forest before descending to the largest expanse of the Gouland Downs. Each thin blade of tussock and tiny herb leaf is cloaked with thick white frost in the vast bowl of darkness. As the Earth turns, sunlight spills into the far end of the Downs. Billions upon billions of delicate, thin tussock leaves sparkle and spit out cold flashes of light. The sunlight slides silently forward and licks fresh frost into light – the visual equivalent of tossing sausages into a pan of boiling oil.

I walk slowly towards dawn. I am not yet out in the centre of this vast crop of tussock when I stop in the shade just in front of the sun line. The frosted tussock dazzles as the sun moves over us. Every tiny, thin blade glints from tip to roots. This is a crop of wands that can be harvested only on a few mornings a year – and on each of these mornings, only within the space of a few minutes.

Far ahead, the frost is melting and the tussock glows orange. Behind, in the vast area of frozen tussock still to be reached, the ground is a whitened yellow. The line of light moves forward and strikes them brilliant white. They become yellow and deepen to orange as it slips onward. Yet the change in temperature that heats the tussock is slight. The sky is blue and the sun is bright. The temperature remains little above freezing.

The rivers are still swollen. The boardwalked detours are beautiful and treacherous with frost, but the swing bridges that preserve dry boots are also now viewing platforms for the dawn. The track is my causeway across a wide sea of glittering blades. If this is what happens when I get up early, then I really must try it more often. Standing alone in the centre of this plain of magic fills my soul.

I have not seen Jane since she left the hut this morning, another twenty minutes ahead of me. I mustn't let her down. Yet, I can't rush these fields of gold. These are Gouland Downs in the sunshine. This is what I came back for. And not only am I seeing Gouland Downs in the sunshine, but something even more breathtaking. So I stop and gawp and dawdle and make gloriously slow progress.

We tend to assume that the bigger a plant is, the older it is. Growth takes time, after all. Yet tussock plants can be up to 300 years old. No higher than a backpack, they could be more than three times as old as your grandparents, or more.

Gouland Downs are an odd sight to the logical mind. Normally, vegetation rises in a set sequence with altitude, from tall forest, to short forest, to shrub-land, to tussock, scrub and finally just a few tenacious lichen. Here, tussock is mixed in with the occasional patch of forest and the treeline climbs much higher up the surrounding mountains. This may be down to human intervention. Maori tribes are known to have razed forests in many parts of New Zealand, where tussocks now grow in place of trees and ferns.

Forest destruction is one of the few environmental crimes listed in the Maori logbook now that Pakeha are tired of being the only ones with inherited guilt. After all, it was the Polynesian settlers who introduced the first ground-dwelling mammals to New Zealand – the Pacific rat and dog. It was Maori who hunted to extinction the large, flightless moa. Europeans messed things up on a much grander scale, but perhaps before we learned whether Maori would succeed in doing the same.

Whether or not Gouland Downs is an untouched wilderness, it's hard to turn my back on it and re-enter the forest for the short wind back up to Perry Saddle Hut. Surprisingly, there is still snow on the ground. These are chunks that iced over during the night following the snow storm and have yet to thaw out after three full days of sunshine. Descending to the Downs the day after we did would have been treacherous.

Jane has left Perry Saddle Hut before I arrive. A cheerful note explains she had to continue because it's such a beautiful day. I sit on the bench outside the hut and eat all my remaining food except my last chocolate bar and the prunes. Then I set off down the long section to Brown Hut.

We took nearly five hours to walk this section last Saturday. I have little more than three hours to complete it now, with only one of the three advantages I should have. I should have a lighter pack than on day one, but I am now carrying several hundredweight of prunes. I should have my last chocolate bar to pep me up, but now I discover that I miscounted and have nothing left but the prunes. My only remaining advantage is the law of gravity.

There is a deep sense of peace to be had from having only one thing to do for a whole afternoon, even when that one thing is to trot-walk seventeen kilometres down a hill chasing the sunset. Strange changes take place in the brain from all these hours of silence, beauty, continuous exercise and faint hunger. For three hours my brain works just enough to keep my legs moving and to wonder occasionally what my mouth is singing and why.

Jane is sitting on the bench outside Brown Hut in the dusk when I arrive. Brown Hut is too smelly to sit inside when it's not raining. Besides, she has disturbed two young Kiwi lads, who were planning to steal firewood from the hut, load up their campervan and camp elsewhere, no doubt illegally. Not quite brazen enough to commit theft with a witness, they use the excuse of stopping to use the toilets, even though Brown Hut is not on the way to anywhere for a campervan.

'Is this wood for general use?' They ask casually, indicating the chests of chopped and stacked wood.

'No, it's for trampers using the hut.'

'That means it's for general use.'

'Yes, if you pay your hut fees,' Jane replies, indicating the box on the wall for tramping tickets and money.

They start loading up firewood.

'We'll pay at our local DOC office.'

Of course they will.

Jane looks genuinely exhausted for once, but smiles when she sees me.

'I knew you'd make it,' she says.

I'm pleased that one of us thought so.

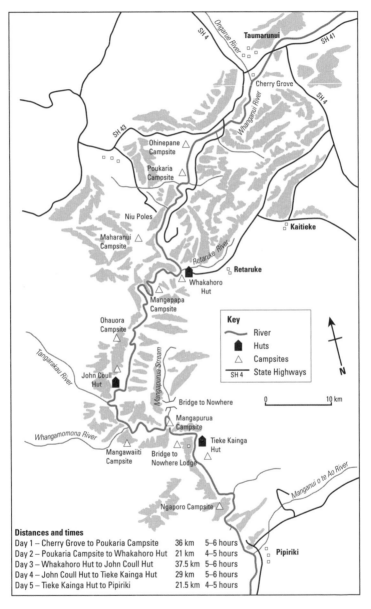

Distances and times

Day 1 – Cherry Grove to Poukaria Campsite   36 km   5–6 hours
Day 2 – Poukaria Campsite to Whakahoro Hut   21 km   4–5 hours
Day 3 – Whakahoro Hut to John Coull Hut   37.5 km   5–6 hours
Day 4 – John Coull Hut to Tieke Kainga Hut   29 km   5–6 hours
Day 5 – Tieke Kainga Hut to Pipiriki   21.5 km   4–5 hours

The Whanganui River Journey

9
Walking on water:
The Whanganui River Journey

In 1999 the Waitangi Tribunal did its best to end one of the longest running disputes in New Zealand's history. It doesn't matter that New Zealand's human history hasn't been all that long. This case ran for more than one hundred years, which is an awfully long time in any lawyer's diary.

The question that the Tribunal tried to answer may be shortened outrageously to, 'Who owns the Whanganui River?' At first glance, this seems like a straightforward question. It isn't. Broken down, each part of the question is almost impossible to resolve. It is the kind of question beloved by very clever and very lazy students, both of whom achieve top marks by ripping apart questions rather than answering them.

In the first place, what is 'the Whanganui River'? Is it free-flowing water, aquatic plant and animal life, a riverbed and banks? Is it a major source of food and water? Is it a place to pray and be cleansed? Is it a being in itself, an ancestor? Is it a hall of many spirits? Does it start with the first melt into mountain streams? Does it end at the sea?

Then, what is meant by 'own'? The European tradition of individual title, or the Maori tradition of collective stewardship? Does ownership presume the dominance of man over river, or the other way round? Is ownership the right to do whatever you want with whatever you own? Does it arise from occupation, use or possession of a piece of paper? Does it preclude the rights of others?

Finally, what is meant by 'who'? An individual or a group? Could it be more than one group? Must an owner be alive, or may they also be dead? Does the answer change over time?

In the end, the answer to the question, 'Who owns the Whanganui River?' was decided to be: the Atihaunui tribes, sub-tribes and families. This is, of course, a vast simplification. Even the short version of the Tribunal's findings ran to fourteen pages and included a dissenting opinion from one of the members of the Tribunal. The full report of findings was nearly 400 pages long and contained several statements to the effect that Atihaunui ownership should not exclude certain other rights such as rights of public access. Moreover, Waitangi Tribunal findings are not legally binding on the government.

So the debate moved into a new era of trying to agree who should be responsible for day-to-day management of the river and how decisions should be made in practice about anything and everything that affects the whole river – from mountains to sea, beds, banks, water, the lot. Emotions still run high over many issues – from gravel extraction, land usage and tourism to the continued diversion of the river's headwaters as part of the Tongariro Power Scheme. This is territory where authors rightfully fear to tread. Not one of my guidebooks mentions the link between the Whanganui River Journey and the Waitangi Tribunal. With just a few pages to devote to the entire five-day River Journey, how could they?

One of the most striking aspects of the Whanganui River Report is the Tribunal's emphasis that their findings cannot be applied to rivers generally. The Whanganui River is a special case. It always has been. It is the longest navigable river in New Zealand and one of the most contentious and controversial rivers in human history.

It should come as no surprise, then, that the Whanganui River defies the first rule of New Zealand pronunciation. Elsewhere, 'wh' is pronounced as 'f', but Whanganui River is pronounced with a hard 'w'. This is the tip of the confusion. The town that lies where the Whanganui River meets the Tasman Sea is called Wanganui. The region in which museum, town and river lie is Wanganui – but the national park that dominates this region is Whanganui National Park. The letter 'h' pops in and out of existence like radio reception amongst W(h)anganui's hills.

The mysterious 'h' probably arose because the original local Maori dialect used neither a hard *w* nor a soft *f*, but a noise like a *w'*, as in W'anganui. It seems that this was too much for the poor Europeans who were writing everything down according to the Maori alphabet they had devised. Fortunately, the different spellings have the same meaning: large harbour or river mouth. The other good news is that the river, town, national park, museum and region are now all pronounced the same: with a hard 'w'. The bad news is that this only comes naturally to a local.

Day one: Rapid learning

At Cherry Grove in Taumarunui, Stewart parks our van-full of gear and takes a look at the river.

'That's good,' he pronounces. 'The level's normal.'

It has rained recently and more is expected. Light, then heavy, if the forecast is correct. It wouldn't be much of a Great Walk without rain, but the impact is more significant than for the other Great Walks. Heavy rain stops a tramper only if it dislodges a few tons of rock and vegetation above her head. Heavy rain stops a canoeist when it causes the river to flood, which is reasonably often on the Whanganui River in winter. Those cattle-flinging February floods happened here. And that was in summer.

We have two weeks in which to complete the Whanganui River Journey, so rain can't deter us. In two weeks' time, Stewart starts his winter ski classes on Mount Ruapehu and won't be free again until spring. It's been a long time since I had a deadline, but two weeks will surely be enough to cover the five-day trip.

Just being here with someone else who's willing to canoe in the cold and wet feels like an immense achievement. It helps, of course, that I'm paying him.

'So, what made you agree to take a complete novice on to the river for five days in the middle of winter?' I ask.

'I've never done it before,' Stewart replies. 'It'll be a good challenge.'

Well, that's honest.

'The main aim,' he continues as we unload the canoes, 'is for neither of us to fall into the river at any point. No one else is out on the river in the next five days, so if we go over we have to self-rescue. And it's going to be cold. If we fall in we may struggle to get dry and warm until the evening. And that's assuming we don't lose gear and we keep our spare clothes dry.'

'We'd better not fall in, then,' I agree.

'We have some options with the canoes,' Stewart thinks aloud. 'We could take one, or both. I'd prefer to take both, so that we have a backup.'

'OK.'

'But you can't paddle one on your own because you've not canoed before.'

No arguments from me. The canoes are more than three metres long, about a metre wide at the midpoint and strikingly heavy even without our ample supplies. A small woman navigating a loaded canoe single-handedly through rapids would want some experience on her side.

'What would you normally do?' I ask.

'Normally I have a canoe to myself and the group doubles up. If there's an odd number, the most experienced one takes a canoe by themselves. I've never been out with a group of one before.'

'Ah.'

We stand and stare at the two double canoes lying side by side on the muddy ramp. At first glance, a canoe journey is a strange candidate for a Great Walk. However, many people do walk on the journey, after they've fallen out of their canoes and before they've managed to refloat. But then, most people canoe here in summer, when the water isn't freezing cold and when it's low enough to stand on the riverbed and still keep your head above water.

I'm nervous – not because of my inexperience, the prospect of the river flooding, the promise of plummeting temperatures, the danger or hypothermia, or the risk of losing gear (or worse). No. I'm nervous about spending five days in the close company of someone else. Moreover, someone I don't know.

I am still trying hard to form an opinion of Stewart. We met for the first time yesterday in National Park Village, the tiny and ridiculously named settlement in the middle of the North Island (it's not in a national park and it's more like a miniature alpine resort than a village). We met for a prep talk and some serious sizing up.

My first impression was of a man who is tall, dark and handsome and has probably been aware of this for quite some time.

'From your voice, I'd figured you for about fifty,' he said, not long after I arrived.

'And you were happy to go out on the river in winter with a fifty-year-old woman?' I mused.

This concerned me. (It was much later that I wondered whether I ought to be more concerned about sounding like a fifty year old.)

'Yeah. Well, we'd talked about the tracks you've done. I knew you could look after yourself.'

A small voice inside my head screamed, 'No! Please don't assume I can look after myself in a canoe. I'm assuming you'll rescue me if this goes horribly wrong!'

We spent the rest of the evening listing and checking our food and equipment, with me asking every five minutes, 'Are we really taking all of this?' and Stewart replying, 'Yeah, we might as well. It's not like tramping. The river does the hard work.'

Yet the river does nothing to help while we spend the best part of two hours constructing and loading our vessel. We use the planks of wood to bind the two canoes together into a canoe-catamaran. We strap most of our luggage into the right-hand canoe. We will sit in the left-hand canoe. The hulls have to be close enough together for strength and manoeuvrability, yet far enough apart for us to be able to paddle in between. Otherwise we'll be turning left a lot.

Our heavily loaded catamaran slumps into the thick layer of silt covering the ramp. We heave and push and lever – and move the whole vessel a metre closer to the river but further down into the mud. We heave again and our vessel doesn't budge. Neither do my legs. I sink up to my shins in river mud.

It takes a full minute to work each leg free for each step. Much unloading, sweating, slipping around in mud and reloading takes place before the canoes are afloat.

'Clean your legs off in the river before you get in,' instructs Stewart. 'We want to keep the canoe as clean as possible.

Marvellous. Wet boots already. Well, I have been dry for the last three days. It was beginning to feel unnatural.

When we push off from the ramp, our paddles almost disappear into the silt and have to be wrenched out at the last moment. Success. We're off. And I have absolutely no idea what to do next.

'Paddle forward on the left,' Stewart says. Then, realising I may need a little more information, he adds, 'Right hand over the end of the handle. Left hand further down, near the blade. Keep your right arm straight. When the paddle goes in the water, use your right arm to lever it through the current. You don't have to pull hard with your left arm. Use the lever.'

This standard stroke feels like a parody of the opening sequence to the 1980s TV show *Hawaii Five-O*, in which a boat-full of semi-clad Polynesian men paddled ferociously to set the scene for the gun-toting, jacket-sleeves-rolled-up, macho shenanigans that followed. It never occurred to me to watch their technique.

'The other main stroke is the draw stroke,' Stewart continues. 'Lean out over the side, put the paddle vertically into the water as far out as you can, then draw it in to the canoe, so you're pulling at right angles to the canoe. Ready? Draw to the left.'

Our vessel swings almost 180 degrees so that we are now facing the right way, albeit on the wrong river. The launch-point at Taumarunui is not on to the Whanganui River itself, but on to the Ongarue River (appropriately meaning 'place of the shakes', although the reference is more to earthquakes than to inexperienced canoeists). Five forward strokes and some quick draw strokes sweep us on to and across the Whanganui River in a rush of speed. A few swift manoeuvres from Stewart somewhere behind me leave us pointing the right way on the right river with the minimum of splashing.

Stewart has far more influence over our vessel than I do and not just because I don't know what I'm doing. He is in the rudder position. One sweep of his paddle can turn our twin hulls more quickly than several of my draw strokes. My job is to keep paddling and follow orders. This is perfect. If anything goes wrong it can't be my fault.

Stewart disrupts this happy train of thought:

'Keep an eye out for rocks and other obstacles. Often they're just below the surface, so they're difficult to see, but they could damage the canoes if we go over them. I can't see as well from the back.'

Surely he's joking?

'Er ... if the rocks are under the water, how will I spot them?' I ask

'Watch the surface. If there's a rock beneath the surface the water dips down and then makes a small wave over it. Tell me if you see that.'

I look at the water as if for the first time. There are waves like this all around. We pass one and there is indeed a rock hidden on the other side. We pass more, but they have no hidden rocks. We ride straight over a few of these while I try to understand what to look for. Is Stewart teasing me? If I were to raise the alarm for every little wave he's described, I'd never shut up. No. He must have given me this role to make me feel I have some involvement, when really I'm just one of the oars.

The first rapid beckons before I've even worked out how to breathe comfortably whilst wrapped in layers and life jacket and sitting on the low prow seat. There are a mere 239 named rapids between Taumarunui and Wanganui; about 120 of these occur before Pipiriki. My guidebook diligently notes that journey times for each section of the Whanganui River Journey depend on how many times your canoe is overturned. I can almost hear it chuckle.

Rapids are universally classified by number, from one to five. (I presume a grading system from Fun to Terror was never seriously entertained.) Grade one rapids are a fun burst of speed for little effort. Grade five rapids are those that the highly experienced may escape alive, but not necessarily inside their craft.

None of the rapids along the Whanganui River Journey are worse than grade two, which roughly means some risk of falling out, but only if you don't know what you're doing. Smugly, I have Stewart for that. Unfortunately, we also have a double hull.

'It's usually best to aim the prow of the canoe into the centre of the 'V' formed by the rapid,' Stewart explains. 'Except, we have two prows.'

When approaching a rapid, the 'V' of smooth-surfaced water is often the only sign of what's to come. It's as if all the well-behaved water is forced into a smaller and smaller channel by mischievous waves, froth, rock and bubbles. The base of the 'V' is where the water flows fastest. The canoeist's aim is to ride through the centre of the 'V' and use its momentum to shoot as quickly as possible through the mess that follows.

Stewart aims the prow of our left-hand canoe for the centre of the 'V'. I keep paddling. Our hulls slap over the waves. Cold water slops over our bows. We paddle as hard as we can, but the currents pull at my blade. I tighten my grip and push through them.

As we slow on the other side I hear a gritty swish-slop behind me. Stewart is bailing us out with a large, sawn-off milk carton. The cap is screwed on, but the original base is missing. Holding the handle, which is secured with blue plastic string to his seat, Stewart scoops up an impressive quantity of water each time. Ingenious.

'We have to be careful not to take on too much water,' Stewart says.

Ah. I had assumed our main risk was capsizing. I hadn't thought about simply sinking.

'If things get difficult I may ask you to jump into the other canoe,' he adds as we swirl over another rapid.

'What would that do?' I ask. Is this another joke?

'It would adjust the weight to give me better steering control.'

'OK.'

Not joking again, then.

We take the second rapid with more aggressive paddling, in retaliation for more waves leaping aboard.

'I'm pleased with the canoes,' Stewart grins. 'This arrangement feels really stable.'

It does. We're both increasingly confident in our craft. I just wish Stewart wouldn't sound quite so surprised about it.

Even in winter the river is a colourful place. The bare willow trees on its banks glow with red and orange tints. As each branch splits upwards into ever-dividing twigs, the halo of colour intensifies. I had no idea that willow trees did this. The reds and oranges of winter willow branches glow against the vibrant greens of farmland pasture and remaining shreds of forest and ferns.

The northernmost section of the Whanganui River Journey passes between hills that have long been cleared of bush and are now grazed by sheep and cattle. These hills are steeply cut, with lots of crinkly lines made visible by deforestation. It is like a mini-Fiordland, not least because we're amongst many waterfalls. They carve intriguing shapes into the rock walls. Some are big hollows like the mouths of enormous caves. One is a whale's fluke in dark wet rock.

The grassy hillsides are rough and deeply lined. A handful of New Zealand's forty-seven million or so sheep turn their backs on us as we drift past. I stare at their bottoms, which is a new habit of mine and one that I blame on Southland's informative bus drivers. Two months ago, I had been travelling through lowland grazing territory between Invercargill and Te Anau near the bottom of the South Island and the conversation in the bus had naturally turned to sheep.

'See the markings on those sheep?' our driver had asked.

Blobs of red or blue paint adorned the backs of many.

'Yes. Is that to show which farmer owns which sheep?' I asked.

'No,' she replied. 'It shows which sheep have been inseminated by which ram. The farmer attaches a special pouch to the belly of each ram. When the ram is doing its business on the back of the sheep, the pressure releases a blob of paint.'

Her passengers stared with fresh insight at the coloured markings, sometimes on the rump and sometimes more than halfway up the back of the docile sheep. She continued, 'The rams don't need paint. They never go back to the same sheep. Scientists have been doing some research into it, trying to work out how the rams know. They reckon it's something to do with smell.'

This made me consider sheep from a new angle. I had stared at those Southland sheep for more than an hour. Had they been 'branded'? If so, how far up their back was the paint? For reasons I daren't consider, this fascinated me.

As we paddle past Whanganui sheep, I check for signs of 'branding' and wonder how New Zealand came to lead the world in women's liberation when its forty-seven million sheep, five million cattle and 2.5 million deer set its four million people a more basic example. In fact, evidence of gender equality in New Zealand is mixed. On the one hand, this was the first sovereign state in the world to give women the vote, and women are clearly evident in all public occupations. In fact, it is common for leaders of political parties – and recently also prime ministers – to be female. On the other hand, average pay rates remain lower for women than men across the vast majority of occupations (sometimes breathtakingly so), the 'national sport' is male rugby and fewer than five per cent of outright farm owners are women. I have met Kiwis who make no presumptions about what a woman can or can't do. And I have met Kiwis with whom I instinctively spend less time.

Stewart sits at the stern, controlling our canoe and directing my actions. I sit at the bow, obeying his orders and feeling unusually dependent on a man. I am no longer in control of my direction or speed and I'm not used to being in this role. What worries me most is not my lack of control over the weather or the mind and moods of the river, but my lack of control over the mind and moods of my companion.

'Stewart, I know this is your job, but it's important to me that you have a good time. I mean it. And I'm not being entirely selfless. If you don't enjoy yourself then I won't either.'

Stewart seems to take this well and we lapse into what I trust is companionable silence. I focus on my paddle strokes. I want to show I can pull my weight. Funny how a need to prove myself reappears in the close company of testosterone.

My next lesson is: Opening and Closing the Day Barrel. We each have two blue, plastic barrels for our personal items. Our Day Barrels are the ones containing anything we think we might want whilst we paddle – hats, gloves, camera etc. These two barrels are secured in the centre of our paddling canoe, behind me, so that we can access them easily (in theory).

The lid of the barrel fits snugly and a metal hoop closes over the join. Closing the hoop tightly is a simple matter of pulling the lever on the loop from one position to another. However, getting the metal hoop to fit properly over both lips on the barrel is an entirely different matter, especially when the contents of the barrel are inclined to overflow and when the protagonist is balancing precariously in the front end of a canoe.

Stewart explains his patented technique for barrel closure. 'Stand on one leg and place your other knee on the centre of the barrel lid to press it shut. Now you have both hands free to work the metal hoop.'

Both hands free, but only one leg to stand on. I decide that I don't really need the items in my day barrel.

To paddle the Whanganui River is to exist within several different time dimensions simultaneously. Looking ahead, we creep slowly towards the next bend in the river. To the side, however, the steep banks of rock and trees slip past more quickly. For a real speed fix, though, look down. Underneath each dip of the paddle, the stones on the riverbed whizz past with heartening speed. Perhaps this is the secret art of canoeing: if the day is dragging, look down; if time is flying, look ahead.

A red van gives me a shock when it appears amongst the ferns growing out from an overhang of rock.

'There's a road up there,' Stewart explains. 'We'll be with it for most of the day.'

It's not one of the world's busiest highways.

We hear a loud, long crunching sound as our sidecar hits a hidden rock square on.

'I'm not sure the spotter's doing her job properly,' chides Stewart, amicably.

The canoe is fine, but I'm not. I really am responsible for spotting rocks below the surface. This is not easy. We're already low in the water, the sun is faint and low in the sky and we're surrounded by currents and small waves, some of which may or may not have rocks underneath them.

An emaciated calf stares at us from a shallow grassy bank where it is stranded between the river and cliffs. Ducks panic at our plodding approach, jumping off the river and flying away as soon as they see us. They must never rest in the summer if they're this jittery. Or do they only expect trouble at this time of year?

Rain sets in early. We see it in the hills in front before it reaches us. It's only a shower and inside it are swallows flitting across the river. Swallows in winter! Black shags fly around us like upended boomerangs. Don't watch the wildlife. Watch for rocks.

Other than our life jackets, we're wearing exactly what we would wear for tramping: warm layers and waterproofs. However, my waterproof overtrousers weren't designed to withstand the pressure of me sitting in a puddle.

'Have you got a wet bottom yet?' asks Stewart.

'Yes.'

'Itchy, isn't it?'

Yes. It is now.

Yet, even in the rain and even with a cold, wet and itchy derriere, I grin. As the hills slowly grow higher and steeper above us, the slanted striations in the rock at eye level show that we are paddling through a tilted world.

At Poukaria campsite we unload our vessel in the dusky light, pull the empty canoes high onto the rocky beach, haul our provisions up the hillside and pitch camp, sweating. As expected, we're the only guests tonight. Stewart spreads our provisions and equipment around the wall-less kitchen area and sets about cooking more food than I would normally eat throughout an entire four-day tramp. He refuses all help, so I huddle on a bench, pile on layers of clothing and retreat inside my hood. Just behind me, rain falls from the roof edge.

I feel a small thud on the back of my hood. The rain must be getting heavier. I put my hand up, but feel nothing except wetness. Stewart proudly serves plates heaped with chicken, potatoes, rice, kumara, carrots, pumpkin and one fried, whole garlic bulb each. We begin to eat.

I don't see clearly what happens next. As I lean forward, two long insect legs appear from the edge of my hood and begin to step onto my cheek. I whack the side of my hood with my hand, then sit very still, not knowing what it was, or where it is now.

A large spider sits in the centre of my plate, dwarfing the potatoes. Thank goodness I saw only its legs up close; its body is enormous. Stewart flicks it onto the grass and we resume eating. Neither of us knows what type of spider it was. I'm happy not knowing. Later, I surreptitiously give all my clothes a shake outside before crawling into the tent.

Day two: Fateful decisions

I wake to the sound of two cars. We're still not too far away from 'civilisation', although the road is on the opposite side of the river, up a steep bank and hidden by forest.

It's not strictly raining, but the forest is wet. I zip my jacket closed over the life jacket and once more lose the ability to bend over. Hauling our bulky, heavy kit down the soft, muddy bank in this fattened and restricted state is not easy. On current evidence, landing and launching canoes requires twice the energy consumed by paddling. It doesn't help that I'm full of Stewart's enormous pancake breakfast. He is scrupulous in sharing the food equally, despite the vast difference in our sizes.

'Wow,' Stewart exclaims from the bank. 'This mist is amazing. You don't get this in summer.'

The river is quiet. A wispy layer of mist hovers above it and seems at once to be rising up and yet not moving. The mist is so delicate that we only see it clearly towards the next bend in the river. In the distance, bursts of weak sun etch out hilltops that look like a full lower jaw of dragon's teeth.

Before we launch, I make two leg-sized holes in a clean, black rubbish sack and pull on my new over-pants, hooking the yellow drawstring through the top clip of my life jacket to hold them up.

'I don't care what I look like,' I say when Stewart laughs. 'If this stops me getting a wet bottom, it'll be worth it.'

'Let's hope the River Fashion Police aren't out,' he grins.

'That's rich, coming from Clown Man!' I retort, smiling.

Stewart's matching waterproofs are red, orange and yellow patchwork. They are deliberately bright, for search and rescue purposes. We laugh at what we look like. I think Stewart's beginning to see the fun side of being away from anyone who cares.

The look and level of the water have changed little overnight. The downward view is still clear to the stones and rocks of the riverbed. The tip of my paddle blade still clatters occasionally against them.

Cut into the sides of these hills surrounding us are some of the most common and yet least remarked-upon features of the New Zealand landscape. They are something between steps and terraces and can cause no end of confusion for the observant visitor.

At Mount Eden in Auckland, for example, everyone who climbs to the lip of this volcano (still officially active, but eruptions unlikely) looks down on to steps cut into the grassy sides of its inverted cone. Visitors are invited to look for the occupation terraces, storage pits and house sites. It seems obvious that the steps and terraces were sculpted by human hands.

These former Maori pas and kaingas (fortified and unfortified sites) are scattered all over the North Island if you know what to look out for (they are rarely signposted). However, once you start looking, it seems that there are few grassy hillsides in New Zealand that *aren't* crinkled with layers of steps or terraces. After months of confusion, I discovered a few weeks ago that many shallow hillside terraces have been fashioned not by the arms of men, but by the hooves of sheep. What were Maori pa sites are now grazing lands – and what were *never* Maori pa sites are now grazing lands.

The hills round the upper reaches of the Whanganui River used to be covered with pa sites. Today they are covered with sheep. The curious canoeist can pass many an hour trying to spot a true terrace from a sheep track. Or staring at the bottoms along it.

Today's rapids seem gentler than yesterday's. Stewart and I are getting used to each other and we're becoming cocky about the stability of our craft. We drift over one of the smaller rapids backwards with neither of us paddling. I'm eating a plate of rice and vegetables and Stewart's head and torso are buried in a crate underneath a tarpaulin in the other canoe.

Rapids seem to work on the same principle as log flume rides: the person in the front gets most soaked. Wave water slops over our prow and trickles down my gaiters.

'I'm fairly lazy about rapids,' Stewart says as we approach another. 'I like to go near the bigger waves to pick up the strongest current, whilst trying not to get too wet.'

Does that mean that if we took the slow route, my feet and bottom might be dry? Grrr.

For those who don't know the Whanganui River and who aren't accompanied by a local, a pamphlet guide describes each rapid in turn and how to approach them. The writing is small, because there are an awful lot of rapids

For the Maori hapu (Maori family or sub-tribe), who lived along the banks of the Whanganui River, every bend, rapid, cliff, cave and waterfall had a name. This was partly for orientation, just as every house has a number and every street a name in a modern town or city. Yet the names also provided practical or spiritual information about the rapid, bend or waterfall in question. Often, what sounds like a dramatic name turns out to be something quite practical and simple: Kowhatupiko (stone at the bend); Tahunaroa (shoal or sandbank); Onepoto (short beach); and Turangahoro (where the landslip stopped). Many are named after prominent plants and birds: Pongahuru (glowing ponga, a common tree fern); Te Miro (a native tree); Te Kowhai (another, noted for its yellow flowers); Kaka (parrot); and Motutara (island gull). Others are more intriguing: Te Moari (the giant swing); Matawhero (red face – which may refer to the papa cliffs, some embarrassing legend, or both); Papakino (one translation is harmful ground); Tokatapu (sacred rock); and Onetapu (sacred sands). Many are beyond my powers of translation. Kauwaewhare, I decide, could mean legless dwelling, dwelling that swims with a foot, dwelling with leg that swims, or cow's foot dwelling. Every one of these sounds like something I would have liked to have seen.

The pamphlet guide to the Whanganui's rapids describes how to navigate them but it would be no good to me. In the first place, it is paper, so I would wrap it in a plastic bag and fold it carefully inside a semi-waterproof pocket, thus maximising its useful life and minimising its usefulness. Worse still, I would never know for sure which rapid was imminent. The pamphlet lists rapids by number and name, but on the river there are no numbers or names – just rocks and water. Some of the rapids are so tiny and tame that I wouldn't know if a sudden spurt of speed had been a rapid or not. I would find myself drifting towards a double 'V', unsure whether this was 'No. 39 – take a left-hand line' or 'No. 40 – avoid drifting to the left'. I would spend so much time trying to count and match the real-life rapids to the pamphlet that I would entirely miss the delights of the river until I fell into them.

Stewart has no need of the pamphlet. I wonder aloud how many times he has canoed this route in order to know them all.

'Oh, I don't know them all. Besides, they change with the weather. Some rapids appear or disappear depending on the height of the water. Sometimes the water covers rocks that you'd have to avoid in drier conditions. Sometimes whirlpools appear where you haven't seen them before. It's always different.'

The banks of the river rise as we move further into a world of mist, rain, waterfalls and cliffs hairy with grasses and pongas and topped off with forest. It feels like another world – or another era in the one we left.

'It's hard to tell if the banks are rock or mud,' I comment to Stewart.

'It's all the same,' he replies. 'It's papa. A type of clay.'

Everything is at an angle, as if I'm not sitting up straight. Striations in the papa cliffs on either side of the river slice into the water at angles. Sometimes there are just six or seven pronounced lines, but occasionally more than thirty, rising high above us. None line up with the surface of the river. We are paddling through a tilted world. On the banks, rocks jut out of the water at even odder angles. On bends and near rapids, banks of pebbles rise out of the water with one side higher than the other. Nothing aligns with the surface of the river. Even the rain doesn't hit it straight.

The most recent flood has pushed flat the first few metres of long grass growing on the steep banks. Nine or ten metres above our heads, occasional plastic bags, scraps of clothing and a pair of yellow, oilskin trousers dangle from tree branches, awaiting the next major flood to continue their journey. Out of sight from the river, we pass the Niu Poles, tall poles topped by ceremonial crosses. A tohunga (a priest, or respected elder) put a spirit into the pole to summon Maori warriors to fight the European settlers in the nineteenth century.

Lunch is so enormous that afterwards I paddle through the rain with my eyes closed, almost incapable of doing anything but digesting.

After a while, I notice again that Stewart isn't paddling. Whenever I turn round, he's doing some gentle bailing, rooting around in tubs for snacks, eating or simply sitting with this paddle across his thighs, watching the water lap by. Perhaps he is taking my request that he have a good time a little too seriously.

However, doing nothing is an entirely legitimate canoeing 'technique'. The Whanganui River Journey is around 145 kilometres long. Over five days, that's an average of less than thirty kilometres per day, on water that travels at an average speed of around five kilometres an hour. This means that a day's 'paddling' can be over in six hours with barely a calorie expended. Moreover, this second day covers just twenty-one kilometres. The river will transport us to today's destination even if we only dip our paddles to steer through rapids. The water really does do the hard work.

I paddle mainly to distract myself from my wet and itchy bottom. Occasionally I kneel up in the front of the canoe to change position. Not scratching requires advanced self-control.

'It's decision time,' Stewart announces. 'We're near the turn-off to Whakahoro Hut. We can stay tonight at Whakahoro, or carry on to the campsite.'

We've been discussing this all afternoon through the rain.

'Whakahoro is the last point on the route that links with a road,' Stewart reminds me. 'If we carry on past Whakahoro and the river floods, we will have to wait at the campsite until it's safe to paddle again.'

I don't want to dictate a decision, but neither do I want to abort the trip. I say something neutral, trying to see if Stewart has a preference. 'Well, it's still raining and it's getting colder.'

'Yes. This rain is here for a while.'

'So,' I attempt to summarise, 'the river is swollen and rising, but we don't know how much it will rise, how quickly it will rise or how soon it will fall again afterwards.'

'No.'

Mangapapa campsite will likely be a few roughly flattened and slightly overgrown pitches halfway up a hillside, with a toilet cubicle or two and an open kitchen area. Whakahoro Hut won't offer much more in the way of mod cons, but it will have a fireplace and it is at one end of a windy, unsealed road that could connect us to some much-needed civilisation if serious winter flooding sets in. Stewart offers another thought.

'The Hut may not be much warmer than the tent, but at Whakahoro there are also the offices of Wades Landing Outdoors. We could throw ourselves on their hospitality.'

My bottom is wet, itchy and cold. Everything else is wet and cold. The hut sounds warm and dry. On the other hand, I am lucky to be here at all and I desperately want to carry on. If we stay at the campsite tonight, we will have to complete the journey because there will be no other way off the river. Even if we have to wait at the campsite for days on end, the only way that Stewart would be able to get back to his other commitments would be by paddling on to Pipiriki with me. However, if we stay at the hut and the river takes days to subside, then Stewart may drive home for the ski season and that will be the end of our attempt.

'So, shall we turn off at Whakahoro?' Stewart asks.

This seems to be Stewart's preference. My bottom, at least, is in full agreement.

'OK.'

In order to reach Whakahoro Hut, we must leave the Whanganui River and paddle a few hundred metres up the Retaruke River. Only, we can't. Facing upstream, our second hull is a liability. We must keep as close to the bank as possible to avoid the strongest currents. However, when one canoe is tight to the bank, the other canoe sticks out into water fleeing the other way.

There are several rapids here. We've become quite good at rapids, but up until now we've been heading in the same direction as them.

We paddle furiously and manage to haul ourselves up to the base of a small rapid, at which point we redouble our efforts and only just remain stationary. When we both realise what's happening, the sudden loss of morale has us slipping back towards the Whanganui, exhausted. Stewart guides us into the right-hand bank as we fly backwards. We hold ourselves with our paddles against the rocks.

Stewart gets out and ties a rope round the front of our sidecar, while I sit and hope that he doesn't drop this slight connection between us. If he does, I'll be back on the Whanganui River within seconds, with plenty of food, a tent, two canoes and nothing but my own limited river skills with which to survive the remaining eighty-eight kilometres of the journey. Don't drop the rope, Stewart.

He tries to pull us up river while instructing me in some furious paddling and levering-off with the end of the paddle. It doesn't work.

'Take this' – he throws me another rope and drops the first. 'Tie it on to the front of your canoe.'

Suddenly I can't remember any of the sailing knots I once learned. Please let this knot hold. Stewart trusts me – and I'd probably be annoyed if he didn't. However, it will now be my fault if I end up drifting backwards alone in our double canoe.

We try the pulling-and-levering thing again and make some progress, until one hull wedges between two large rocks. We move backwards and try again, with the same result.

'Get out of the canoe. Quick as you can.'

I scramble out on to the rocks and the lighter load enables him to jerk both hulls around the rocks.

'OK, now take the rope, head upstream and pull us up from there.'

I attempt to do as instructed. The physical conditions are not conducive to the work. The large rocks under my feet are slippery, uneven and mostly submerged. The rope wraps itself around my limbs. The rain is heavy, cold and obscuring visibility. My rubbish-sack underpants restrict movement above knee level.

I pull back my hood so that I can see what Stewart is doing and hear what he needs me to do. Alas, slightly improved visibility does nothing to stop my right foot from slipping along the top edge of a rock and sliding down into the river. The riverbed is not deep at the edges and I get a firm footing, but there is neither means nor point to getting my foot quickly out of the water. I experience the now familiar moment of intense awareness of dry foot, followed by a sudden and equally intense awareness of river in boot.

I plunge my left leg into the river as well and wade upstream, hauling on the rope while Stewart pushes the hulls out and around rock obstacles. He wobbles on the rocks, looking extremely dry.

'OK, that's the worst of them behind us. Now, throw me the rope and climb back in.'

I check he has the rope before stepping into the front of the luggage canoe.

Suddenly, our ship shoots out towards the middle of the river, taking my left leg with it.

'Whoooaaaaghhh!'

I clutch the boat with both hands, right leg trailing in the water, torso hovering between canoe edge and river.

Stewart takes up the slack on the rope – just in time to stop me falling. I use the tension to haul the rest of me into the boat, where I collapse into the sidecar and laugh and laugh. Weakened, I haul myself over to the rowing canoe as Stewart throws first the rope and then himself into the sidecar. We have just negotiated rapid number one.

We paddle furiously again and gain some ground on the current, only to approach rapid number two. This time we steer into the left bank and I hop out with the rope and into cold, whizzing water up to my knees. That's it. Now I know I must have been a horse in a previous life. First the raw carrots and now towing boats.

I haul our vessel upstream while Stewart sits in it, fending it off from the worst rocks with his paddle. Another large rock sits squarely central, such that it cannot pass between our canoes and the canoes cannot both pass on one side of it without being literally in the middle of the river.

Still dutifully under instruction, I provide tension on the rope while Stewart stands with one foot in a canoe and the other on a rock. Wobbling, he physically lifts one canoe up and over the rocks. I watch and wait, impressed by the audible effort and scraping. Stewart sits back down in the rowing canoe, shouting, 'Forward – quickly! Keep pulling!'

I leap on to the next submerged rock, but my foot slips. I flop chest first into the water. Another rock breaks my fall and the combined padding of clothes and life jacket prevents bruising. I push myself back upright, expecting a great wave of wetness to slosh through the layers of clothing. Amazingly, it doesn't. I seem to have flop-pushed most of the water away from me on landing. Still, I've amused Stewart. Both of us are now laughing.

Before we resume our efforts I unzip my jacket, pass my un-waterproof camera to Stewart and take off my restrictive bin-bag miniskirt. Now physically unhampered by anything hanging off me and mentally unhampered by any remaining thought of staying dry, I splosh along, hauling our ship – and Stewart – up river.

We make real progress in this manner, although I still can't see the landing. We take another rest, which is almost as tiring as not resting, because we have to fight to hold the canoes steady. Stewart is confident that we are almost there.

'The landing is on the opposite bank. Once we're up with the next rapid, you get back in the canoe and we'll ferry-glide across the river.'

This sounds like an attractive manoeuvre. I particularly like the word 'glide'. Gliding is not a word I associate with drowning.

The concept is to paddle at a forty-five degree angle to the oncoming current, finishing further upstream and on the opposite bank from where we started. Stewart does the steering. Somewhat inevitably, my role is to paddle furiously.

In the middle of the river, the full force of the current is impressive. We slosh and heave our way across it, with our arms moving at double speed and our ship moving in slow motion. We most certainly do not 'glide'. We do end up on the opposite bank, but downstream of our goal and entangled in heavy undergrowth.

We pull on overhanging branches to haul ourselves upstream, but make no progress. Stewart jumps out of the canoe on to the steep, silty, overgrown riverbank. I hang on to the undergrowth, perfectly calm and waiting for the next part of the plan.

'We'll have to leave the canoes here. You get out while I hold on and then we'll pull them as far up as we can.'

Somehow we find the energy to haul our heavy ship out of the water, lodge it in between tree trunks and climb up through the undergrowth. It is about 800 metres from the landing to the hut. For each of these 800 metres water gushes out of every gap in my clothing and washes chunks of the unsealed road down into the river.

'Well,' I venture as cheerfully as I can, given the prospect of having wet feet for several days, 'at least we're not at the campsite tonight.'

'No. I don't think we'll be going anywhere for a while.'

Oh no. I want dry feet, but I want to finish this journey more. Is Stewart wimping out?

We pass Whakahoro Hut and arrive at the offices of Wades Landing Outdoors, where Robyn opens the door.

'Hell, what happened?' she asks.

Everything is decided quickly. Stewart commandeers Steve, the owner of Wades Landing, to help him rescue the canoes. Robyn plies me with towels and stands me in front of a heater. We will stay here until the river is safe for us to resume the trip. I hope that means tomorrow.

Robyn, is slim, tiny and one-eighth Maori, with long, dark hair, beautiful brown eyes and lots of freckles. She is stunning. And here she lives alone in the offices at Whakahoro, population under ten. An unsealed road leads some twenty-five kilometres to the next nearest settlement, but is frequently closed in winter. This next nearest settlement is Kaitieke – population around one hundred, spread over a seven-kilometre radius.

Whakahoro comprises these offices, the DOC hut, one farm and two other buildings. The offices of Wades Landing include a couple of rooms that we improvise into sleeping quarters for Stewart and me.

'Did you see the dent in the bridge?' asks Robyn as I hug her gas fire.

'We didn't make it as far as the bridge.'

'Have a look when you go back. The old bridge was further upstream to the one that's there now. There was a flood in 1941 and loads of logs and debris got trapped by the old bridge. It gave way eventually and swept straight into the new bridge. The new bridge held, but it's got a great dent in it.'

The dent in the main arch of the bridge is around fifteen metres above the normal river level. Fifteen metres qualifies as a decent flood around here.

'The water level we've had for the last two days has been much lower than I expected,' I say. 'I've read that there used to be paddle steamers on the Whanganui, but I don't see how. We hit the bottom just using our canoe paddles.'

'The normal level used to be about a metre higher,' explains Robyn. 'A lot of water has been diverted for the Tongariro Power Scheme. The local Maori say the loss of its waters makes the river sad,' she adds. 'This makes them sad.'

The Tongariro Power Scheme is a leader amongst New Zealand's controversial hydroelectricity schemes. Since the 1970s it has diverted headwaters from the Whanganui River via Lake Taupo into the Waikato River. With a few enormous sweeps of an engineering pencil, it edited New Zealand's longest river, longest navigable river and largest lake.

Those from whom the water was taken – the Whanganui Maori – feel a spiritual loss from the stolen force of the river. They have spent more than thirty years cataloguing and campaigning against the practical impacts: depleted fish stocks; pollution; damage to vegetation and banks; and navigational difficulties. By the time the Waitangi Tribunal convened to consider the claims of the Whanganui tribes, there was rather a lot for them to consider.

Meanwhile, the Waikato Maori weren't pleased either. Lots of extra water doesn't make their river 'happy' because the additional flow doesn't belong to that river. And goodness knows, in a country like New Zealand and in a lush region like the Waikato, the average annual rainfall leaves no practical need for the extra millions of cubic tonnes of water that swish down from Lake Taupo each year after twizzling the turbines.

Tonight, water is in plentiful supply in Whakahoro. It rains heavily as Stewart, Robyn and I eat another of Stewart's rugby-team dinners. It rains heavily as we talk into the night. It rains heavily as I lie on an old mattress in my remaining dry clothes.

Day three: Going nowhere slowly

In the morning, the rain has stopped but the air is a wet tea towel. Stewart, Rob and I crowd round her internet connection watching the weather forecast and the published water level at Pipiriki, the end point for the Whanganui River Journey.

'The level is already seven metres,' says Stewart. 'It was twelve metres at the height of the February floods and the forecast says more rain is due. We're not going back out on the river today.'

'You're welcome to stay here,' says Robyn.

'Tomorrow looks better,' I try. 'Forecast shows only cloud.'

'Yes,' agrees Stewart, 'but we don't know how quickly the water level will drop. We'll have to wait and see.'

The catchment area of the Whanganui River is enormous. It can be raining hundreds of kilometres away to flood the river a day or two later. When it rains everywhere, the river can rise more than five metres in less than a day. We check several local area weather forecasts to second guess the movement in river levels over the next few days. Part of the problem is that much of the vegetation in the catchment area has long since been cleared. Where once moss, ferns and tree roots soaked up the heavy rainfall, now tufts of grass take a few quick sips before drowning.

Stewart is worried. There are no entry or exit points from the river between here and Pipiriki, some eighty-eight kilometres away. Once we relaunch from Whakahoro, our only emergency strategy will be to hole up at one of the huts or campsites for however many days it takes to wait out a flood. (That is, assuming we made it to one of these sites.) Whakahoro has, at least, a road out, even if it is unsealed, long and frequently closed in winter when bits of surrounding cliff slide on to it.

I am worried. We are running out of time to complete the journey. Stewart doesn't seem keen to go back out on to the river and I can't tell if this is entirely because of the weather.

Robyn has no worries.

'We'll be right,' she grins. 'You can wait it out here.'

She lifts the lid on an enormous freezer and shows me her winter supply of carcasses. There is enough meat to feed us all until spring.

We wait. We chat. Robyn and Stewart watch films on the satellite TV. I raid the small bookshelf and read about the post office that used to exist here and was also known as Wade's Landing. The mail was delivered by a woman who completed a forty-five-mile journey by horseback twice a week, for which she was paid £5 a year.

In the dull afternoon light I pull on soaking boots and investigate the Mangapurua Track, a forty-kilometre tramping track from Whakahoro to Mangapurua Landing, which we will see further downstream if ever we relaunch. The mud is deep enough to bathe in. Gunshots within the surrounding bush are my excuse for turning round after only an hour.

At Whakahoro the population has doubled. Seven men have arrived, with four dogs, assorted crates of gear and two four-wheel drive vehicles, each with jetboat and trailer attached. The men set up camp in the DOC hut. Four months ago, I would have nodded a silent greeting from this safe distance. Now I go over and introduce myself.

They are Steve, Steve, Glen, Glen, Jason, Colin and Blair. The group splits naturally around the two jetboats, one red, one blue. In the red team are Steve, Steve, and Glen, who lean on their jetboat, drink beer and are happy to chat.

The first Steve is the natural leader of this group. He is the oldest and is the one who invites me to join them for a drink. He leans his hefty frame on his jetboat and tells of the regular repairs he makes with assorted improvised household objects.

The second Steve is wiry, jumpier and with a mischievous sense of humour that he's happy to sharpen on a stranger.

'Why are you fucking canoeing down this river in the middle of fucking winter?' he laughs.

'What did you say your name was, again?' I say.

'Steve,' he answers, rolling his eyes. 'He's Steve. I'm Steve. Bloody stupid poms.'

'Oh yes. Other Steve.'

'Fucking "Other" fucking Steve?!'

He's grinning. We both are. The name will stick.

'Where are you guys from?' I ask.

'Murupara,' answers Steve. 'Have you heard of Te Urewera National Park?'

'Certainly have. That's where the Lake Waikaremoana Track is. I hope to tramp there, if I ever get off this river.'

'Well, Murupara's the last town on the way to the lake from the west,' Steve replies. 'It's difficult to get to. Last town on State Highway 38 before the park.'

'It's a shit-hole,' adds Other Steve.

'It's a Maori town,' Steve says. 'We're about the only whites there. And it's changed a lot over the last few years.'

'Fucking Waitangi,' Other Steve interjects. 'Every fucker thinks he's a right to claim whatever he wants.'

'I've nothing against the Maori elders,' Steve adds. 'The older Maori are wise. They're well respected. But the young ones are different. They're out for everything they can get and they don't want to give anything in return. They think they're "owed" by the Pakeha.'

This is the flip side of the positive discrimination that tries to balance out past injustices and insensitivities inflicted by Pakeha on Maori. However, not everyone thinks the claims process works well. Not all claims made to the Waitangi Tribunal will be upheld. And not every generation views the issues in the same way.

I change the subject and we talk about their jobs. Glen, it transpires, is a possum hunter. He has a gently handsome, bearded face and deep brown, friendly eyes. He talks quietly and confidently about his job, but only when asked directly.

'I get dropped into the bush to work a particular territory.' He means by helicopter.

'First thing I do is build myself a shelter for however long I'll be out. That can be a few months. Then I trap and kill as many possums as possible. The aim is to clear the area, though they'll come back from outside once you leave.'

'And you work alone?' I ask.

'Yeah. There are other guys doing the same thing, but we each have our own patch.'

I know I like Glen. He doesn't need to talk to be friendly, but when he does talk, it's fascinating. He has the quiet charm of a man who is deeply comfortable with his own company alone in the bush for extended periods of time. I'd like to learn more about him, but suspect I never will.

'What are you hunting here?' I ask.

'Whatever we can fucking hit,' laughs Other Steve.

'Goats mainly,' answers Steve. 'We came this time last year. Goats bloody everywhere. Must have hit at least twenty a day.'

'Didn't have to leave the boat,' smiles Other Steve. 'They were all over the fucking banks.'

'These guys will use the dogs,' adds Steve. 'They're hunting pigs.'

The blue team are four lean men whose names I don't catch at first because they are busy unloading, sorting and cleaning gear. As they disappear and reappear from inside the hut, they look over occasionally and nod. I interpret this as the height of friendliness for a group of armed men who've just been disturbed by a foreigner – and a female one, at that.

'Are you going out today?' I ask. The afternoon is young, but the light is already dim under dark clouds.

'Nah. No point getting wet today,' Steve replies. 'We're here to have a good time. We'll go out tomorrow. Want to come with us?'

'Thank you, that's a great offer. But I'm hoping to be back in the canoe again tomorrow.'

I leave shortly afterwards, so as not to trespass too long on their all-male weekend.

'Hopefully see you on the river tomorrow,' I say as I head back up the short track to another bowel-expanding dinner and more discussions about the river level.

Day four: In the line of fire

I wake several times in the night to find the familiar drum of heavy rain on the walls missing. Just after dawn, low clouds merge with the hillsides and shake a light rain on to everything. Stewart squashes my optimism.

'We're not going anywhere today,' he announces. 'I've checked the forecast and the river level. It's up even more than yesterday.'

Nothing I say shakes his resolve. Robyn and I eat breakfast glumly, until an idea strikes me. I run down to Whakahoro Hut.

'Is your offer still open?' I ask Steve.

He nods. 'Go get your gear.'

'Are you sure?' I ask. 'I don't want to cramp your style. Weekend away from the women, and all that.'

'Fuck off and get your gear,' grins Other Steve.

'We'll be off in about an hour,' calls Steve as I run back up the track.

Robyn dresses me. On her instruction, I wear all my warm clothing and all my waterproofs. To this she adds goggles that cover half my face, a life jacket and an enormous pair of bright yellow plastic trousers. They are too big by a factor of almost two in every dimension. When I pull them fully up they reach to what would be my breasts if any of us were still capable of spotting these. The only way of holding the trousers up is by clamping them between life jacket and waterproof jacket. Bending down to take up the reigns on my still drenched boots leaves me purple-faced and pained.

Robyn grins and I suddenly remember what it's like to feel self-conscious about clothes. Maybe Robyn and Stewart are having a spot of quiet fun with me to relieve the boredom.

'Are you sure I need to wear all this? The guys won't be dressed like this, will they?'

'Hell, no,' she smiles. 'They'll be jealous, mate.'

I waddle down to the hut. There is no dress code. In any case, I already stick out.

On their invitation, I propel myself up into the front of a jetboat and we drive down to the ramp. In the first boat are four pig hunters, four dogs and four rifles. In the second boat are three goat-hunters, two rifles and me.

Once we pick up speed on the river, cold air and light rain become shards of glass slicing cheeks and mouth. Underneath my many layers of bulky clothing, the rest of me is merely cooling and slightly damp. Nice one, Robyn.

The river is considerably higher now than two days ago. We fly upstream, dodging logs and slithering around on eddies and rapids. The boat slips and twists as Steve skates us up rapids and around debris and submerged rocks.

Hmm. I bet my travel insurance doesn't cover this. Oh well. Why would I even worry about that any more?

Like so many of life's most cheek-flattening diversions, the jetboat is a Kiwi invention. Others include the bungy jump and something called a zorb, which is a large plastic sphere into which the thrill seeker is strapped before being pushed down a mountain, across a lake, into a volcano or suchlike. The joyrider (and I use this term in its widest sense) assumes the position of Da Vinci's Vitruvian Man in the pocket of air at the centre of the zorb, surrounded by a thick outer layer of bounciness. For extra excitement, water is injected into the centre of the zorb, as if the height of mankind's thrill-seeking ambition is to feel what it's like to be a lost sock in a washing machine. If you were to pop in some soap, you could kill two birds with one stone for the average backpacker.

Compared with the zorb, the jetboat seems the height of practicality. It can navigate shallow waters because it has no propeller. Power comes from a jet of water, produced by the engine sucking water in through one tube and expelling it again at high speed through another. Steering is also controlled by the jet, which enables playful jetboat drivers to execute 360 degree turns and other manoeuvres normally seen at stock car rallies. Unfortunately, this also means that the slower a jetboat travels, the more difficult it is to steer.

An interesting rule of river etiquette that arises from this is that canoeists should give way to jetboats. After all, you want a jetboat driver to be in the greatest possible control of his craft. You don't want him to slow down. On many stretches of water (for example, anything with rapids), it is highly unsafe for a jetboat to slow down or stop. Drowning or overturning a canoeist is a small price to pay for the well-being of those in the jetboat and most canoeists on the Whanganui River in summer must bow to this law of the jungle.

The first jetboat in the world licensed to carry passengers operated from 1958 on the Whanganui River. Today, jetboats are thrown around most rivers and lakes on the main tourist circuit in New Zealand, filled with up to fourteen gurning passengers. The jetboats belonging to The Boys From Murupara are much smaller. Glen and Other Steve are squashed in the back as they would be in a sports car. When Steve eventually cuts the engine, they sit up on the back of the boat with their feet on the back seats, cracking open the beer and ammo.

The plan is to drift downstream, drink beer, shoot things and steer round logs as necessary. Glen and Other Steve use a paddle to steer us, between taking shots into the undergrowth. Occasionally Steve has to fire up the engine to manoeuvre us away from rock outcrops in the raging current.

'Here you go,' Other Steve says to me. 'Your turn.'

He passes me his rifle as if we've been sharing it for years – and I take it from him as if it's the most natural thing in the world.

Now, no one with whom I've worked or socialised over the last fifteen years would assume that I know how to handle a rifle, never mind hand me a loaded one within the confines of a small boat on a swollen river. However, I do know my butt from my elbow. For two years in my mid-teens I was a foot soldier in the UK's Air Cadets. Mostly this meant handing out programmes at air shows and marching up and down in drill halls to teenagers' barks, but occasionally we were allowed to strip, load and shoot a few weapons at some appropriately inanimate targets. And, boy, did we make the most of that.

Drifting along the Whanganui River, I am now fifteen years out of practice. Yet, a man I met only yesterday has just handed me a rifle and assumes that I know what to do with it. I don't know why he would think this. At no point have I mentioned my drill-hall past, which I'm sure they would find deeply hilarious. Nothing about a short, twenty-first century British woman naturally screams 'hunter'. I assumed that I was joining them as an observer. Wasn't that obvious? I've spent the last decade living in a city and wearing suits, for goodness' sake.

Only now do I realise that, yesterday, this hunting party did not meet someone wearing a suit. They met someone who was walking down a muddy track, alone in the rain in the tiny four-building settlement of Whakahoro. They met someone who talks knowledgeably about the backcountry of New Zealand, goes canoeing in winter and likes a good laugh. Someone who is happy to wait out a minor flood in an isolated spot. I begin to see myself as they might see me. Of course this person can handle a rifle.

But can I? I like the fact that they've given me a gun. I don't want them to regret it.

The first problem is finding a target.

'Where are all the fucking goats?' moans Other Steve.

'It's not like last year,' agrees Steve.

The banks of the swollen river are goatless, giving me a chance to consider how I feel about shooting a live target. The answer being: completely fine. I eat meat (though not yet goat) and I'm comfortable with killing it first. I'm not saying it would be a pretty sight if I tried to kill a cow, but I'd cheerfully give it a go. Moreover, hunting wild goats in New Zealand feels like doing the country a favour. It's not just goats. DOC is happy for recreational hunters to kill any number of pests – deer, sika, tahr, chamois, possum and feral pigs as well as goats. If you love the forests of New Zealand, then killing the pests that eat them is only polite. Besides, I'm a little intoxicated by all the testosterone. Bring on the goats.

My first target becomes visible from within the ferns on a steep bank. The gun explodes and the goat disappears.

'I think you may have hit its arse,' says Other Steve, as we all peer to see how far the goat has run.

Steve steers the boat into the bank. Other Steve, Glen and I jump out. We scramble up the bank, which is steep, deeply uneven and full of snagging vegetation. There is no trace of the goat or any blood. Had there been blood, the plan was to follow it and make sure that the goat was dead. Goatless, we scramble back down, gracelessly slithering off the grass and mud back into the boat. Glen waits to push us off from the bank but inadvertently slips up to his waist into the water. Considerately, he pushes us off before extricating himself.

A short way downstream, we pull into the bank again. Last year they found an open meadow full of goats here. Steve waits in the boat as the three of us crawl/run up the forested cliff. I can barely raise my legs above knee-height for all the layers I'm wearing, but I'm determined not to be left behind.

We find a mother and baby goat grazing in the open over the brow of the hill. We creep closer, vaguely using two trees for cover.

'You take the shot,' Other Steve whispers to me.

Glen crouches down in front.

'Lean the rifle on my shoulder.'

I do as he instructs, peer through the sights, push the air slowly out of my lungs and squeeze the trigger.

Then we're off. The goats are running. We're running. Glen takes a shot. We all carry on running. Halfway across the clearing we realise we're not going to get the goats and stop, panting. Then Glen sees something much smaller running across the field, curses and chases after it.

'I'm supposed to be on holiday,' he says as he stares out the possum and we join him, surrounding it.

Possums are sluggish during the day. It trembles on the grass between the three of us, clearly looking for a way to run but knowing we have it surrounded. Glen picks it up by the end of its tail, so that its front paws are still on the grass.

'This is a good way to handle them,' he explains. 'It keeps their paws on the ground and away from your arm. They've got a vicious grip. If they get their claws into you, they'll do some damage.'

He hands me the end of the possum's tail. The possum shifts its weight but stays otherwise still, its front paws clutching the grass. Its whole body is tense and we're both waiting for what happens next. Glen takes it back from me. With the end of the tail in one hand, he steps one foot onto the possum's head, holds its jaw against the ground at an angle, pulls a long knife from a side pocket and cuts its throat. The cut is so clean and deep that the possum's head flops back and I see its spine.

For many long seconds, the possum's dead body visibly shrinks. Logically, this must be the result of relaxing muscles and escaping air. I wonder, though, whether I'm watching a possum soul drift away. I don't feel guilty. On the contrary, I have just played a part (albeit an exceedingly minor one) in the death of a possum. I am one step closer to becoming a Kiwi.

We slither back to the boat, with Other Steve laughing at my failure to hit either of the goats. ('Fucking useless pom cunt,' delivered and received with a big grin.)

Downstream we spot a couple of goats on the opposite bank and Steve grabs Glen's gun. He takes one shot and goes to reload, but as he pulls back the bolt, it jumps up and falls into the river. The goat trots away, unharmed.

'Shit.'

'Fucking cunt. Did you see that?'

'Was that the bolt?' Glen asks, peering overboard.

We now have one gun between four. There's not much that can be done about a missing bolt, even though these guys are all clearly adept at running repairs on rifles.

We have more luck on the next bend in the river, where a high rock shelf juts out from the main bank. Two black goats are busy grazing on this bench and we drift to within about fifteen metres before they notice us. Other Steve squeezes the trigger and hits one squarely on the backside. It springs upwards and he hits it again. The goat lets out a strangled bleat-howl as it is hit for a third time. It looks round, then runs straight out into thin air, bounces once off the cliff and falls into the river in front of us. It sinks quickly. We cheer loudly.

Our final tally for the day is: one possum, one goat. The goats were safe with me, but I haven't disgraced myself completely – the goats were fairly safe with all of us.

Steve fires up the engine and we speed downstream to our appointed rendezvous with the blue boat. Two of the blue team are waiting on a pebble bank with two of the dogs. We keep them company in the cold and dimming light.

'We dropped them off down there a few hours ago,' they explain, pointing to the next bend in the river. 'They were going to go up over those ridges to flush out as many pigs as they could, then drop down and meet us here.'

They are half an hour late. The guys shoot a couple of air shots to see if they can get an answer. After the short echo dies away into the steep valley, we hear nothing but the river and the new rain. No rifles are fired, no dogs are barking.

'We'll get back and get the food on,' says Steve after another fifteen minutes.

'Yep. No fuckin' sense us all standing out here in the fuckin' cold and rain,' agrees Other Steve.

'Don't wait too long,' Steve warns the others as we push off. 'Make sure you get back before dark.'

We leave them standing on the bank on a bend in the river, surrounded by cliffs and hills and dusk. We sputter and slip our way back upstream, numb with cold and ready for a hot meal, but at the Whakahoro jetboat ramp we encounter a problem of our own. The river level has lowered during the day and the bottom of the ramp is thick with silt. Glen jumps out onto an adjacent bank and climbs up and over to fetch the four-wheel drive. Ten minutes later he hasn't returned. I follow him over the bank, where I find him trying to extract the four-wheel drive from more mud. He looks genuinely pleased to see me.

'Here,' he says, throwing me the keys. 'When I say go, reverse hard.'

He rips up some of the nearby undergrowth and stacks it under the back wheels as I climb inside and work the gear stick. Glen knows without asking that I can reverse this vehicle out of the mud if he just throws me the keys and helps get the wheels some traction. I'm just one of the boys. It feels marvellous.

My driving is better than my shooting and we are soon back inside the hut. However, it is dark outside, the rain is relentless and heavy and none of the others has returned.

'Stupid fuckers,' says Other Steve. 'They didn't want to leave without Colin and Blair and now they'll all have to spend a night on the fucking river.'

'Yeah. It's too dark to land a boat on that ramp now,' Steve agrees. 'Even if they could navigate up the Whanganui in the pitch black, they wouldn't find this river or the ramp. They've left it too late.'

I run up to the office to let Robyn know that four men and four dogs are missing. There's nothing we can do in the dark, but we gather maps for a search in the morning. Stewart has driven out to National Park Village to spend a night at home, but we'll call him for help in the morning.

Back in the hut, Steve and Other Steve are full of stories of reckless car journeys, accidents with weapons and stupid things done with cars and weapons when drunk. Fortunately, none of the hurt inflicted in the stories is to anyone except the perpetrator. This means I can sit, roaring with laughter at the crazy antics of grown men, without having to suggest sparing a thought for any innocent victims.

'One of my mates,' laughs Steve, 'got so drunk at a party that he decided to go out to his car to have a nap. He fell straight asleep, but was woken by a hard object digging into his ribs. So he pushed it away and fell back to sleep. Unfortunately, it was the handbrake.

'While he slept his car rolled backwards down the road and into a ditch. He didn't wake up until the morning and took ages to work out where the hell he was. He went back to the party and accused us of dumping his car, with him in it. Eventually he remembered what he'd done.'

Other Steve takes a turn. 'When I was a kid, I tried to make a silencer. I'd seen one on the TV and thought "that's just a piece of rubber fucking tubing". So I got a piece of tubing and fixed it to my gun and fired a shot out of my bedroom window. There was this enormous fucking boom! I threw the fucking gun under the bed, switched on the TV and pretended it wasn't me.'

In between bursts of laughter, we hear the sound of an engine outside.

'Hell – that's not the boat, is it?' Steve says and disappears outside.

He takes the jeep and returns not long afterwards with Glen and Jason, who are streaming with water and extremely cold.

'We waited as long as we could,' Jason says sombrely. 'It's fucking dark out there now. Could barely see the river, never mind the banks. Had to crawl back, with just enough juice to steer. Bloody miracle we got back.'

'No sign of Colin and Blair?' asks Other Steve.

'No. We fired a round off every half hour, but heard nothing back. We'll search in the morning.'

They tuck into the enormous stew. Those of us inside the hut are warm, dry, well fed and horribly aware that the others aren't. Rain lashes the hut, with no sign of letting up. Hopefully, they're not injured, or worse.

'I had a narrow escape once,' confides Glen. 'I'd been working a patch with a river running through it. I'd been crossing the river at a particular point for a while, carrying traps. The water was often up to my waist, but I could get across by really kicking off on the bottom with each step, to push against the current.

'Then one day, I took the next step and there was no bottom. I went in over my head with my full pack on. I managed to kick off against the bottom and came up to gasp a breath before going down again. I tried to keep going in the same direction by swimming across, but I kept sinking. I got fewer and fewer chances to take a breath. So I went under and released my pack.

'I was still fighting the current and getting pulled under. Each time I went under, I was going lower and lower and could see the surface getting further away. I burnt my muscles away with the effort of pushing up from the rocks at the bottom, but I couldn't get above the surface any more. The currents were carrying me along the bottom.

'I had to relax to get past that burning need for air in the lungs. It took a huge effort to stop panicking. I thought to myself, "If this is the end, I don't want to go out in a panic." And I knew it was the end. I couldn't fight it any more. I remember thinking, "I've done everything I wanted to do, except watch my son grow up."

'I was angry about that, because I grew up without my Dad, but even this didn't give me enough strength. I remember feeling surprised – I'd thought that I'd die in a car crash or in the bush, given my history. I started to black out. I was so relaxed. I just gave in to it.

'Then a big current picked me up and hurled me up to the surface. Right where I came up was a big rock with a crack in it. I threw my arm out into the crack and made a fist to wedge myself there. It nearly ripped off my arm, but I had no muscles or energy left to do anything else. I stayed wedged on that rock until I could move again. Then I crawled up on to the rock and out on to the bank.

'Weeks later I'd just stop in the middle of something and wonder how the hell I was still alive.'

Silence has fallen in the hut. Outside the rain and wind lash the darkness.

Day five and beyond: Rescue and disaster

When I reach the hut in the morning, the guys have already been out on the river. Steve and Glen are outside.

'It's all right – we've got them.'

'Are they OK?'

'Well, they're still alive, but they're pretty pissed off. Apparently they were stood on a bank a couple of bends further down the river, while we were stood upstream waiting for them. Bloody crazy – Jason drove up and down the river checking different banks, but they were one bend further down from where he stopped looking.'

'What did they do for shelter?'

'Not much. Blair had a lighter, so they got a fire going and bunked down with the dogs. Thing is, they had a lot of weed on them, so they smoked that all night. When we found them this morning, they were angry as hell, but also completely stoned. They're in there now, sleeping it off,' he adds, indicating the hut.

The mood in camp is grisly. Relief that Colin and Blair are safe has quickly given way to recriminations and hangovers. To compound the dampened testosterone, the Whanganui wild pig population is undented.

'River's up from yesterday,' says Steve. 'There are trees, logs and cattle floating down it. You won't want to take your canoes out today.'

Stewart calls to check how we're doing and report that the river level at Pipiriki is up to nine metres. We're still grounded.

The hunting party leaves, but not before they've extracted a promise from me that if I'm ever in Murupara I'll look them up. Hell, if I'm ever in Murupara the beers will be on me.

For now, though, my Whanganui River Journey is over. Stewart returns to Whakahoro the next morning with his decision that we can't go back out on the river for at least another few days. He drives me back to National Park Village, where we part. Tomorrow, Stewart will be taking people over the Tongariro Crossing, which now requires crampons and a guide. I am heading to Rotorua, to check out the smelliest place in New Zealand and dwell on the diminishing hope that the rain may stop.

In Rotorua, my daily routine becomes: check weather forecast, call Stewart, extend stay in Rotorua, retreat to hot pool. Floating in warm water looking up at the stars, I let go of the dream of completing the Great Walks. I'm not sure Stewart is keen to complete the journey. I don't know why, but I sense it's not entirely weather-related. We chat every day, but increasingly about his other ventures rather than river levels and weather forecasts.

On the fourth day, I make my usual call.

'Hello – only me. How're things?'

'Hi!' he replies. 'I'm glad you've called. We might be on for tomorrow.'

Day three again: After the flood

Relaunching our vessel proves almost as difficult as getting to the ramp in the first place. Stuck in the mud, I laugh until I'm no use to anyone. I'm so happy to be back here. Once we push off, we will surely complete the remaining eighty-eight kilometres to Pipiriki because we will have no choice but to let the river take us there. I'll be finishing this 'walk' even if they have to pull me off the beach at Foxton with the rest of the driftwood.

It takes more than an hour to pack and relaunch, the flood having left several feet of mud behind. We discard the tent and one canoe, but even our lighter vessel sinks into the silt. Robyn, Stewart and I heave and strain at the canoe, wrenching it up as we sink beyond our knees again in mud.

Shortly after we have waved goodbye to Robyn my bottom is wet and itchy again but I couldn't care less. The river has changed utterly since our last day's paddling. It is higher, faster and now a light chocolatey colour. We stare concentratedly along the surface trying to avoid logs and other debris.

Numerous pumice stones swirl along with us. They have been swept all the way from the headwaters of the river in the volcanic centre of the North Island. This is the route carved out by Taranaki on his flight from the Mountain Clan. The lumps of variously coloured pumice stones are our visible link to the ancestors of the Whanganui iwi (tribe).

These days Mounts Tongariro and Pihanga act like a long-settled married couple, which is more than can be said for Stewart and me.

'It's not so bad,' Stewart says of the river conditions. 'I've been out when it's been much higher and faster.' He points at a waterfall tumbling off the bank. 'I've seen the river almost two metres higher against that.'

I can't quite believe what I'm hearing. For a whole week he has counselled against us coming back on to the river because of the water level. Yet now we are here he loves the speed of the water and is almost bragging that he's done this in much worse conditions. Still, at least we're back on the river.

A few kilometres downstream we pass into the dramatic heart of the Whanganui River Journey. We've been away from the river for eight days but we are already immersed in this new world. We are surrounded by dramatic waterfalls and whirlpools. Several times we paddle over small whirlpools to a very satisfactory suck-squelch noise. Small side alleys and crevasses in the rocky banks are now hanging valleys of silt and mud, cut through by streams and waterfalls draining away the deluge. These hanging valleys make us feel even lower down, although the river level has risen due to the flood.

The walls of our private valley rise higher and higher. We gaze up into foliage and crevasses at the many different kinds of waterfall: burst water mains gushing out from gaps in the rock; long, white fishing lines cast down; giant snail trails slithering over glistening rock; and some that puff so much from within their caves that they sound like paddle steamers from years long past.

As the cliffs rise higher on either side, the channel narrows and the river bends sharpen. An outcrop of rock looks like the sharp prow of a supertanker, with us the tiny dolphin in its wake. Beyond the prow we pass the bulging rock hull, overgrown with lichen and forest and waiting rediscovery.

Soon, we are creeping into a fleet of anchored ships. Horizontal striations in the rock look like the timbers in the sides of ancient galleons. Each bulge of rock is the hull of a great ship looming above us. We're paddling into a fleet of galleons at anchor in an enemy harbour. Each vine hanging down from the cliffs is part of the rigging. Each waterfall is the result of some sailor high above sluicing the decks. If we break the silence we will be found out and fired upon.

We stop for lunch at the Ohauora campsite, which is conveniently positioned just past a large bend in the river, between two rapids and opposite a distracting cave. Marking the pebbled landing point is a row of kayaks, whose paddlers we find after scrambling up the hill to the campsite shelter. They are a group of teenagers and their guide is from the local OPC – the Outdoor Pursuits Centre. Stewart knew they'd be on the river with us for these last three days. This is one of the reasons we left our second canoe behind.

They are leaving as we arrive and we have the ghostly harbour to ourselves once more when we relaunch. However, after only half an hour or so, we see them in front.

'Let's pass them,' instructs Stewart and starts to paddle hard.

Wow. So *this* is what it feels like when Stewart is paddling fully. We fly past the kayaks and slow into the quiet world beyond. I love the feeling that we're the only people here. I can't help thinking, though, that we could have let the group stay far ahead of us if we wanted the river to ourselves. Only when we reach John Coull Hut do I realise why Stewart was so keen to pass the kayakers. Stewart is a first-sleeping-bag-out person.

There must be a reason why the person with whom I am bound on this journey is the kind of person I have most difficulty understanding. My priority was to paddle through our sunken world undisturbed by such reminders of modern life as brightly coloured kayaks and noisy teenagers. I was happy to stay on the river while the light was still good, enjoying the sensation of being tiny and isolated on our liquid highway. His priority was to be first to John Coull Hut, to get the pick of the bunks.

I still don't understand this first-sleeping-bag-out behaviour. It seems pointless. The 'best bunk' is invisible until after midnight – particularly tonight, when there will be more bunks than people. I see no point in unrolling our sleeping bags in triumph until such time as we know the exact position of all the smelliest feet and the loudest nasal passages. If I'm the first to claim position, the only possible advantage to be achieved is to find a place by a wall, so that I know I won't be flanked by smelly snorers on both sides. Yet, chances are that my wall spot is a cold one and that I will find myself in an echo chamber between the wall and the booming snorts of the person on my warm side.

Maybe I'm missing the point. Maybe when you know a hut well, you know its secret vortex of warmth and silence. Or maybe there is some tramping gadget I've yet to discover, which, when attached to an unrolled sleeping bag on a fresh bunk, emits a warning smell that deters newcomers from claiming the neighbouring bunk. For now, though, I take my position on a top bunk under the sloping eaves. I am soon pinned to the wall by the stench of teenage boy sock.

The teenagers are deeply excited at the prospect of meeting local Maori at the Tieke Marae (meeting area) the following evening. Normally the marae is unoccupied in winter. However, a film (*River Queen*) is being shot soon on the river, so the marae may be in use.

'What's your song?' they ask us, as they discuss the protocol of the powhiri, or Maori greeting ceremony.

'Um … I don't think we have one,' I reply, glancing over at Stewart, who is deep in conversation with the other guide and busy frying three more whole bulbs of garlic.

This hut has a box of books, but they're mostly trashy romances and probably more for burning than reading. The intentions book is far more interesting. Every group up to the end of May lists canoeing or kayaking as their Main Activity. Hit June, though, and the entries are all about shooting and hunting.

Day four: The middle of nowhere

'May I steer for a bit, today?' I ask Stewart as we load the canoe under promising sunshine.

Stewart is reluctant, but has few reasons to object. The river level is falling, he's happy with my paddle technique, the kayakers will help us if we tip over and we are now familiar with our canoe and each other.

We push off with me at the stern and Stewart squeezed into the prow. We are immediately wobbly. Stewart steers automatically, even from the front. I feel him shifting his weight quickly as he takes wide strokes on either side of the canoe. However, with both of us steering, the canoe swings wildly from side to side. It's like wrenching car wheels ninety degrees to the right in order to perform a simple overtaking manoeuvre.

'Paddle left! Paddle right!' Stewart shouts as we wobble and swing. Is that panic I hear in his voice? He starts to curse.

'I'm not happy,' he announces. 'We need to switch back.'

I feel like shouting, 'If you'd just paddle and let me steer, we'd be right!' I don't. There's no point. Stewart's not comfortable up front and is not open to persuasion.

'OK. Well, it's your decision,' I reply evenly.

As we pull onto a pebble bank, I'm amazed at myself. I'm angry and frustrated, but I know that getting upset with Stewart won't change his mind. It would only make the day worse. A younger me would have said something. As we pull away again, I'm still frustrated, but glad I've managed to bite my tongue.

On this fourth day, the Whanganui River is joined by several large tributaries with large names – Tangarakau, Whangamomona, Mangawaiiti, Otumangu, Mangapurua and Mangatiti. The side alleys offer tantalising glimpses of worlds even more lost than our own gorge.

Today, the chocolatey Whanganui River is so full and quick that the water from the Tangarakau struggles to push its way in. The currents swirl and slide into each other. It's an extremely strange sight. Where the two rivers collide, the clearer water in the tributary is being stopped and pushed back on itself by the greater force of the Whanganui, so that the water level in the tributary is higher than the main river and is certainly calmer, almost lake-like. The height difference is barely a couple of inches, but clearly visible from canoe level.

With Stewart back in rudder position, the mood in our canoe improves so much that we sing as we take our first detour of the day, up the Tangarakau River. Our singing is not a spontaneous, Mary Poppins-style celebration of the wonderful world around us. It is a serious attempt to find a song for this evening if we do find ourselves participating in a powhiri. Whilst maintaining a steady rhythm against the current, we sing our way through our personal musical catalogues to try to find our greeting song. Stewart's offerings are from The Eagles and The Rolling Stones, but the furthest I go back is to a wobbly Motown. The local wildlife covers its collective ears at our attempts to bridge the sixteen-year gap between our musical educations. We eventually settle on a clichéd 'Michael Row Your Boat Ashore', but make up some new verses. Stewart's are unrepeatable.

The Tangarakau is narrower and more placid than the Whanganui. The surface is so calm in places that it's hard to tell where the hanging forest ends and the hanging forest's reflection begins. It's strikingly easy to paddle upstream with only one hull. The sides are strewn with logs and we use the slipstream from these obstacles to help us up the rapids. Staying in the lee of a log just a few inches thick enables us to keep the canoe stationary for a quick rest while a fast rapid rages on either side. Twice we inadvertently beach ourselves, because the water is cloudy even here, but it's nothing that a bit of wiggling and shoving and laughing can't resolve.

Our second detour of the day is where the Mangapurua Stream meets the Whanganui. We see a track carved into the bank and whiz to a halt.

'Watch out for that iron rod,' I call to Stewart as he sweeps our rear end round so that we're facing upstream.

'Nice one,' calls Stewart. 'I hadn't seen that.'

The few inches of iron sticking out above the surface of the river is all that's visible of an iron mooring post driven into the bottom of a concrete landing ramp. In summer the ramp and post are both clear of the water. We tether our canoe to a handy log and set off up the well-cut track, which ends forty minutes later at the Mangapurua settlement.

Here, tiny side trails into the undergrowth are marked by wooden signs.

Other names are still clearly legible amongst the lichen and rot, but little remains of the small houses themselves. The first settlers came after the First World War. By way of reward for surviving campaigns such as that at Gallipoli, returning soldiers were gifted land here. If they could win fresh battles against the undergrowth and the weather, they had the promise of land and a living for the rest of their lives.

'The men came first,' Stewart recounts, 'to clear their land and build a dwelling. Many of them were young and newly married.

'There's a good story about one of the English wives. After two years of waiting, she took a ship to New Zealand. Then a carriage. When the carriage could get no further up the valley, she used donkeys – and saw one of the donkeys slip and fall to its death. She came the last part on foot, to find a hut with little more than four walls and a roof. Whereupon, she rolled up her sleeves and asked her husband what he wanted for dinner.'

At one time, just under fifty returned servicemen and their families lived in this valley. The remaining handful left in 1942, long after the majority and after the government refused to maintain the tricky access road any longer. The settlers couldn't win against decreasing soil fertility, decreasing prices for pastoral products in the 1930s depression, increasing erosion and bush regeneration, and problems of access. How nice to be in a part of the world where we've tried but failed to bend the environment to our will.

Yet, the Mangapurua Stream valley is still spanned by the bridge that was built to the settlement, now called The Bridge to Nowhere. I cross to the other side, where a narrow track leads off into the middle of Nowhere. Beyond Nowhere, forty kilometres and three days away, is Whakahoro.

Our tramp brings a breakthrough. Stewart talks of his broken marriage, the mistakes he made and how he's changing from the person he used to be. I tell him about my failed pursuit of the Young Professional Dream, my hopelessly inadequate sex life compared with his prodigious efforts and my complete uncertainty about what comes next. By the time we return to our canoe, we both know more about each other than is entirely sensible but I've discovered the things about Stewart that I needed to know: the bits I admire.

Excluding detours, our paddling time to Tieke Marae is less than three hours: half the time required on the 'normal' river level.

We are met at the small mooring beach by two girls from the OPC group.

'We're going to greet you,' they say, running back up to join the others.

After more than twenty-four hours' rehearsal, the OPC group had arrived to find the marae deserted. If it had been occupied by the local hapu someone would have met them, like this, to tell them that the powhiri will commence when they walk up to the marae entrance. Undeterred, they now intend to stage an entire powhiri to greet us as new guests on the marae.

The group stands on the terrace at the top of the path. One of the boys – their chosen warrior – moves forward, slaps his chest and utters a few loud 'U-u-ha's'. Without taking his eyes off us, he places an axe on the open ground between us and his group. Still without taking his eyes off us, he moves backwards to rejoin his group.

Stewart moves forward to pick up the axe. He must do so without breaking eye contact – a crucial point of etiquette sadly lost on early European arrivals to New Zealand. To break eye contact at this point is to suggest disrespect or dishonourable intentions. Better to be scrabbling at the floor trying to get a grip on a gift than to do so.

Next they sing us their song, led by one of the girls. She is Maori and has spent most of today teaching the song to the others. She has a simple dance to accompany it and some of the other girls follow the movements. Even the boys sing along in a voice-breaking, abashed but determined manner.

There is no way that Stewart and I can respond to this with 'Michael Row Your Boat Ashore', even with all the best hallelujahs we could muster. So I tip my head back and attempt the call that should be performed by the female elder in both groups during the powhiri – the karanga. Fortunately, I've participated in Maori greeting ceremonies before (albeit at the back of very large and extremely touristy groups) and I know that the karanga is a high, sustained call around one note, using a pronounced vocal wobble, for which I'm sure there's a technical term. I don't know what words to use (or even if there are any), so I imitate the long vowel sounds I've heard elsewhere. From the looks on the faces of our hosts – and the sidelong glance I get from Stewart – it seems I do a passable imitation.

Our hosts tell us of their ancestors, meaning their mountain and their river. Ancestors – both human and other – are an important part of Maori tribal identity. The welcome onto a marae comes from more than just its living members. The respect we must show is to all our hosts, which includes those who lived here formerly as well as the ones we see now.

'My mountain is Ruapehu,' Stewart leads for us, 'and my river is the Whanganui River.'

'My mountain is Snowdon,' I follow (painfully aware that Snowdon barely qualifies as a mountain here), 'and my river is the River Severn.'

At this point, the powhiri breaks down because Stewart and I haven't brought a koha, or gift, for our hosts. Stewart's not sure whether he can lay the axe back down as our gift in return, or whether that constitutes some sort of snub. They're all smiling and laughing, though. One of the boys comes forward, Stewart hands him the axe and they help us cart our still hefty crates of gear up to the hut.

The exact protocol for a powhiri differs from tribe to tribe. We have skipped a few of the more common stages such as story swapping, food sharing and the hongi. The hongi is one of the New Zealand tourism's poster images: two smiling New Zealanders pressing their noses together. It would help, I think, if there were some footnote to these posters to explain what is actually going on. After all, New Zealanders are renowned for their total fixation on the sport of rugby and some may interpret this nose-butting business as a violent sports-related practice. Instead, the hongi is a gentle pressing together of nose and forehead, often accompanied by a civilised handshake. It represents the sharing of knowledge and breath of life. It comes after the warrior challenges in the powhiri, once the hosts and guests have already established that they're going to eat together rather than attack each other.

Thus, with honour intact and noses unbroken, Stewart and I enter Tieke Marae. The main area encompasses several small wooden huts, a large DOC hut and a meeting house around a central lawn. Nearer the river is a campsite. However, the boundary of the DOC campsite and hut at Tieke Marae has been one of the more recent causes of tension between Whanganui Maori and Pakeha. It's not at all clear whether there is a boundary, or whether DOC built the hut on Maori land.

Day five: An unexpected detour

'Do you want to have another go in the back?' asks Stewart as we conduct the now familiar decathlon of loading and launching a canoe.

'Absolutely. Only if you're comfortable with that, though,' I add.

We set off with me in the stern, but I can tell that Stewart still isn't comfortable up front. As we manoeuvre round several small rapids he makes wide, steering strokes just as I'm making similar strokes from the back.

'Shall I tell you what line I'm taking as we go?' I ask. 'Then you'll know what I'm doing and you can tell me when I'm going wrong.'

I focus hard on the movement of our canoe through the water and provide a running commentary on what I see and the lines I'm taking.

'OK, you can shut up now,' laughs Stewart after about twenty minutes.

I do, and discover that the canoe's not rocking any more.

The level has dropped slightly from yesterday, but the water is still cloudy and fast. Small whirlpools open and close on eddy lines between different currents. Fast currents dominate mid-river. Where the river collides with bends and outcrops of rock on the banks, currents swirl back upstream, creating pockets of seemingly calm water. Near the bigger bends in the river, big sucky whirlpools open and close. The river is not one entity at all, but a moving plait of hundreds of different currents.

We avoid a couple of whirlpools only with hard paddling. The back of the canoe gets sucked into a small one, making a huge plughole sound – but stronger paddling pulls us clear.

'Are you up for an adventure?' asks Stewart.

'Yes.'

He helps with a left turn into the Manganui o te Ao River and directs us on to a pebble bank.

'I've always wanted to come up here,' Stewart says as he climbs out. 'I've been up past the first rapid, but never round that bend,' he adds, pointing a few hundred metres further upstream, where water is foaming out from behind a large cliff.

The rock walls of this gorge are the highest and most sheer we've seen yet – probably seventy metres up, if anyone were to measure. Between us and the bend are several fierce rapids. These are far worse than anything we've yet attempted – even travelling in the conventional downstream direction.

We unload all our gear, except for the spare paddles and long rope. With a light canoe and Stewart back in the driving seat, the plan is to spend about an hour travelling as far upstream as possible – and then to see how quickly this river can return us to where we started. There is a good chance that we will capsize coming back down the river even if we don't on the way up. However, we both have last day fever. And we trust each other.

We paddle furiously up the first rapid. I kneel high in the prow and dash my paddle through the waves as if my life depends on it. (It doesn't entirely. We would need to be extremely unlucky to both capsize *and* injure ourselves so badly that we couldn't crawl over the rocks to the bank.)

'Yee-hah!' I whoop as we conquer the first rapid with brute force.

This is gloriously different from our battle with the Retaruke River all those days ago. We push, lift, paddle and inveigle our way past the rapids in one long hit of adrenalin. We carry and shunt the empty canoe over rocks in sheer delight that we can now actually pick it up. We stop before each rapid and discuss the best approach. We paddle until my arms burn and my knee bones reshape to fit the prow of the canoe. And within an hour we have made it round the bend.

Other human beings must surely have stood here before us, but it doesn't feel like it. During five days on the Whanganui River we have seen only seven hunters and eleven others, but that feels like a state highway compared with where we stand now. From around seventy metres above us, a slim waterfall tips over the edge of a cliff and slithers down the rock that it has been wearing smooth for aeons. Rapids rage on either side of us. Stewart and I stand, panting and grinning at each other.

'Time to go back down,' he says after a few minutes.

He describes the line we're going to take. We will have no thinking time once we push off. Stewart will not only have to steer, but also tell me what to do.

I obey his every instruction completely and quickly as we shoot back round the bend.

'Forward left! Forward left! Draw to the right!' Stewart shouts over the roar of water.

We execute a ninety degree turn mid-rapid as we pass the glorious waterfall. No time to look. Just enough time to register that the waves to either side of me are at the same height as my head.

'Forward left! Hard left!' yells Stewart.

We crunch to a halt near our belongings. We're wet, but we didn't tip over.

Grinning, we reload, relaunch and slip back round on to the Whanganui River. Soon, the galleons of rock and high halls of forest are behind us and we are once again paddling between low, sheep-grazed hills. We holler exuberantly into the echo wall of rock near Pipiriki, but we know the journey is nearly over. We'll soon be leaving our controversial host.

'What are you doing next week?' asks Stewart as we haul our belongings out of the river for the last time.

'Walking round Lake Waikaremoana, I hope. Why?'

'I've got a few days free and I reckon we could do a trip down the

Manganui o te Ao River. I've wanted to try canoeing down that river for ages. I don't know anyone who's done it, but it looks passable. I don't think any of the rapids would be any worse than the ones we took today. We could use the tent and start a few days upstream.'

What a difference five days have made. I'm hugely flattered and sorely tempted. We discuss possible dates, but can't find any that match. I don't entirely mind. Stewart is a strong personality, but every personality seems strong these days. I miss the feeling I get when I don't talk to anyone for hours or days on end.

Besides, there's somewhere else I really want to be next week.

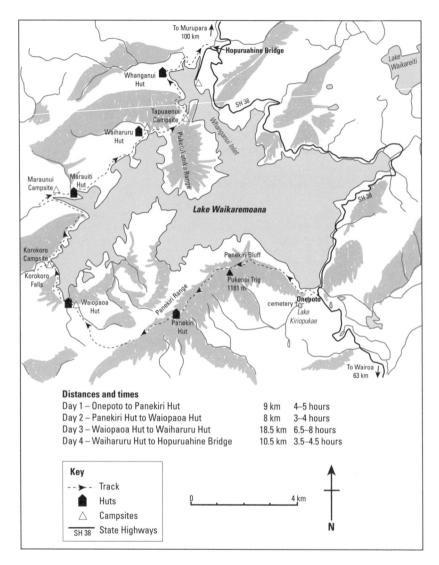

Distances and times

Day 1 – Onepoto to Panekiri Hut	9 km	4–5 hours
Day 2 – Panekiri Hut to Waiopaoa Hut	8 km	3–4 hours
Day 3 – Waiopaoa Hut to Waiharuru Hut	18.5 km	6.5–8 hours
Day 4 – Waiharuru Hut to Hopuruahine Bridge	10.5 km	3.5–4.5 hours

Key

- --->-- Track
- 🏠 Huts
- △ Campsites
- SH 38 State Highways

0   4 km

N

Lake Waikaremoana

10
Alone at last: Lake Waikaremoana

> *Final additions to kit*
> ⚬ Firelighters
>
> *Finally, some kit I no longer need*
> ⚬ Canoeing gear and guide

'Are you on your own?' asks Steve as he picks me up with the mail in Wairoa, a town of some 5,000 people near the top of the 150-kilometre crescent of Hawke Bay on the east coast of the North Island.

'Are you on your own?' asks John as he picks me up from near Onepoto the next day.

I try, again, to explain that I really do want to tramp this way, I really will be all right, it's not at all lonely, it really is enjoyable. As so many times before, my audience is unconvinced. I fall back on the only comment that seems acceptable, 'I'm sure I won't be entirely alone. There are always other people on the track or in the huts.'

'We took one guy out, but two days ago, so you won't see him. There's no one else that we know of and we're about the only outfit that goes out there at this time of year.'

Bliss. I can't believe I'll be so lucky as to have the 2,127 square kilometres of Te Urewera National Park to myself for four days. He can't believe I consider that lucky. Still, he's happy to accept my money in return for the promise to meet me, in three days' time, at 2.00 pm at Hopuruahine Bridge. If I really am to be alone until then, I hope nothing goes wrong with my watch.

Second only to the Rakiura Track, which lies beyond the southern tip of 'mainland' New Zealand, the Lake Waikaremoana Track is the least frequented Great Walk. This is surprising, given that it is on the far more heavily populated North Island, only about 300 kilometres from Auckland and 400 kilometres from Wellington. It is one of only two overland Great Walks on the North Island and the other, the Tongariro Northern Circuit, receives more than thirteen times its number of visitors. What keeps this track so well hidden?

For a start, 212,672 hectares of forest. Lake Waikaremoana lies near the southern boundary of Te Urewera National Park, which is the North Island's largest remaining area of forested wilderness. It is not possible to 'drop in' here on the way between major towns or cities. Special effort and a store of provisions are required in order to approach the lake. The nearest main settlements are Murupara, one hundred kilometres away to the north-west, and Wairoa, sixty-three kilometres away to the south-east, linked by wriggly State Highway 38. It took me half a day just to reach Wairoa.

Day one: Bluff and puff

The first people I meet are dead. I wasn't expecting them, but then I doubt they were expecting me either. An early sidetrack leads to the small Lake Kiriopukae and just before this lake an old, overgrown trail leads towards a gap in the trees. Past the gap is a small cemetery. The few graves still discernible are variously marked, mostly in stone. They have no obvious link, other than names that all sound European. One grave is of a nine-month-old baby. Another is that of Private Michael Noonan, a member of the armed constabulary, shot in 1869 whilst carrying dispatches from Wairoa to Onepoto.

He was almost certainly a victim of the New Zealand Wars – a series of violent clashes between Europeans and Maori. The cause? Land. Or, rather, land and everything that went with it: food, water, shelter, materials, authority and cultural values and protocols. The Tuhoe tribes of Te Urewera were heavily involved in fighting against government forces. Onepoto was something of a local stronghold in the fighting, but the struggle ended with government success and much Tuhoe land was confiscated.

I linger so long at the graveyard and lake that it's late morning before I even begin this track's big ascent. I'm having trouble getting started on this mountain because it will be the last and I no longer want to finish the Great Walks. I'm beginning to have some pretty wild ideas about my life and I'm intrigued to see how much wilder they can get.

Perhaps I'm suffering from chronic withdrawal of advertising. No one tries to sell me anything here and no one has a message for my subconscious. How can I make positive decisions about my life in a marketing vacuum? I've even begun to believe that I don't need anything other than basic food, water, practical clothing and a shelter at night.

Of all the climbs on all the Great Walks, the ascent of Panekiri Bluff has the most daunting collection of place names. The first viewpoint I'll reach is Te Rahui, which means a mark of warning to trespassers and the boundary of a sacred place. Further on lies Pukenui, or the 'large hill' (and if I've learnt anything over the last few months, I've learnt that this really means 'enormous mountain'). Later still – and just before tonight's hut – is Puketapu, meaning a hill that is sacred or forbidden. And here I am, with no knowledge of the local protocols that should ensure my safe passage.

Ignorance is not a valid defence. I recall a conversation with an extremely helpful lady at the Whanganui River Maori Trust Board. She was so friendly and helpful that I asked her a huge question. 'Do Maori New Zealanders go tramping like Pakeha New Zealanders do?'

'In a different way,' she began her reply. 'I go tramping, but when I tramp I am making the journey for a particular reason. So, for example, I go tramping in Tongariro National Park, because that is the source of my river.'

'Have you ever been to Fiordland?' I asked, thinking of the Kiwi trampers I had met there who had described the Milford Track as 'something every New Zealander wants to do before they die'.

'No. I would be more cautious about tramping around land that is not my tribal land. It wouldn't stop me going. I would like to visit Fiordland, but if I did, I would make contact with a local tribe and I would only go tramping accompanied by someone from that tribe. They would know the right protocols.'

I wonder what the right protocols are here and what may be the penalty for failing to observe them. I find one answer quickly: pain.

I had thought I might be better at this by now. Another 600 metre climb?

No problem. Why, I'll even pack some extra carrots. Stupid me. Months spent tramping have not changed this packhorse into a bird.

Yet, the signs are there that I have become a tramper: I no longer worry about carrying too much gear; I eat better in the bush than I do in towns; I clean the huts more diligently than my own home; I pick up litter from the tracks; and I prefer going up to coming down. With the possible exception of this particular up.

This section of track is an endless series of false summits and the trees here are all jokers. I look up and spur myself on with the determination not to rest until I'm up there by that tree, where this particularly steep section levels off. When I reach the tree I see the track rising up behind it in another surge for the sky. Still, this isn't too bad. It's only for another twenty metres or so, until that tree ... and so we continue until I hear the trees whispering, 'They're taking gullible out of the dictionary.'

This trail is well maintained in the sense that there's rarely a point when I can't see the next orange triangle marker on a tree somewhere ahead. However, this is the narrowest, most overgrown and most difficult Great Walk I've encountered and the track is covered in debris from winter storms. Part of my time is spent moving aside fallen branches. The track becomes a ladder woven from tree roots. Its rungs are neither neat nor uniform. Frequently the next step is higher than my knees. I place my hands on the ledge above, stretch a leg up to meet them, do a vertical push-up with my arms and kick off with my trailing leg from the step below. If I swing my shoulders in the middle of this manoeuvre, I can tip the balance of my pack weight to propel me forward and prevent me from falling backwards off the trail.

I am beginning to think that this track wasn't built for people of my size. Almost every step requires a testing straddle or abnormal stretch. The forest would be a perfect place for this yoga-ing if I wasn't also carrying all my belongings. Several times I balance in the middle of a root ladder and puff just at the thought of the effort required to take the next step.

The side of the Panekiri Range up which I am crawling is an enormous inland cliff. Its near vertical face is the southern boundary of Lake Waikaremoana, rising about 600 metres up from the lake. After three hours the first viewpoint is a small sandstone theatre with soft golden blocks on to which I gratefully collapse, leaning back on my pack and feeling my shoulders tremble with freedom. In front of this tiny, semicircular gallery the stage plunges down to the lake. To the left is the face of Panekiri Bluff. As the name translates, it is an immense sandstone forehead overlooking Lake Waikaremoana and beyond, northwards over the ripples of all the mountain ranges in the Park.

The wilderness and grandeur of Te Urewera National Park are not well served by its name. Here we have the North Island's largest forest reserve and New Zealand's fourth largest National Park. It is bigger than the whole of Mauritius and is the home of the 'children of the mist', the Tuhoe tribes. It is full of sacred places and protected species. And its name? Like many of New Zealand's National Parks its name is Maori. However, whereas others hint at features of their lands (glowing skies, strong south winds, a treasured possession or a large harbour) the name Te Urewera comes from the unfortunate fate of an elder who was jeered by his sons and fell onto a lit fire. It means burnt penis.

I don't know what possessed the National Park gazetteers in 1954. Perhaps they didn't realise what the name meant, or perhaps they thought that no one would ask. Either way, it's a good job the track leaves little room for focus on anything but the next step.

More often than not, tramping in New Zealand requires tackling the worst climbs on the first day with a full pack. Where a Great Walk has a big climb near one end, that becomes the most popular place to start. I have been drawn into this masochistic behaviour. On the Kepler, the Routeburn, the Heaphy and now the Lake Waikaremoana Track I have tackled the hardest climb with the heaviest pack. The Rakiura and Abel Tasman Tracks are a little unfortunate in this regard because they don't have any big climbs at all. The Milford Track lets the side down a bit because it has an enormous climb, but right in the middle. This leaves the Tongariro Northern Circuit, where I dutifully completed the first section to Mangatepopo Hut, only to discover that most people ignore that bit in favour of heading straight for the climb up Mount Ngauruhoe. Is it just me, or would it be easier to break our knees quickly with a hammer? Or strap our hearts to some live electrical wiring?

There are two benefits to inflicting this strain upon ourselves. The main one is that on the first day of a tramp you have a genuine shot at knowing what the weather will be like. This makes it the only day when you have a good chance of a 'guaranteed' view from the top. The second benefit is that it gets it over with.

One of the great wonders of tramping alone is that moaning becomes pointless. Misery loves company, to the extent that when it has no company it shuts up. Being alone saves me from misery. And goodness knows, it saves a potential companion from despair. I could moan to a tree (and I've tried), but this stops being a proper moan because I can't help laughing at myself for talking to a tree.

After the sandstone theatre, the ridge ascent continues in slightly less vindictive mood. The track runs along the top edge of an enormous block of sandstone that tilts into the Pacific Ocean at Wairoa. The prickly bushes by my right leg are comforting because they make me feel as if the narrow path is set back from the very edge. Then I realise that they are growing out and up from the side of the cliff, their roots a couple of metres below my feet. The illusion of forest on either side is comforting, but only that. These cliffs deserve the name bluff.

Lake Waikaremoana is thought to have been created when the end of one of Te Urewera's mountain ranges dropped off, largely damming the Waikaretaheke River. Forget that. A Maori legend provides a much better explanation for the many-tentacled lake. Its main protagonist is Hau-mapuhia, the daughter of Maahu. Hau-mapuhia rebelled at her father's order to fetch water. Annoyed, he drowned her. The dead Hau-mapuhia became a taniwha, or monster, and tried to escape to the sea. She surged north and west, but was blocked by mountains. Then she fled east, but when the sun rose she hadn't reached the sea and was turned to stone. Her attempts to escape are what carved the many arms of Lake Waikaremoana (literally, 'sea of dashing waters'). Her stone form is the dam that holds the lake. Meanwhile, her similarly rebellious siblings were turned straight to stone by their father and are the rocks in the lake called Te Whanau a Maahu (the children of Maahu). The nineteenth century might have deemed Maahu a strict disciplinarian.

Lake Waikaremoana is shaped exactly like five failed attempts to find a way through the mountains. In the summer it is criss-crossed with water taxis, kayaks, canoes, motor boats and water skiers. Today, throughout my five hours of sweating and straining, I see one tiny wooden boat creep across the lake like a water boatman on a star-shaped pond. See? Someone else *is* here. They're only about 600 metres below and a couple of kilometres away from me. We're almost a crowd.

All afternoon the sun seems to be just about to set. It is, of course. I'm thirty-nine degrees into the southern hemisphere on 1 July and deeply relieved to reach Panekiri Hut without the aid of torchlight.

The Guided Walks do an excellent line in spectacularly positioned huts. Any hut is spectacularly positioned when it is at the end of a hard day's tramping. Yet, some stand out: Mangatepopo Hut in its valley of volcanoes; Luxmore Hut in the belly of Fiordland; Mackenzie Hut enclosed by mountains; Awaroa Hut on the creeping inlet; Saxon Hut across the ghoulish downs; and now Panekiri Hut on this sacred hill.

I am its only occupant. I busily do chores and drink hot tea to keep warm without having to resort to using the gas heater, which would be a waste of resources for one small person in a hut built for thirty-six larger ones.

The temperature drops to near freezing but to stay inside would mean missing the extraordinary events taking place outside. I don't know what magic has brought me to be here on this clear night with the solar system lined up so as to provide a sunset across the centre of the lake on one side and a full moon rise from the Pacific Ocean almost directly opposite and at exactly the same time. Across the lake and over the mountains to the north, the sky is a layer of clear orange rising to pale yellow and then pale blue rising to deep blue above me. There are only a few breaths of cloud around the sunset horizon – right on the edge of view, looking like another distant mountain range. To the south, the sky is a thick layer of pink, rising to pale blue. The unimaginable space of sky above me is just that: space.

On the grass next to me, my moon shadow makes funny shapes, excited at seeing me for the first time. The forest on either side of this clearing is shadow. Lake Waikaremoana shimmers grey against its black edges. A sliver of shore juts out into the water like a black dagger. Overhead the southern hemisphere night sky shows again just how crowded the universe is and makes me wonder whether everything isn't bigger and better on this side of our planet.

Few tangible thoughts enter my head as I stand with numb fingers and toes, numb cheeks and nose, cold legs, trembling stomach and no intention of giving this up for warmth. By 9.00 pm the frost is so thick that I could make a snowball by running my hand along the wooden rail outside the hut. I am nearly 1,200 metres high on a clear winter's night. It's cold.

In all the years I've been learning about the world, no one has ever mentioned the astounding skill of being still. Can you imagine it? 'Now class, we're going to spend the next hour learning how to think and do absolutely nothing.' It would never make it on to any approved curriculum. Perhaps it should. Stillness is probably the greatest discovery I have made on the Great Walks.

It helps, of course, to be standing on a mountain being treated to two of the most spectacular sights our planet provides. Suddenly, I wonder whether anyone else is out there within the thousands of square kilometres of forest, also standing and admiring the display. This is the closest I come all night to remembering that there are other human beings in the world. It soon passes.

Day two: Descent with modification

I recently read somewhere that, 'In the course of an average lifetime you will, while sleeping, eat seventy assorted insects and ten spiders.' My night in Panekiri Hut has surely elevated me to above average status. There should be a separate statistic for trampers. 'In the course of an average tramper's lifetime you will, while sleeping, eat 350 assorted insects and sixty spiders, and be run over by twenty-seven mice. You will also, under cover of darkness, be woken by 135 snorers, see two million glow-worms and kill six possums.'

The hut has been warmed in the night by the arrival of thick cloud. However, it is still cold enough that once I disentangle myself from my many sleeping layers, the best way to keep warm is to tramp.

Substantial sections of all the Great Walks run through forest. This one is no different, but I'll never tire of being inside New Zealand forest. Rather than becoming bored with these views, I miss them when I'm not here. Besides, each of these forests has its own unique parts. Here it is a high-level meadow, thick with the kind of grass that cows eat only in advertisements.

Around 1,000 metres high, all around is lush greenery even though the temperature is little above freezing. No tree trunk or branch is directly visible beneath warming layers of moss and lichen, but their leaves are bright green and naked. Large swathes of the forest floor are thick meadows of rich grass. It is the last thing I was expecting to see at this altitude. Every available inch of ground, trunk and branch is cloaked in moss.

Unique amongst plants and animals, human beings seem to be the only living beings that require clothes to survive. Some creatures grow fat for warmth, but we do that and still need clothes. Living in a city, I never thought to question this. Out here, it feels silly. Nothing else has to keep stopping to pull jumpers and jackets on and off as it ascends and descends.

Hypothermia is one of my top ways to die. I don't plan to use it, but I can think of many worse and few better ways to go. Mild hypothermia is apparently like being drunk: the victim becomes clumsy, irrational and confused and is likely to deny there's a problem. Call me a wimp, but I prefer denial to panic in the face of impending expiry. Meanwhile, the worse the hypothermia gets the less conscious the victim becomes. By the point of cardiac arrest, the victim is unconscious – and thereby, I assume, not particularly aware of what is about to happen. 'Drunk' and then dead with the minimum of fuss.

My only fear about hypothermia is of getting to the severe stage and being rescued. This would mean a long, painful hangover and the potential loss of digits or limbs. I don't plan to get that cold. Still, if I were to get hypothermia here no one would be along to thaw me out until at least Monday. Three days away.

As I play snakes and ladders along the top of the Panekiri Range, I think about other types of death. If concentration lapses or a knee gives way I could easily fall and I don't know how many of my limbs would be in working order by the time I came to a stop. The possibilities are rich.

I have known this all along. Yet here the risk seems more acute. Here the track is tricky and I am genuinely alone. Moreover, I never believed I would complete all of the Great Walks – at least not without injury. With just three days left, the odds are shortening.

I consider the main possibilities for injury and my strategies for dealing with them. The ones where I end up unconscious are easily dealt with. Next come scenarios in which I am unable to walk but can otherwise move to unpack my backpack and construct shelter. The worst outcome is to be conscious but unable to move. Then I would certainly die, helplessly and slowly – and not until I had been crawled over and potentially nibbled by the forest's permanent inhabitants.

Yet, even my worst case scenario doesn't scare me. To die out in the open is much better than dying in a car or an aeroplane or a hospital. To be plant or animal food is infinitely preferable to being popped in a casket and burned, or buried where fertiliser isn't needed.

Being unafraid to fall means that I don't. It helps, of course, that I focus my attention back on the track now that I've considered death and realised that it's nowhere near as scary as it used to be. My only remaining worry is about someone else putting themselves at risk to save me. If I get into trouble, I am my own responsibility. I don't want anyone else endangering themselves on my behalf. It is deeply comforting to know that the first rule of search and rescue is that no rescuer must put themselves at risk.

The main dangers for a tramper in New Zealand are generally self-inflicted and can be avoided with a little care and attention. Hypothermia or exposure, dehydration, malnutrition, twisted ankles, snapped ligaments, cooking fuel explosions or asphyxiations, giardia, and knocking yourself out on any number of obstacles in the dark are all avoided by the tramper who has the right equipment and knows how to use it. Evading self-inflicted injury allows the tramper to savour the dangers for which few preparations can be made: landslips, rockfall, floods, volcanic eruptions, avalanches and so on. Even an event as simple as a branch falling from a tree could be fatal if delivered with a sense of timing.

Te Urewera's speciality is earthquakes. Notices in the huts advise on the steps to take in the event of an earthquake. (I don't know if they work, but it's reassuring to have a strategy and perhaps this is their main purpose.) First, move to high ground. This must be at least five metres above lake level, but the higher the better – presumably so that you might have a chance of surfing the wave of any collapsing earth. I assume that the quality of the high ground is important. For example, Panekiri Hut lies at 1,180 metres, but on a ridge. A decent earthquake last night would have seen us tobogganing down the hillside with no means of braking at the five-metre mark.

The second earthquake stratagem is to keep away from large trees, which may shed their branches or themselves on top of you. If avalanches ever accompanied earthquakes, then I would be immobilised – torn between advice that tells me to run away from large objects and to use them for shelter. Still, being immobilised is probably the best one can hope for in the middle of earthquakes and avalanches.

The final – and perhaps most important – piece of advice is to stay where you are for at least fifteen minutes after the last shock. In other words, if your strategy has worked so far, don't blow it all by sauntering off along ground that may not yet have settled down. Even if all you want to do at that point is to tiptoe quickly away.

New Zealand is sometimes known as 'the shaky isles' for its frequent earthquakes. Every year it has thousands of them, although most are too small or too distant to be noticed by its human inhabitants. This still leaves plenty that are hard to miss. The most damaging within the last one hundred years occurred less than seventy kilometres from where I'm currently standing, in and around the town of Napier in Hawke's Bay. Photographs of Napier in 1931, immediately after the quake, resemble pictures of Warsaw after the Second World War. Well-constructed chimney stacks and the odd wall were the skeletal remains of a town that is now a cheerful pastel-coloured Art Deco show-town. This suggests that a good earthquake strategy in a built-up area is to hide inside the nearest chimney.

In a world that measures its disasters in terms of human death toll, many of New Zealand's biggest disasters have been landscape upheavals. The 1931 Napier earthquake killed 258 people. In 1953 a lahar from Mount Ruapehu swept away a railway bridge moments before a train arrived, killing 153. Perhaps this one of the reasons why New Zealanders are so friendly. After all, why be wary of each other when we can all have a much greater fear about what the rest of the planet is up to?

The knee-grinding descent from the Panekiri Range is steep and not entirely stable, but it isn't quaking. The rocks I pass have some kind of mauri, or life force. Every day in London I walked past beautiful blocks of stone and never, ever even remotely thought to put my hand on them as if they were alive. Is this the slow madness of spending too much time alone, or is there more to it than that? I stop whilst still a few hundred metres above the lake and sit down intending to give further thought to what I should do after Monday. But as usual these days, I don't do any constructive thinking or planning. I sit, smiling, still, silent and happy.

Shallow footholds between tree roots are still the main feature of this track. I wonder how trampers with feet bigger than size five negotiate the steepest sections. Several hundred metres further down, the tree root ladders give way to sweeping aristocratic staircases of tree roots, which deliver me to my next residence, Waiopaoa Hut.

I'm no longer alone. The small wooden hut is filled with food, logs, pans, fishing gear and bits of things like batteries and engines. Squeezed into the remaining space are two men who could hold back the front row of any rugby team. They smile greetings but leave just as I'm arriving. Shortly afterwards I hear a boat engine start up and travel out on to the lake. I've no idea how they fitted their gear and themselves into that small boat I saw yesterday. I'm alone again, thank goodness. I need some time to remember how to make conversation.

Waiopaoa Hut is set back from the lake shore, within the forest, and takes its name from the stream that joins Lake Waikaremoana at this western extremity, meaning something like 'smoking waters'. A short walk brings me to a quiet spot overlooking reeds and water, with high forest to the side, lit by low mid-afternoon sun. I am still inside the glorious torpor induced by thirty-six hours alone inside wilderness.

A torrential but silent downpour strikes the lake. Thousands of fat ripples plummet onto the previously calm surface. Yet the downpour makes no sound and, when I hold my face and hands up to the grey clouds, I feel no rain. On the water, vast squadrons of insects and water boatmen and are zipping around in their dusk exercises.

When the men return to the hut they laugh at my small torch and switch on a large bulb they have installed on the ceiling, with a wire trailing across the room to a battery half the size of my backpack. Conversation is minimal until they produce a pack of cards. Now I remember how to talk because I have something practical to say by teaching them Arsehole. Soon I have remembered enough about human interaction for us to be ganging up on each other, swapping rude jokes and giggling at points scored. I am shocked to discover that they are teenagers. I've never seen teenagers this big before.

Day three: Calculated risks

This is my last full day's tramping and finally I am awake and ready to leave a hut in the morning before the Kiwis. Admittedly, these particular Kiwis are teenage boys, mildly hungover and more interested in maintaining their fishing tackle than tramping into the cold forest. Nevertheless, they are Kiwis and they are still in the hut when I leave and I feel I'm beginning to make progress.

In a second radical departure from tradition, the flat section of track between here and Korokoro campsite, three kilometres away, is genuinely flat. I have descended from my last mountain and the remaining half of this track hugs the lake shore like a dotted guideline for nimble fingers to create a cut-out-and-keep model of Lake Waikaremoana.

This western end is almost a separate lake. A narrow channel connects it with the rest of Lake Waikaremoana, somewhere to the north-east and invisible from here. The sky is overcast but light, the water is calm, the track is flat and rootless and I am on my own again.

At the junction with a sidetrack to Korokoro Falls, I turn off from the main track but leave my pack behind. I stuff an energy bar and water bottle into my pockets and prop my pack up against the signpost, making sure to tuck attractive foodstuffs down to the bottom and pull both pack covers tightly around the battened-down backpack. I should only be about thirty minutes. My pack will have to fend for itself while I'm gone.

The side track along Korokoro o whaitiri stream leads through a patch of forest given over entirely to rimu trees. Always delightful as individuals, a whole grotto of them is like an explosion in a lace curtain factory. I would not be in the least surprised if a troupe of elves or witches were out there in the dark gaps visible from the track.

The 'stream' is more like a river. After about thirty minutes the track runs out at its bank. I peer upstream, expecting to see the falls that mark the endpoint. I see several deep and swift rapids, but no falls. I stare again, mesmerised by the speed of the water, which is around ten metres wide and too deep to guess.

As I turn, perplexed, I notice what looks suspiciously like an orange triangle on a tree on the opposite bank. Strung up next to it is a metal guide wire leading to another tree somewhere behind me. I consult the map and it does indeed look as if the tiny dotted red line crosses the thin blue line. I must cross.

To do so I must be absolutely sure that I will make it. Or, I must be absolutely sure that I accept the consequences of falling.

I step up on to the first of the boulders that I might use as giant stepping stones while I make my decision. The boulders are too far apart to be anything but leaping stones. Some are submerged under inches of racing water. The guide wire is floppy. For balance I shouldn't use it, but for morale I keep one gloved hand circled loosely around it.

I jump carefully between boulders, pausing on each one to plan the next step. Good old boots, with their firm tread. Yet I reach the other side, only to discover that it is an island. A narrower but deeper section of the river lies on the other side, but with no guide wire. By the time I reach the far side I want the falls to be worth all of this, yet somehow no longer care. I hear a bigger rush of water for the first time, but the orange markers continue up a ten-metre scramble and I still see nothing but rock and forest.

Then I do. And the sight has me grasping for the nearest tree trunk for balance. According to the map, the vertical drop down which the water plummets is twenty-two metres high, but I don't know how anyone could possibly have measured it. A wide, deep river has been cut off in mid-air. Around it is dense forest and below it vertical rock and more dense forest. The only possible approach is from below, where any boat would be crushed to pieces shortly after the driver's ears had burst from the noise. I am standing about one hundred metres away and about halfway up and I am surely the closest it is possible to get to Korokoro Falls.

Standing behind a tree, the noise is just about bearable. Peeking out, the sight added to the noise is more powerful than my knees can take. Even after fifteen minutes, chocolate, water and rest, I can barely stand upright when I look directly at the falling water.

I turn back reluctantly and find my pack undisturbed, an hour and a half after I left it. To remind me that daylight is a rationed commodity that I shouldn't be squandering, the clouds darken and it begins to rain. I trot off along today's remaining fifteen kilometres, still elated from the energy of the falls.

The track winds up and round the crinkled edges of the lake and in places it is possible to see out and into the many bays that are the edges of Lake Waikaremoana. It has no sandy beaches, but strips of shale or reeds glow in the intermittent sunshine and remind me of the bays in Abel Tasman National Park.

If the lake were raised back to its original height, these strips of beaches and reeds would be covered. In 1929 Lake Waikaremoana joined the wave of New Zealand's power-generating lakes. However, you could be forgiven for not noticing. The power stations and pipelines are tucked away from State Highway 38 to the south-east and the lake doesn't normally fluctuate beyond a three-metre range, which is roughly what the annual rainfall here could achieve.

A few kilometres further on, the track passes through private land and next to a scattering of private houses that look empty for winter. These are little more than huts, but with signs of amenities not available to trampers, including TV aerials: another echo from the Abel Tasman Coastal Path.

Every Great Walk is represented along today's route. Spiders' threads across the track represent the Routeburn. From the Whanganui River there are pongas, with their long, brown beards of dead leaves hanging down underneath the living branches. The absence of birds is the Rakiura. Underground streams, collapsed sections of track, bouncy wooden swing bridges, fallen trees, and moss and lichen are the Kepler, Heaphy and Milford. Still wondering whether I might yet slip and fall, each of the Great Walks flashes slowly before my eyes.

At Marauiti Hut I should acknowledge the dim light and spend the night here instead of pushing on for another six kilometres to Waiharuru Hut. I don't. Rationally, I tell myself that if I stop now, I won't be able to meet my lift tomorrow. I would need to leave before dawn in order to complete the remaining distance before 2.00 pm, but I am alone and without an alarm clock, so this would be impossible. However, I carry on also because I am still high on adrenalin and because this is my last full day and I don't want it to end.

I find myself scrambling over slippy rocks in dim light, following a headland just a few metres up from the lake's surface. *Now* I want this to end. I curse myself for being on this part of the track in the dusk. I curse myself even more when the track moves back into the forest. Although my ankles are safe, the tree cover removes almost all the remaining light and I stare wide-eyed for obstacles by my feet. My situation worsens still as I discover a large section of track that has collapsed and a marked diversion that runs out with a leap across a waterfall, and a climb up a near-vertical muddy bank that leaves me shaking.

I don't want to have to use my torch. If I were to switch it on, everything outside of the small spotlight would instantly become dark. Under trees at night I'm still wary of something leaping out at me, but I would rather see a dark shape jumping than not see what hit me.

I trot along, using every raw carrot I've ever eaten to dilate my pupils into those of a morepork. Adrenalin provides the speed and focus I need to reach Waiharuru Hut in the moonlight, now pushing out from behind clouds.

Waiharuru Hut is the size of a health club on the lake shore. One cavernous building contains forty wooden bunks that are spacious, new and accompanied by thoughtful storage spaces. A second aircraft hanger is given over entirely to kitchen facilities and both of these structures are raised on patterned boardwalk with railed verandas providing views out over the lake. Toilet cubicles are at a discrete distance, like the rows put up for rock concerts. These are the kind of facilities that might exist on the Milford Track if only the valley floors there were wide enough.

Echoing around inside the private spa are two boys, aged eleven and nine, and their father. They live nearby and the boys are 'excited as'. (Lots of Kiwi sentences end like this. Things can be 'sweet as', 'big as', 'crazy as', or pretty much anything else 'as'. The only rule is: never finish the phrase. Never say 'sweet as sugar' or 'sweet as that first beer after a long day's cattle droving'. Just say 'sweet as' and stop. Thus, these two boys are not 'excited as two young Kiwis on their first fishing and tramping trip with their father'. They are 'excited as'.)

We form a small, candlelit huddle at one end of one of the hangars and play guessing games until it's time for the boys to go to bed and for me to stand on the veranda and gaze out at the lake like I'll never see it again.

Only after I've seen more shooting stars than I have wishes for, and when my fleece and cheeks are damp with frost do I bunk down for the last time.

Day four: The end of the road

In the morning I don't want to pack up and leave. I'm still feeling emotional, but I'm also delaying the one-hundred-metre climb up the lowest end of the Puketukutuku Range, which pushes out deep into the lake on this northern side. The climb is tough because I move slowly. I don't want to finish the climb because I don't want to finish the track.

I still don't know what will come next. Surely I can't return to a city of more than seven million people, when three people in a hut built for forty now feels like a crowd. I want to stamp my boots and refuse to leave this space and wilderness. I am saved from slumping into a rebellious heap by the example of two young boys carrying packs as big as themselves and tackling the track as if this were the greatest privilege known to man. I think it may well be.

By the side of the track here, a fence runs through the forest. Next to the fence are traps – wooden box tunnels with bait to tempt pests such as stoats. This is the northern perimeter of the Puketukutuku Peninsula kiwi reserve. The reserve is surrounded on three sides by the lake and at this narrow end by the fence. On the other side of the fence from the track, kiwis can walk tall, with their bottoms held high.

I don't see any. I don't expect to any more. Not only are kiwis nocturnal, but I've seen the statistics now and I know why the nation is concerned. It is estimated that before we humans arrived, these islands held up to twelve million bobbing kiwi bottoms. Current estimates put the total at less than 60,000. For two varieties the figure is 300 or less.

Human beings have a lot to answer for in terms of endangering and destroying other species. Into New Zealand we brought stoats, rats, possums, ferrets, cats, rabbits, goats, deer, dogs, pigs, chamois … and, well, ourselves. These animals have attacked the kiwi, takahe, kakapo, New Zealand pelican, flightless goose, New Zealand swan, Haast's eagle and many other bird species now extinct, including, most famously, the moa (a large, flightless bird that could weigh more than 250 kilograms). To complete the circle, the human beings introduced have attacked the stoats, rats, possums, ferrets, cats, rabbits, goats, deer, dogs, pigs, chamois … and, well, ourselves. Realising that the stoats, rats etc. were a bad idea, we look back now on our nineteenth-century selves and think how little we knew. My, weren't we silly. Thank goodness we've stopped that kind of behaviour.

Yet, new species are imported into New Zealand all the time. They're just not as obvious these days. They are poked and prodded in laboratories and they are mostly tiny, such as the insects currently munching broom and gorse, which are invasive weeds in New Zealand. Research is being conducted into viruses or parasitic worms that could reduce possum fertility. Maybe we'll succeed in cancelling out all our past mistakes. Or maybe our twenty-third-century selves will look back and think, 'possums were a mistake, but they were nothing compared with what came afterwards.'

The forest through which I'm walking doesn't feel like it's a field of war. It feels calm and permanent. It's hard to appreciate that we've meddled here. Daytime birdsong gives no hint of the grinding of possum jaws in the darkness.

The track descends into Tapuaenui Bay, whose name denotes a place of great sacredness. It is one of the larger indentations in the northern tentacle of the lake, which is called Whanganui Inlet. Fittingly, this is the place where I shall finish my Great Walking.

I remain fascinated by the names on the maps of New Zealand and the great chasm they reveal between Maori and Pakeha traditions. Maori gave names to places based on their physical and spiritual features. Maori names do sometimes incorporate a human name, but the person is usually a legendary or mythical figure. In sharp contrast, so many Pakeha place names are frequently the graffiti of the men who felt they had discovered them. They are like spray-painted signs saying 'I was here' or 'I'm sucking up to my boss'.

The Remarkables, in the South Island, are one of the best exceptions to this rule. Peaks of schist rising almost vertically up to 2,324 metres from the shore of Lake Wakatipu, they are deserving of their name. Yet, the most remarkable thing about the Remarkables is not their height, their jagged lines, or their undisputed dominance over everything below, but the fact that they're not named after a European explorer.

Yet the names given to features of the landscape in the explorers' own homelands were practical, descriptive names. The highest peak in Scotland, Ben Nevis, means 'mountain by the river Nevis' and Nevis probably derives from a Celtic word meaning 'moist' or 'water'. The highest peak in England, Scafell Pike, likely means 'hill with a summer pasture'. Wales' highest, Snowdon, means 'snow hill'. And so it goes on: big mountain (Ben More), grey mountain (Ben Glas), grassy lake (Grasmere), winding river (River Wear).

European naming habits, once in New Zealand, perhaps acknowledged that voyaging to this other side of the Earth and scaling these mountains, discovering these passes, climbing these volcanoes and charting these seas and lakes were all great feats of human achievement. I'm not disputing that. Yet it seems to be missing the point.

Crossing these seas and mountains is a great feat because we are so much smaller than them. And because we are so much smaller than them, it is silly to give them our names. Even 'big hill' or 'fast water' is better than Mount Mackenzie or, arguably, Sutherland Falls. Silly also to call vast tracts of forest 'burnt penis', but fortunately Te Urewera is an aberration. Land of the long white cloud, glowing skies, sacred hills, treasured possessions … now that's more like it.

The highest mountain in New Zealand is the pinnacle of this debate. It has two names: Aoraki and Mount Cook. The latter honours a brilliant European navigator, explorer, astronomer and captain. James Cook bequeathed to the world an extraordinarily accurate chart of New Zealand (amongst other places), a fascinating log of his journeys and an example of empathy and respect in dealing with other peoples. If any European should share their name with the highest mountain in the Southern Alps, then Cook is surely the greatest contender. However, when you stand near the mountain itself, his life and achievements are not what spring to mind. The mountain is surrounded by others almost as high, but a halo of cloud or vapour often encircles this peak only. To spend just ten minutes looking upon it in silence is to sense a power and majesty that no human being will ever achieve. Its Maori name, Aoraki, means 'cloud piercer'. I rest my case.

The final few kilometres of the Lake Waikaremoana Track alternate between open, grassy flats and forest hugging the shoreline. I'm singing now. I can't help it. I haven't slipped or fallen and I'm just a few, almost genuinely flat kilometres from the end.

As I have tramped my way round New Zealand, I have asked many people what is meant by the term 'Great Walk'. I have enquired at the main DOC offices in Wellington and Auckland and in some of the smallest backcountry DOC outposts and in huts along the way. What qualifies these nine tracks to be Great Walks and therefore disqualifies all the other challenging, beautiful and shocking multi-day tramps in which New Zealand specialises?

There have been times when I've thought that the idea was either to kill off tourists, or convert them into hardy Outdoors People, worthy of mingling with the locals. Trampers and track workers have offered me speculative answers: these routes are the most popular, the most spectacular, the best equipped, or simply the most expensive. One DOC employee winked at me and replied, 'It's to get more money out of the tourists.'

Brian Dobbie provided the answers. Brian has worked for DOC since before 1992, when the Great Walks were set up. He explained that Great Walk status was bestowed on eight tracks in 1992 because these most popular multi-day tramping tracks were being adversely impacted by people camping indiscriminately near or off the track. Great Walk status came with a hut/camp fee system requiring trampers to purchase passes and stay only in huts or designated campsites. DOC has since developed and implemented service standards for huts and tracks, and higher standards distinguish the Great Walks from other multi-day tramping tracks.

According to DOC's visitor strategy, there will be no more new Great Walks. The standard of the tracks and facilities on the Great Walks has been criticised by some keen backcountry enthusiasts as being too high. For me and my boots, it has been a great start to the rest of our lives.

My relationship with my boots has long since surpassed that of mere boot and wearer. On the eve of every tramp I have spent many happy moments alone with my naked boots and a bottle of aqueous wax. I have worn them every day for the last 124 days. If they were to be lost to me now I would feel as a lover torn from the object of her affection.

My boots protect me. Wearing them I am confident, free and capable of anything. Without them, my feet and ankles would be shredded, chipped and torn. Without them I would slip from wet rocks and my knees would buckle under the weight of my pack. Without me, they would be – well, clean. Only after we met did we both realise our full, mud-spattered potential.

The attraction is partly chemical. With every hour we have spent together, they have come to smell more and more like me and I have come to smell more and more like them. We have achieved the nasal equivalent of being able to finish each others' sentences.

It wasn't always easy. In those early, heady days of our romance, we had to learn to fit together. Much has been written on the subject of 'breaking boots in' by people who know a lot more than me about these things. But 'breaking boots in' makes them sound like wild horses in need of a good sitting-on. I don't feel like that about my boots. If anything, they broke me in.

They brought me into a world where human beings are not the number one priority. A world that asks no more than that you pass by without disturbing it. Such an enormous responsibility for yourself and to the world around you. Yet, simultaneously no responsibility for anything else. Life becomes hugely more enjoyable when basic things like staying alive and watching water fall provide a sense of achievement and privilege.

I have had butterflies in my stomach and gone weak at the knees. I have cried and laughed, been excited, exhausted, nervous, delighted, hot, cold and calmed. Few people have ever made me feel like this, but all the Great Walks have. Wherever I go next, my boots are coming too. New Zealand has plenty more tramping tracks. Maybe I'll fall in love with my homeland if I walk round its quieter corners. And there are still those last few kilometres of the Heaphy Track. I think I may have left them deliberately.

The track ends with a final long, bouncy, wooden swing bridge. In the river below, a trout swims to stand still in the clear and lightly stained waters running into the lake. On the far side, the beginning and end of the track is marked by the usual wooden board, to which are pinned a few notices, and a roof for shelter in emergencies that require only your head and torso to stay dry. As usual, the road adjoining it is unsealed and empty.

For once, I am early. I look around for a good place to sit and find none. The choice of views is between a wall of rock or roadside scrub. I shed my pack and, sitting on the edge of the road, lean against it. Twenty minutes after my scheduled rendezvous time, a van pulls up, but with it comes another. From the vans climb about twenty people, mainly sixteen and seventeen-year-olds, with three teachers.

The teenagers jostle excitedly, comparing their kit and making endless final adjustments. The track and huts will be theirs for the next four days. They shout and laugh about who has the best provisions, who will climb Panekiri Bluff first and who will complete which sections of track the fastest. The teachers and I smile silent hellos. When they finally set off, the group takes nearly fifteen minutes to travel its first fifty metres, because each tramper must bounce across the long, wooden swing bridge one at a time.

11
Some statistics

Pack weight
At the start of the first tramp: 12.5 kilograms
By the end of the first tramp: 8.5 kilograms

At the start of the final tramp: 16 kilograms
By the end of the final tramp: 11.5 kilograms

Number of kilometres walked
If I had just walked the main tracks and not done the Heaphy twice, I would
have tramped around 535–565 kilometres (depending on which track guides
and maps are correct). Adding in the side tracks and the 'extra Heaphy'
brought me to around 640 kilometres.

Number of days/nights spent in the bush
Thirty-eight days and twenty-nine nights.

Favourite comment from a fellow tramper
'Awesome views!' (Uttered with a smile from within the cloud atop
Mackinnon Pass on the Milford Track.)

Favourite track
Not a question I like, but almost everyone asks this, so here's my answer: the
Heaphy. For its length, its peace, its four different worlds, Gouland Downs
on a clear, frozen, winter's dawn and the people in the town near its northern
end.

Day that I most wanted to be over
My final day on the Milford Track. It wasn't the dripping boots, wet sleeping
bag, sleep deprivation, sandflies, speed-trampers or hidden views that got me

down. It was standing in the Milford Sound tourist centre surrounded by staring tourists.

Day that I never wanted to end
The second day on the Routeburn Track.
  If I must bow my head, let it be to the mighty mountain. (Maori proverb)

Oddest person encountered
A number of contenders: Dutchmen who need to complete a four-day tramp in two; those who said I was sexy through three-day old sweat; Leon, for going into a wilderness to meet people; Jane, for tramping whilst on an elimination diet; the middle-aged Kiwi couple who walked fifty kilometres in winter to have sex in private; and the hut warden who did screeching kiwi impressions and told us all off in the nicest possible way. In the end, though, the winner was undoubtedly: me.

Offsetting carbon emissions

New Zealand is a long way from anywhere. The nearest significant land masses are Australia, some 1,600 kilometres away, and Antarctica, around 3,000 kilometres away. From the UK, the distance is around 19,000 kilometres as the crow flies (although, goodness knows, he wouldn't).

The vast majority of people travelling to New Zealand no longer go by boat. Instead we use possibly the highest polluting form of travel we have yet invented – the aeroplane.

Whilst tramping the Great Walks, I carefully stuck to pre-designated tracks, made sure I didn't damage any vegetation, and picked up litter dropped by others, but I couldn't miss the obvious fact that just by going there at all, I was not helping the natural environment, which I was so enjoying, to survive.

Sadly, the best way of minimising the impact is not to go at all. The next best thing that I have yet discovered is at least to offset the high carbon emissions that my trip generated.

There are many good organisations that work to offset or neutralise our carbon emissions and that have clear, well-explained websites, with easy-to-use calculators for individuals who care about the cost of their trip beyond the price of the ticket. The best websites I have found not only help you calculate the impact, but convert this into a monetary amount and explain the projects they run, for which your money could be used.

The following is a short list of the sites I have personally found to be the most useful. The comments included below are my opinion only.

Landcare Research New Zealand
www.carbonzero.co.nz

Landcare Research operates CarboNZero®, a programme designed to make it easy for individuals and organisations to minimise their climate change impacts. It has calculators tailored to different needs: home, business, school, travel and tourism. The travel and tourism calculator incorporates calculations for transport, accommodation and recreation activities. It is easy to use and also outlines the current project in which payments are invested – with the added bonus that these tend to be native reforestation projects in New Zealand.

More about the full process of measurement, management and offsetting of CO_2 emissions can be found at www.carbonzero.co.nz

More general information about Landcare Research can be found at www.landcareresearch.co.nz

Climate Care
www.co2.org

Calculators for household, car and flight emissions, with information on the methodology used and projects in which to invest. It also has gift offsets and quick offsets.

The Carbon Neutral Company
www.carbonneutral.com/calculators/index_shop_calculator.asp

Calculators for flights, domestic travel and households, with choice and explanation of projects in which to invest.

Trees for Life
www.treesforlife.org.uk/tfl.global_warming.html

Only deals with transport emissions, but does at least cover air, car and train/coach.

Sustainable Travel International
www.myclimate.co.uk

Only deals with air travel emissions, but explains the projects in which money is invested.

Note: the online calculators use certain assumptions to calculate the carbon emissions your travel has generated and to estimate the cost of offsetting this. These assumptions may differ slightly between organisations and websites.

Further reading

The following is my personal selection from the wide range of good books available about the Great Walks, tramping and New Zealand's natural environment and human history.

General
DOC parkmaps, guides and visitor centre displays are full of fascinating as well as necessary information. Log on to the vast and well-structured website, www.doc.govt.nz, or go to the nearest DOC visitor or information centre. A list of visitor and information centres and their locations is available from www.doc.govt.nz/About-DOC/Contact-Us/index.asp

The Penguin Natural World of New Zealand edited by Gerard Hutching, Penguin, 2004
This is an informative, fascinating and gloriously illustrated volume dedicated to everything a tramper could hope to hear, see or walk over in New Zealand – and more. It is easy to dip into and then impossible not to read from cover to cover.

The Reed Dictionary of New Zealand Place Names by A.W. Reed, Reed Books, 2002
Explains the meanings and origins of the names of New Zealand's cities, towns, rivers, lakes and mountains. It includes both English and Maori place names and is particularly useful for those who don't speak Maori.

New Zealand – The Great Walks by Alexander Stewart, Trailblazer, 2004
New Zealand's Top Tracks by Mark Pickering, Reed Books, 2002
These are both guidebooks focusing almost exclusively on the Great Walks.

The Reed Book of Maori Mythology by A.W.Reed, revised by Ross Calman, Reed Books, 2004
or a shorter alternative,
Maori Myths & Legendary Tales by A.W. Reed, New Holland, 1999
An absolute must for anyone who can't live on a marae and hear its stories as they ought to be heard.

The Penguin History of New Zealand by Michael King, Penguin, 2003
Making Peoples: A History of the New Zealanders by James Belich, Penguin Books, 1996
These are very readable accounts of New Zealand's history since human beings arrived.

The Treaty: Every New Zealander's Guide to the Treaty of Waitangi by Marcia Stenson, Random House, 2004
Provides a clear, high-level explanation of this complex debate.

The Treaty of Waitangi by Claudia Orange, Bridget Williams Books, 1987
An authoritative work by a renowned New Zealand historian.

For detailed insight into the Waitangi Tribunal and its impact on modern New Zealand, visit www.waitangi-tribunal.govt.nz.

The Lonely Planet Guide to Tramping in New Zealand by Jim DuFresne, Lonely Planet Publications, 2002
This is the tome carried by most non-native trampers in New Zealand, covering the Great Walks and many, many more tracks besides.

Other books on which I variously relied as I tramped included:
Native Trees of New Zealand by Andrew Crowe, Viking, 1997
Penguin Pocket Guide to New Zealand's Native Birds of Bush and Countryside, Penguin Books, 1996
How To Shit In The Woods: An Environmentally Sound Approach to a Lost Art by Kathleen Meyer, Ten Speed Press, 1994

Specific tracks

The Chopper Boys and The Helicopter Hunters by Rex Forrester, Penguin
    Books, 2002
Contains matter-of-fact tales that must make every reader admire, marvel
and wonder over the lives of Fiordland's former army of airborne deer
hunters.

For Milford Track enthusiasts who can't get to the archives to read Blanche
Baughan's article, 'The Finest Walk in the World', *The London Spectator*,
1908, a fair alternative is:
Out of the Mountains by Iris Nolan, Reed Books, 2002

Old Tasman Bay by J.D. Peart, Cadsonbury Publications, 1998
The Enchanted Coast by Emily Host, John McIndoe Limited, 1976
Both contain fascinating accounts of incidents in the lives of some of the
first residents in Abel Tasman National Park.

The Heaphy & Its People compiled by Barry Chalmers, available from the
    Last Resort, the Information Centre or the Karamea Museum, all in
    Karamea
A fascinating collection of newspaper articles, maps, early track accounts
and biographies of those who have lived and worked on the Heaphy Track.

The *Waitangi Tribunal Report* should be at least dipped into by anyone
canoeing the Whanganui River Journey – it's long, but it could easily be
longer and it is extremely well written. The report can be found on the
Waitangi Tribunal website www.waitangi-tribunal.govt.nz.
    Other books I used to research the Whanganui River Journey included:
Woven By Water: Histories from the Whanganui River by David Young, Huia
    Publishers, 2004
Kaitieke: The District, The People, The Schools compiled by Wilf Couper and
    Ron Cooke, C & S Publications
The Bridge To Nowhere by Arthur P. Bates, Wanganui Newspapers Limited,
    1981